THE RADICAL ACT OF LISTENING

The Radical Act of Listening: Making Documentary and Investigative Theatre explores best practices in the field of Documentary and Investigative theatre and offers readers a how-to guide for making their own work, written by a leading practitioner in the field.

This book looks at how listening can radically bring about change through documentary and investigative theatre. It examines the mechanics and value of listening and how theatre practitioners can use these skills to create theatre. What does it mean to *really* listen, especially during a time when everyone is shouting? Can we listen without an agenda? Can we take what we hear and find ethical ways to share it with others so that we capture nuance, complexity, and contradiction, i.e., all things human? In exploring these questions, author KJ Sanchez shares conversations with peers and fellow artists who work in the fields of interview-based and non-fiction art practices, to look at what it takes to be a great listener and a great theatre maker.

Featuring key artists, themes, and practices, this book is written for students and practitioners interested in creating documentary and investigative theatre, as well as other interview-based art forms.

KJ Sanchez is a professional playwright and director. She is an Associate Professor and head of the MFA Playwriting and Directing programs at the University of Texas, Austin. She is also the founder and CEO of American Records, a theatre company dedicated to making theatre that chronicles our time and serves as a bridge between people.

"Ground-breaking theatre-maker KJ Sanchez has given us both a manual and a manifesto. Her comprehensive knowledge of the art of the interview is delivered here in clear and lucid terms, braided with inspiring examples (from her own career, and from other leaders in the field) of how private reflection can be transformed into public artistry. Sanchez never loses sight of the fact that the true 'heroes' of this work are those being interviewed; those brave and vulnerable enough to give testimony in the courtroom of their own lives. A moving, bracing, and indispensable book for theatre-makers and citizens of the world alike."

Steven Dietz, *Playwright/Director*

THE RADICAL ACT OF LISTENING

Making Documentary and Investigative Theatre

KJ Sanchez

NEW YORK AND LONDON

Designed cover image: Khristián Méndez Aguirre

First published 2025
by Routledge
605 Third Avenue, New York, NY 10158

and by Routledge
4 Park Square, Milton Park, Abingdon, Oxon, OX14 4RN

Routledge is an imprint of the Taylor & Francis Group, an informa business

© 2025 KJ Sanchez

The right of KJ Sanchez to be identified as author of this work has been asserted in accordance with sections 77 and 78 of the Copyright, Designs and Patents Act 1988.

All rights reserved. No part of this book may be reprinted or reproduced or utilised in any form or by any electronic, mechanical, or other means, now known or hereafter invented, including photocopying and recording, or in any information storage or retrieval system, without permission in writing from the publishers.

Trademark notice: Product or corporate names may be trademarks or registered trademarks, and are used only for identification and explanation without intent to infringe.

Library of Congress Cataloging-in-Publication Data
Names: Sanchez, K. J., author.
Title: The radical act of listening : making documentary and investigative theatre / KJ Sanchez.
Description: New York, NY : Routledge, 2025. | Includes bibliographical references and index.
Identifiers: LCCN 2024012860 (print) | LCCN 2024012861 (ebook) | ISBN 9781032567860 (hardback) | ISBN 9781032567839 (paperback) | ISBN 9781003437154 (ebook)
Subjects: LCSH: Documentary plays. | Theater and society. | Listening.
Classification: LCC PN1953.5 S26 2025 (print) | LCC PN1953.5 (ebook) | DDC 792.2/2--dcundefined
LC record available at https://lccn.loc.gov/2024012860
LC ebook record available at https://lccn.loc.gov/2024012861

ISBN: 978-1-032-56786-0 (hbk)
ISBN: 978-1-032-56783-9 (pbk)
ISBN: 978-1-003-43715-4 (ebk)

DOI: 10.4324/9781003437154

Typeset in Garamond and Scala Sans
by KnowledgeWorks Global Ltd.

Contents

Acknowledgments   vii

    Introduction   1

Part I
Essays   5

1. A bridge between people   7
2. Listening, memory, and *ReEntry*   21
3. Listening and reconciliation   47
4. Tell them I was here   68
5. The ethics of listening   92
6. Studs   127
7. Listening as civic engagement   141

Part II
Interviews   175

8. Leigh Fondakowski, *The People's Temple*   177
9. Les Waters   185
10. Steve Cosson, The Civilians   191
11. Sara Zatz   200
12. Mark Valdez, serving community   213
13. Christine Simonian Bean, dramaturging the "truth"   224

| 14 | Idris Goodwin, telling the story | 235 |
| 15 | Larissa FastHorse, Ty Defoe, and Michael John Garcés | 244 |//

INDEX — 255

Acknowledgments

I'm immensely grateful to those who generously gave of their time and expertise:

Cristina Alberini, Christine Bean, Nawar Bulbul, Steve Cosson, Ty Defoe, Larissa FastHorse, Leigh Fondakowski, Michael John Garcés, Idris Goodwin, Saengmany Ratsabout, Daniela Schiller, Mark Valdez, Les Waters, Nikki Yeboah, and Sara Zatz. I'm equally grateful to the hundreds of people who, over the years, gave me the chance to listen to their beautiful stories and allowed me to represent their lives and experiences on stage.

Many thanks to Michael DeWhatley and Ashley Malafronte for their invaluable assistance in securing permissions, checking citations, and copy editing.

And last: special thanks to Richard Huntley, for 26 years of love and support.

INTRODUCTION

As a playwright, my mission is to write plays that chronicle our time, plays that serve as a bridge between people. The core of the work comes from interviews. Essentially, I'm a professional listener. Listening is a muscle like any other; it takes time and consistent practice to be a good listener. I used to pride myself on my listening skills. I used to believe that everyone had a great story to tell as long as I took the time to listen. I used to believe that I needed to hear all sides of any story in order to best serve and reflect what I saw and heard. Then, over the past decade, as extreme political rhetoric and hyperbolic echo chambers of disinformation escalated, I hit a wall. I had a serious crisis of faith. As the floodgates of fearmongering and intolerance opened, my lifelong commitment to listening fell apart. I was no longer interested—no, it was worse than that—I *couldn't* listen to some voices anymore. What does a professional listener do when she can no longer listen? I lost my buoy, and my artistic process came to a crashing halt. All of my work was based on the radical power of listening, and I no longer knew how to hear.

After months of panic, I had to stop and take stock. I had to go back to the very start of my career and map out my process from there to here to remember why I fell in love with the art of listening in the first place. I needed to start a new search, a new look at how the act of listening can radically bring about change. This book follows that map, marking the patterns, lessons, methods, and techniques I picked up along the way. I'll share some of my favorite interviews from the last twenty years of my work and conversations with my peers who work in Investigative and Documentary Theatre, and I'll go back to some of my heroes of the art form to look at what it takes to be a great listener. And in sharing this with you, I hope to find my own capacity to listen again.

The first seven chapters of this book follow my own investigations rather than chronological order. My research and playwriting embraces a discursive process and similarly, in this book, I invite you to follow me down circuitous and tangential paths. I intentionally do not start with an overview of the genres of documentary and investigative theatre but instead offer such in a later chapter because—like most of us who make theatre that chronicles real people and real events—I started with content first, and then form came second. I didn't really understand what documentary theatre was until I had something to write about. The form was simply the best possible vehicle. The last seven chapters contain interviews I have conducted with some of my favorite practitioners today.

I invite you into this book as a confidant, peer, colleague, and friend. Though you will find many helpful tips for making your own work based on listening to others, this is not a "one-size-fits-all how to make a documentary or investigative work of art" textbook. I will cover subjects such as interview techniques, narrative structure, sampling found material, history of the forms, and the ethics of telling someone else's story, but I offer these slowly; I gained my own insights over decades of trial and error and stumbled-upon epiphanies, and I share these with you in the same cumulative mode. I hold off until chapter six to discuss the many aspects of the ethical practice of sharing someone else's lived experience because everything that comes before is the groundwork for such essential consideration.

It may take a minute to get used to my casual, anecdotal tone, as my intention is that this will be a conversation, not a lecture.

I will explore the mechanics and value of listening. What does it mean to *really* listen, especially during a time when everyone is shouting? Can we listen without an agenda? Can we take what we hear and find a way to share it with others so that we capture nuance, complexity, and contradiction—i.e., all things human? Can we listen to the quietest voices? The voices that get suppressed, the voices that have given up because they think no one wants to hear? By listening and then reflecting on what we hear, we all—whether a playwright, composer, public advocate, teacher, journalist, ombudsman, scientist, or simply someone, like me, who desperately wants to remember how to listen—have a chance to say to others, "We see you. We hear you. You matter." What could be more radical than that?

PART I
Essays

1
A BRIDGE BETWEEN PEOPLE

I grew up on a ranch in a tiny township called Tomé in central New Mexico. Tomé is where my family has lived for 13 generations. If anyone ever asks me if my parents were immigrants, my usual reply includes a few jokes about us settling in New Mexico (then called New Spain) right around the same time the Pilgrims were landing on Plymouth Rock and that we never crossed a border, the border crossed us. I'm the last of 12 kids and, though born on a ranch, I was a terrible cowgirl. Back in the late 1970s when other kids of my age were riding in rodeos or raising livestock to take to the county fair, I would spend hours every afternoon out wandering the *llano* behind our ranch. The *llano* is the flat high desert plain between Tomé and the Manzano Mountains. Most readers will have likely seen this particular *llano*. If you ever watched *Breaking Bad*, many of the scenes in which Walter White goes to meet the drug dealers out in the middle of nowhere—those scenes were shot on the very land that used to be my *llano*.

I would come home from middle school, have a fried bologna and mustard sandwich, watch *Gilligan's Island*, and then go out to wander the *llano*.

I would spend hours out there just walking around daydreaming and making up stories. I would pretend to be the people I saw on TV. I watched all the talk shows of the day and would pretend to be the host interviewing guests. My favorite was to pretend I was Dick Cavett interviewing Dolly Parton. I was in *love* with Dick Cavett. I wanted to *be* Dick Cavett. He was charming and funny and had all the things I lacked. He had nerves of steel with a calm and warm demeanor. He could just sit there and smile and come up with a clever joke and an even more clever question, no matter how cranky or agitated or outright hostile his guests could become.

Cavett, who once said, "it's a rare person who wants to hear what he doesn't want to hear," had talk shows with various names that aired on various television stations including ABC, CBS, PBS, USA Network, CNBC, and TMC and spanned from 1968 to 1995. His talk shows ranged from half-hour format to 90 minutes, aired from several times a week to bi-monthly or monthly. Sometimes he had multiple guests, while on other occasions, he had just one guest for the entirety of the show. For example, in 1974, comedian and actor Carol Burnett was his only guest for the entire 90-minute program—no musical interludes, no sketches or top-ten lists as we see in talk shows today; this was just Carol Burnett and Dick Cavett *talking*. Cavett interviewed not only film stars and television celebrities but also writers, musicians, athletes, politicians, and thought leaders. He had guests who agreed with his political point of view, but he just as often had guests whose politics or belief systems were in direct conflict with his own. He also had guests who were in opposition to each other as a way of creating an open forum to discuss pressing issues of the day. For example, in 1972 his two guests were young John Kerry, arguing against US involvement in Vietnam, and John E. O'Neill, arguing for the war in Vietnam. Years later, Kerry would run for US President and O'Neill would found an organization that opposed his candidacy.

There are three central tenants to Cavett's abilities as a talk show host that exemplify the radical act of listening:

1. **Gain one person's trust, and they will bring everyone else.** How do you gain someone's trust? It begins with being authentic. Be yourself; don't try to be who you think the other person wants you to be. Janis Joplin was on Cavett's show, and—though he was seemingly straitlaced, clean-cut, and rather square, and she was, well, Janis Joplin—they really hit it off. Because he was goofy, nerdy, and didn't try to be hip, he put Joplin at ease. In fact, she was so charmed by him that she came back two more times and told her friends that she liked him, trusted him, and found him actually pretty cool; and after that, everyone came on his show: Joni Mitchell, Sly (of the Family Stone) David Bowie, George Harrison, and John Lennon and Yoko Ono, to name just a few.
2. **Context is everything.** Cavett always made sure he knew enough about his guest so that his questions were connected to who they actually *were*. They weren't generic questions, because he had enough knowledge of who the person was/is and where they were coming from. This knowledge also helped frame the interview for his viewers; he helped his audience set aside their pre-conceived ideas and listen without assumptions or agenda. A great example of this is from July 7, 1969 when Cavett's guest was Jimi Hendrix. In his introduction, Cavett highlighted the fact that Hendrix was a paratrooper in the 101st Airborne Division. Years later, Cavett said that the reason he stressed this in his introduction was that he didn't want viewers seeing Hendrix, in a silk flower-print shirt and flashing the peace sign, to make assumptions about who he was as an American and patriot.
3. **Take your time.** Cavett had to fight to keep the long-format talk show. Even when you are as skilled as Dick Cavett at asking questions, it takes time to get to the really good stuff. Cavett's interview with George Harrison is a fantastic example and I recommend watching it. At first, Harrison is surly and does not want to be there. He keeps responding

with edgy, biting comments, but Cavett keeps his cool and responds very gently, with great patience, stays present, and sticks with the questions. Finally, after at least 20 minutes of very awkward conversation, something unlocks, and it becomes a terrific interview.

In 2016, Rico Gagliano and Brendan Francis Newnam, hosts of *The Dinner Party Download*, had Cavett on to talk about the art of listening. They asked him about that particular interview with George Harrison, and how he managed to pull it off. Cavett says:

> The best thing you can do is, and it sounds so silly, try to listen to what the guest is saying. When I first did the show, I thought, "What a nightmare! I'm going out there to do 90 minutes of television, improvised, and I don't know when to throw to commercial. And I don't know what's going on. And oh, my God, I'm talking to this guest here, but maybe I'm supposed to be in a commercial now." And you look over at the guest, and the guest's lips have stopped moving.
>
> And you have no idea what you were talking about, or what they were talking about, and it's really scary.

Cavett seemed to relish the really scary moments. For me, this is key to making work that chronicles real events. It's essential to go toward what scares you. One of my first documentary plays sat squarely in the center of some of my biggest fears. As I noted in the introduction, I will invite you to travel down tangential roads, but I promise you, we'll get back to the subject at hand. This is one of those tangents: My family, along with nearly everyone in our little town, was involved in a major land feud. As I was growing up, Tomé had a population of less than 2,000 people, and everyone was, basically, related. Tomé was first settled in the 1630s and was formed as a documented land grant in 1731 when the Spanish government gave this massive track of land (250,000 acres) to about 30 families. These were my ancestors, who were a combination of Pueblo Indians, Sephardic Jews, and German merchants.

The Tomé Land Grant continued for centuries as a communally owned land grant—from 1731 all the way until the 1970s. If you were born in Tomé and your family was from Tomé, then you inherited a share in this property. Tomé, like all of what would later become the state of New Mexico, was a Spanish Territory. It was a Mexican Territory for 36 years after Mexico claimed independence from Spain and then became a US Territory when the United States invaded in 1846. Over the centuries and under three different governments, the Tomé Land Grant remained intact. The size diminished, as segments of land were lopped off and sold to pay for maintenance or taxes. But nonetheless, for nearly 300 years the people of Tomé shared the land grant. By the time I was born, the land grant was about 47,000 acres of land, still a rather impressive piece of property, shared by decedents of the founding families. Aside from the fertile Rio Grand River valley on one end and the mountains on the other, the majority of the property was high desert, very dry, and very sandy. This is the very land that recently served as the backdrop for *Breaking Bad*; under a huge blue sky surrounded by nothing but desert sage, that great expanse of nothing—that was our Tomé Land Grant. The only way to get much use out of the land was to graze cattle. If you could afford cattle, you could get something out of the land.

Then, in the 1950s, and lasting until the late 1970s, a feud broke out over the rights to the Tomé Land Grant. Everyone sued everyone; lives were threatened, and families were torn apart. Sometimes the battle lines cut right through nuclear families: A cousin of mine did not speak to his brother for 13 years, even though they lived right next door to each other. All told, there were over 100 lawsuits. Ultimately, everyone lost. The suits made their way to the State Supreme Court where the judge threw out centuries of precedent and decided that the entire land grant was null and void. And just like that, the land was gone. People were left with nothing but their rancor and hatred for each other.

My father was one of *Tomeseños* at the center of this war between families. Half of the town thought he was a hero fighting for the poor and the other half thought he was the devil himself, who was only out for his own personal gain, obsessed with power.

Growing up, our house was command central for meetings about the Land Grant and the stress on my parents—waist-deep in lawsuits and trying to run their own business to provide for their 12 kids—was palpable. That's when I headed out to the *llano* to pretend that I was Dick Cavett ... far, far away from the fighting and worry.

I never expected to be a playwright. That was out of the realm of possibility. Most of us *Tomeseños* became cowboys, land developers, or worked for the Catholic Church. Somehow, through a series of accidents, I found myself in theatre. I stumbled into it and fell hard and fast and deeply in love with it. I have always loved everything about the problem-solving of rehearsal, and I found a particularly deep love for making plays, especially plays about real people and real events.

When I was about 25 and starting my professional theatre career in New York, my father passed away from a stroke after surviving two heart attacks. No doubt the stress of so many years of court battles and personal threats had an impact on his health, as it did on most of the patriarchs of Tomé, many of whom, like my father, died at a relatively young age. A few years after my dad passed, my mom came to visit me in New York, and one night she said, "Honey, somebody needs to make a book or a movie or something about everything that happened. You should write it all down." And so, I did. I pulled out a tape recorder and started asking her questions. I knew I couldn't do this alone; the subject was far too personal, and I knew I needed collaborators to help me approach the material with expansive listening. So I got a grant and found a theatre company in Albuquerque called Working Classroom,[1] and together we went to Tomé, interviewed *Tomeseños* who had been involved in the feud, and made a play about it called *Highway 47*.

My first rule of engagement when making a documentary play is, "It ain't about me." I have no interest in putting my own opinion, my own agenda, or my own politics or beliefs on stage. I want to put the opinions, agendas, and politics of the people I interview on stage instead. This ethos probably sounds impossible when working on a story that was so deeply personal, but it was in fact the only way into and through this story. And, believe it or not, setting my own feelings aside was easier than I thought because my feelings were rather ambivalent. My mother's family was on one side of this feud, my father's on the other. I was stuck right in the middle. And I needed to stay right there in the middle, the only way to honestly hear both sides of this story. I worked with Working Classroom's ensemble of actors; I shared with them the interview techniques I was using and we went to Tomé to interview my father's friends and foes alike. For those who were my father's friends, I would introduce myself as Gillie Sanchez's daughter; and for those who were his enemies, I introduced myself as Cipriana's child. My mother was one of the kindest, most generous humans on the planet, and no matter what they thought of my father, they granted me an interview because of their affection for her. When trying to gain access to a closed community like this one, the key for me is this: If you earn just *one* person's trust, they will then vouch for you and introduce you to others.

What can you do to earn that trust? Here are a few suggestions:

Meet that person on *their* turf. When you set up the interview, ask them where they would prefer to meet, and what is most convenient and comfortable for them. This is incredibly helpful because the location the person might choose will inform what they tell you. For example, one of my father's enemies chose to meet me at the town cemetery. As we visited graves, he told me stories about each person buried there and we realized that many of his great, great grandparents were also my great, great grandparents. This commonality bridged so many gaps for us. On another occasion, a matriarch of the opposition wanted me to go to her home. *Tomeseños* are very hospitable people, and so she offered me coffee and cookies. We talked about her *biscochitos* recipe, which was quite like my mother's recipe, and through this talk of cookies, we found common ground.

Be transparent about what you are doing and why you are doing it. With this particular project, I explained that my mission was to capture the *whole* picture, not just my dad's side of the story, and that I wanted to share the *whole* story with a larger audience. This play had the potential to be part of the historical narrative of Tomé, so people agreed to be interviewed because they wanted to make sure that their experience and family's role in this feud was properly chronicled.

Be a compassionate, non-judgmental listener. Do your level best to leave your own opinions and judgments at the door. If the interviewer shares how they feel about something with the interviewee that will always impact what the interviewee might say. Here's an example: If I were interviewing, say, a guy named Fred, and Fred started our session by saying, "Sorry I'm late, my dog died this morning and I had to take care of that." Now, in an effort to gain common ground, I might tell Fred how sad I am to hear this news, I might tell Fred how much I love dogs, I might show Fred a picture of my own dog, or talk about how sad I was when my dog died. All of this will affect what Fred says next regarding his dog. He knows I love dogs so that will impact anything I ask him about the dog. However, if I remain a compassionate, yet non-judgmental listener and simply ask, "Tell me about your dog?" Who knows what Fred might feel free to say? He might say, "Actually, it was my ex-wife's dog and I hated that dog so I'm glad to finally be rid of it," something Fred would probably not have said if he had known how much I loved dogs.[2] A productive interview is an interview in which the interviewer in not defining what the interviewee can or cannot say. If one of the *Tomeseños* thought that I was angry at them for their position toward my father, it would color what they shared with me. It was vital that I helped them understand that I wanted to hear it all, the good, the bad, and the ugly.

Leave your notebook at home, keep your list of questions in your back pocket, and just *listen*. If you are worried, you will not remember anything, bring a small, unobtrusive audio recording device with you, turn it on, set it aside, forget about it, and just listen. If you have a notebook out or a list of questions, people might likely feel they are being quizzed and can become self-conscious. I avoid using video cameras because I find some people become self-conscious and can't forget about the camera. We are all familiar with the reality show confession booth and interviews with video cameras can easily get performative.

Don't go fishing, let them lead where the interview goes. This requires faith and trust. The best material comes from tangents, from stories that at first might seem like they have nothing to do with the subject. If I went into an interview with what I would consider a fishing question—like, "Tell me how you feel about what my father did"—the answer would likely be short and obvious. So instead, I started with very open-ended questions and then let them lead the way from there. Let's say that I was interviewing Fred because I was making a play about the emotional fallout between couples living together during the COVID pandemic and Fred is a lawyer who specializes in divorce. My impulse in asking Fred for this interview might be because I want to hear from him whether his workload had increased or decreased and if the pandemic played a role in any of the divorces he is working on. So, Fred comes in and the first thing he brings up is his dog dying. My rule of thumb is to follow *whatever* is offered. If I ignored the mention of the dog, or said, "That's too bad, but anyway, tell me about your work as a divorce lawyer." The natural organic flow of the interview would come to a crashing halt. It would feel jarring and I would likely lose Fred's trust. What I must do is have faith that if I follow Fred's lead, we will eventually get back to the subject. I must always remember that everyone I interview is a human being with particular given circumstances and lived experiences, and those circumstances and experiences always inform why they do what they do, and that is what I am really there to uncover—not only the "What happened?" and "What do you do?" but also the "Why do you do what you do, and how does that inform what happened and what you did?" So, if Fred mentions the dog and I follow, asking about the dog, "How long have you had this dog?" or "Was the dog sick?" or "Was this an accident?" that tells Fred that I am truly present in at the moment, with him wherever he goes. Following their lead always pays off. Fred might tell me that the dog belonged to his ex-wife, he might then tell me about their marriage, about their painful divorce, which might ultimately loop back to his work as a divorce lawyer and then to the subject at hand. All I had to do was ask, "Tell me more?" or "Oh, what was that about?" or simply just sit there and listen, truly listen.

A person can feel when you are *really* listening without judgment or agenda, and when they feel that, they trust that they can speak candidly and freely and will tell you anything.

In short, you earn someone's trust by putting aside your own needs and agenda and being present and ready to go wherever they lead you. For *Highway 47*, little by little we earned the trust of a handful of *Tomeseños* who in turn vouched for us and opened doors we could not have opened otherwise. Little by little, the people I listened to felt they could tell me the story from their personal perspective, even though they knew who my parents were.

I'd like to note here that I offer these strategies as just the beginning of the covenant we create between the people we listen to and the work we make. My plan is not to *win* their trust just to get the good stuff for my play. My hope is to *earn* their trust. The first step is to listen without judgment, without agenda, and then, of course, I try my best to honor that trust by never intentionally misrepresenting them on stage. I have no interest in twisting what someone has said to prove my point. In fact, we don't need to because the real is always so much more interesting—to me, at least—than anything I could make up. But honoring the trust we have earned is something we cannot take lightly, and the ethics of representation will be covered in Chapter 5.

In my typical playwriting process, while I am conducting interviews, I am also doing extensive research. For *Highway 47* much of this research was at the New Mexico state archives in Santa Fe. When comparing archival documents with how the land grant feud was covered by the press, I discovered that the reportage was spotty, incomplete, and at times misleading. I rarely found a newspaper article that clarified the story or leaned into the complexities of the truth, but rather, many articles embraced bias or oversimplification. This less-than-accurate reportage amplified the disinformation and fueled *Tomeseño's* hatred of one another. I took this research and sampled it, putting it right into the play, so that the audience could see the marked differences for themselves. I then took the transcriptions from our interviews and sampled those as well. For this project, instead of identifying who was on which side of the fight, I took stories from both sides and made characters that were amalgamations of both experiences. For example, I took two interviews from two *abuelitas* on opposite sides of the fight and made one character, The Grandmother, who spoke text from both interviews. I wasn't sure if this would work. The only way to know was to wait until opening night and see what the audience made of it all.

This was a nerve-wracking wait. Not only was I worried about what the audience might take away from the play but we, myself and the producers of Working Classroom, became more and more nervous about what the *Tomeseños* might think. People in Tomé knew about the play, and they bought their tickets for opening night. Given the history of violence, our fears were real. The artistic director of Working Classroom received a phone call from someone vaguely threatening trouble if the play was not "right." Opening night came, and the theatre was filled with *Tomeseños* there to see if I had kept my word, if I would tell the *whole* story.

Rather than describing the performance or the audience's response that night, I'll share one anecdote that speaks to how the play was received: A week or so after opening, my mother got a call from the matriarch of the family who would have been considered one of my father's most fierce enemies. She had seen *Highway 47* and called my mom and invited her over for coffee. They hadn't spoken in decades, they barely glanced at each other in church, but one Saturday afternoon they sat down and had a little coffee and *biscochitos* and had a nice long visit.

It's easy for me to be cynical about art and its value to society. When I hear someone talking about how art can change the world, I can't help but cringe. It sounds naïve to me. But I can say without any cringiness that this play had an impact on our town. It wasn't earth-shattering, it didn't fix what happened, it didn't bring the whole town together in one glorious, healing reunion. It didn't even reach everyone, but it helped build a small bridge between a few people. Listening can in fact repair what is broken, one cup of coffee, one *biscochito* at a time. Not always, sometimes listening can open deeper wounds ... and that in itself can be a different kind of bridge.

In 1971, Dick Cavett hosted one of the most tension-filled, edge-of-your-seat 90 minutes of live impromptu conversation that ever aired on television. His guests were Janet Flanner, the

WWII war correspondent and narrative journalist who for five decades wrote for the New Yorker under the nom de plume Genêt, and the writers, thinkers, verbal brawlers Gore Vidal and Norman Mailer. Mailer was said to be drunk and had head-butted Vidal in the dressing room before the taping. Vidal had recently written a scathing review of Mailer's book about "women's lib" calling him a chauvinist and rolling Henry Miller, Mailer, and Charles Manson into one persona: "The Miller-Mailer-Manson man (or M3 for short) has been conditioned to think of women as, at best, breeders of sons; at worst, objects to be poked, humiliated, killed."[3] Mailer came out onto set, shook hands with Flanner, shook hands with Cavett, and turned his back to Vidal. Cavett's brilliance was to not ignore the snub or make a joke about it but, with all the ease in the world, to address it. He asked what happened, if they are not friends. He did not bate Mailer, he simply wanted to know. And from there Mailer was off, attacking Vidal as being an "intellectual polluter" and a hypocrite of tiny intellect. Flanner interjected, saying she's bored with Mailer's boorish, pugilist behavior, and Vidal deflected every insult with beautifully crafted comments that elicited applause from the live audience. Mailer kept swinging wildly, trying to insult not only Vidal's intelligence, but Flanner and Cavett's as well. Cavett threw himself into the fray by trying to follow one of Mailer's attempted jokes that seemed to fall flat, when Mailer told Cavett, "Why don't you look at your question sheet and ask a question." Cavett didn't move, was very quiet, then looked down, took a breath, and said, "why don't you fold it five ways and put it where the moon don't shine." The audience erupted in applause, and Mailer was knocked over. Mailer then turned to the audience and asked them why they're rooting against him, and the voices of men and women rang out, some shouting that he's just being rude, others calling him a chauvinist pig.

I realize that this is an odd example for me to include in a chapter about building bridges, when I have been making the case for the value of remaining a non-judgmental listener, but Cavett, in this segment, teaches me another value—to always be authentic. Cavett takes great effort to remain neutral, but when insulted, he wasn't going to pretend that it didn't happen.

He had to be himself. And he had to let the conversation go where it was going to go. Toward the end of the segment, Vidal finally stopped deflecting and took a stand. He told Mailer that he excoriated him in this article because he was sick of Mailer's love of violence and glamorization of murder: "The country has had quite enough of that!" The audience burst into applause. At the very end, Cavett made no attempt at tying the night up in a neat bow. He didn't try to get them to shake hands and part as friends. He let the open wound just sit there. That was the moment the country was in—people were taking off the gloves, there were bullies and intellectual snobs and people fighting for equality and civil rights, and there were performers making the most of the mayhem. And I think Vidal tapped into some real truth when he said people were sick of it. That truth rings true today.

This was clearly not a bridge that led to healing. Was it even a bridge at all? Maybe not. Or if it was, maybe it was a bridge toward what many artists and activists are trying to do today by bringing all the rough stuff into the light, with its complexities and contradictions and hypocrisies. We cannot revise the real to make it more palatable. Speaking only for myself, all I can hope for is to listen and let what I hear take me where it will, whether that's a happy place or not, and then to share what I hear with others in the hope that the work can build tiny bridges toward healing or honesty or, at least, recognition. *Listening* is the first step toward building those bridges. When I was a child, Dick Cavett helped me escape my reality, and then when I grew up to become an artist, he became a role model for me so that I could go back and see what I didn't want to see, teaching me how to listen to what I did and did not want to hear.

NOTES

[1] Working Classroom is a 30-year-old arts organization in Downtown Albuquerque, New Mexico with a mission to cultivate "the artistic, civic, and academic minds of youth through in-depth arts projects with contemporary artists to amplify historically ignored voices, resist systemic injustices, and imagine a more equitable society."

[2] This specific example, "my dog died this morning" was originally (many, many years ago) shared with me by Steve Cosson, founder and Artistic Director of The Civilians, who in turn heard this from director and former member of Joint Stock Theater Company, Les Waters. More on both of these artists and the lineage of interview techniques in later chapters.

[3] Vidal, Gore, *In Another Country*, The New York Review, July 22, 1971.

BIBLIOGRAPHY

Cavett, Dick. *Talk Show: Confrontations, Pointed Commentary, and Off-Screen Secrets.* New York: Times Books, 2010.

Cavett, Dick. *Brief Encounters: Conversations, Magic Moments, and Assorted Hijinks.* New York: Henry Holt and Co, 2014.

"Dick Cavett Waxes Poetic on Playing Himself" The Dinner Party Download, American Public Media, April 29, 2016. https://www.dinnerpartydownload.org/category/interview/.

Ebright, Malcolm. *New Mexican Land Grants: The Legal Background.* Albuquerque: University of New Mexico Press, 1987.

"Prime Time: Jimi Hendrix's US Network Television Debut", The Dick Cavett Show July 20, 2021. https://www.jimihendrix.com/editorial/prime-time-jimi-hendrixs-us-network-television-debut-the-dick-cavett-show/.

Sanchez, K. J. Highway 47, Directed by KJ Sanchez, Working Classroom. Albuquerque, New Mexico, April, 2005.

2

LISTENING, MEMORY, AND *ReENTRY*

When we listen to someone and they tell us their story, this exchange between speaker and listener often involves the speaker remembering something from their past. Whether it is something that happened five minutes ago or 30 years ago, the speaker is drawing on memories as they talk and we listen. The act of listening triggers the retrieval of memories.

There is a revolution taking place in the field of neuroscience. A revolution that is as important to how we relate to the mind and memory as the industrial revolution was to how we relate to work and the physical world. Part of this revolution began in the 1970s with Dr. Elizabeth Loftus, whose research suggested that a person's memory of an event can be influenced and altered by external forces. Her research showed that eyewitness accounts can be manipulated during interrogation, depending on who is asking the questions and how the questions are asked. In one of her earliest experiments, Loftus showed subjects recorded videos of car crashes. After an interval of time, the subjects were then asked to recount what they saw and estimate the speed at which the vehicles were traveling. When the questions included words like "collided" or "hit each other" speed estimates were on average 32 and 34 miles per hour, respectively. However, when the prompt included the phrase, "smashed into each other" subjects remembered the cars were traveling faster and estimated speeds on average at 41 miles per hour. They even recalled seeing shattered glass when the question's language was more suggestive of violence, though there was no shattered glass in the video. Lotus wrote, "these results are consistent with the view that the questions asked subsequent to an event can cause a reconstruction in one's memory of that event."[1] Lotus' work has not been without detractors and critics but her impact on how we understand memory is significant.

When I was in college back in the 1980s, the general, average-undergraduate-with-a-budding fascination-with-neuroscience understanding of memory was that we have a thing called short-term memory that is then consolidated into long-term memory, and once that memory is consolidated into long-term form it becomes something concretized, permanent, and difficult to change. We used to think of memory as fact, as this little piece of information that is stored in a safe-box in our brain, and every time we retrieved it, that memory could be relied upon to be true and accurate. Today, neuroscientists like Dr. Cristina Alberini, Professor of Neural Science at New York University, and Dr. Daniela Schiller, Head of the Affective Neuroscience Lab at the Mount Sinai School of Medicine, are continuing the examination of memory. Though their work and conclusions are different from one another, they are both looking at some of the systems involved in memory and memory recall at the synaptic level, the center of the making of memory. As Dr. Schiller told me:

> It started with some findings in animals. The initial evidence was that when an animal was confronted with a reminder cue, a cue that reminds the animal of a negative event that it had learned about, the neural representation of the memory became unstable. And then it had to undergo again the process of re-storage, which is not identical, but it looks quite similar to, as if you're encoding a new event. But it's a memory, right? So, it's not a new event, but it's going to look similar, so it was termed reconsolidation.

Dr. Schiller went on to explain to me that, though there is significant research with animals (studies in the tens of thousands), there are also studies of humans (in the hundreds). All these studies combined are indicating that when we remember, when we retrieve a memory, that memory can, at times, once again be in a vulnerable state, and therefore subject to change. A memory can be open to influence, chemical or suggestive, and when we retrieve it, depending on its strength and what kind of memory it is, that memory can get reconsolidated. So, in lay terms, some of the memories that we remember the least often are possibly the memories most true to the actual event, and some of the memories we recall often are likely being reconsolidated and therefore far less likely to be perfectly accurate. Dr. Schiller's research suggests that some memories are far less reliable than we might think. I asked her ...

KJ: So, do people come up to you and say, you know, *(laughs)* "you're ruining everything because we don't know what's true anymore?"

Dr. Schiller: Yes. I think that most reactions are like: "it's terrible." But I understand that. It is scary because it's like everything you thought true is maybe not true. We don't test our memories on a daily basis. We actually rarely compare notes. We just assume that everybody remembers what we remember. And when you do have situations of comparing notes, it's kind of depressing because the other person says, "No that never happened" or they would remember it differently.

There's also contamination between partners. If you sometimes think it's your memory, but actually it's another person's memory. So, we never really test it. We just assume it's all true. But I found it liberating because memory is this chain. If you assume that what happens is who you *are*, that is very deterministic. But if it's not true, then you're free, you know? You can break those chains.

Also, it's not that everything is lost. It's more that the accuracy of it and the emotional tone and meaning of it is what is constantly dynamic.

KJ: So, for example, if I keep remembering a moment when I felt humiliated and shamed by someone, instead of thinking that that's an accurate memory, am I really just determining what my future is going to be? For some reason I want to always be angry at that person, and so I will always reconstruct that memory in that way

Dr. Schiller: That's exactly what you want to escape and that's kind of the trap we're in now because we think we *are* what we *think*. But actually, what you can say to yourself is, "Oh, now I'm a person who feels humiliation when I think about this event. But I can have, actually, a completely different perspective of that event."

And you can feel compassion toward yourself for being in that situation and then say, "Okay I'm in a good place now. This is the person I am. So ..."

You see what I'm trying to say? Memory tells you, really, who you are *now*.

It's an *experience*. Memory is an experience.

I imagine that our ability to have compassion for ourselves, as we relate to our past via memories, waxes and wanes depending on the memory.

It's important to note that some memories are less vulnerable to reconsolidation than others: Traumatic events are webs that live in many different parts of the brain all at once, because there are physical and emotional dynamics connected to those experiences. Memories of traumatic events—events that are connected to severe physical, psychological, or moral injury—are much more complicated to negotiate. Dr. Schiller's laboratory at the Icahn School of Medicine at Mount Sinai recently collaborated with researchers at Yale University on a study of 28 participants with diagnosed post-traumatic stress disorder (PTSD). Post-traumatic stress (PTS) is a normal human response to either experiencing or witnessing a traumatic event. These normal responses—anxiety, changes in mood, flashbacks, nightmares and other intrusive thoughts—make it difficult to adjust back to everyday life. However, these symptoms tend to fade as time passes. PTSD is diagnosed when these symptoms do not fade away but continue to disrupt daily functioning.

Dr. Schiller and her colleagues published their study on November 30, 2023 in *Nature Neuroscience*. In this study, the 28 participants, all diagnosed with PTSD, underwent MRI brain scans as they listened to previously recorded interviews in which they either discussed a sad, yet not traumatic event, like the passing of an elderly relative, or recounted the traumatic event connected to their PTSD diagnosis. When each subject recounted the sad but non-traumatic event, the MRI scan showed increased activity in the hippocampus, the area generally associated with retrieving and consolidating memories. However, when the subjects listened to the pre-recorded narration of the traumatic event, the increased activity was not in the hippocampus but rather in the posterior cingulate cortex (PCC). As Dr. Schiller explained in an interview with the *New York Times*, the PCC is the area of the brain associated with "processing internal experience" in the present.[2] This study suggests that traumatic memories live in a different part of the brain than non-traumatic memories and that traumatic memories are processed not as memories at all, but as an experience that is happening, again, *in the moment.* This study might have profound implications, as the hope is that therapies can help individuals move these memories from the PCC into the hippocampus, where they can be organized like all other memories.

There is also the issue of lost memory. Dr. Cristina Alberini's research at New York University is working on just that. Her laboratory's website lists their mission:

> Our laboratory focuses on the biological mechanisms underlying memory. In particular, we aim to identify and characterize the mechanisms which control long-term memory formation, storage, retrieval and reconsolidation. Memory is a fundamental and well-conserved biological function, but also a critical component of our human identity. Understanding the biological processes that allow for the formation and storage of long-term memory is important in order to develop strategies to modify memory strength.

> The knowledge gained from this understanding may lead to therapeutic approaches for memory loss including those which occur during aging, in Alzheimer's and other forms of dementia, as well as for memory disorders caused by pathogenically strong memories, such as those associated with post-traumatic stress disorder (PTSD).

I first got to know Dr. Alberini's research after she had seen a play I co-wrote and directed, *ReEntry*. *ReEntry* is based on interviews with Marines returning from combat deployment and includes discussion of PTSD. The genesis of *ReEntry* was personal experience: I have several brothers who served in the military during the US war in Vietnam, and I have seen first-hand the grip such an experience can have on a person's life. Because of my brothers' experiences, I was curious about warfighters who at the time were serving in the US wars in Iraq and Afghanistan. I asked the actor/writer Emily Ackerman[3] to write *ReEntry* with me, as Emily has two brothers who at that time were in the Marine Corps and had served combat deployments in Iraq. We began research after the US invasion of Iraq and spent two years—2006 and 2007—interviewing warfighters who had recently returned from combat deployment. Nearly all of the dialogue in *ReEntry* came from transcriptions of those interviews. One of the individuals I interviewed was a US Marine Corps (USMC) colonel whose battalion led the invasion of Iraq. I, like many other Americans at that time, hoped the war in Iraq could be over relatively soon, and so I asked him what he would do next. He told me:

> I tell guys, I mean, "who's got a crystal ball up your ass? Raise your hand. If you don't, then you don't know what's coming next." And if you had told me on ten September 2001 what was gonna happen, who woulda predicted that? So, uh, we've got five thousand years of recorded military history, "What's in your wallet?" And that's kinda where I am. If I stay in the game, and we really are in this thing for fifty years, you know, someone's gotta get ready for the next one. Intellectually, emotionally, spiritually, somebody has to be the next generation of leaders.

When this commander said we'd be "in this thing" for 50 years I thought, "That's absurd; just not possible." Jump forward to today and, well, maybe more of us should have listened to what these boots-on-the-ground warfighters were telling us about US engagement in Iraq and Afghanistan. I wonder where we would be if our elected leaders were as honest with themselves about our timeline as those doing the fighting. They knew how protracted and complicated the wars in Iraq and Afghanistan would be, and we were simply not listening to them.

The title of our play, *ReEntry*, came from a term used in space travel. It is the process of a space craft returning into Earth's atmosphere after being in outer space. *How* a capsule reenters Earth's atmosphere is critical: If the angle of reentry is too steep, the capsule gains too much speed, which generates too much friction, and the craft will burn up. If the angle is not steep enough, the capsule will bounce off of Earth's atmosphere and get sent back into space. The return has to be just right for the craft to make it back. NASA scientists, engineers, and mathematicians spent so much time, energy, and resources getting a manned ship into outer space, but it was only at the 11th hour that they figured out how to get that ship back home safely. This seemed to me the perfect metaphor for returning from war.

When Emily and I began our interviewing and writing process, all we knew is that we wanted to interview combat veterans and we wanted the play to be about coming home from war.

When conceiving a project, I find it helpful to start with four steps:

1. Identify the subject of inquiry.
2. See, read and study everything I can find on the subject: Newspaper articles, plays, books, movies, podcasts, etc.
3. Based on my opinions and feelings about the work that is already out there, create a list of do's and don'ts and rules of engagement.
4. Find an organizing question, an umbrella inquiry under which all other questions will sit.

We had the subject: Coming home from war. Given that less than one percent of US citizens were serving in the military when our troops invaded Iraq, we believed our play could serve as a bridge between those doing the fighting and the rest of the country they were fighting for.

We then set about building our do's and don'ts and rules of engagement. We watched and read as may war plays, books, and movies as we could. From this we knew:

- Verisimilitude is essential.
- No actors in uniforms—there are far too many movies and plays out there where you see actors in ill-fitting uniforms and helmets too big for them (and *why* don't actors *ever* buckle the straps on their helmets?).
- No scene where the lights go out, then come back up, revealing a soldier with bloody hands looking up at the sky and screaming, "*Why????*" And no scenes in this vein.
- If we can already easily find the information in the news, it doesn't need to go into our play.
- If actors are going to represent the veterans we interviewed, they would need to go thru rigorous and deep training to do so.
- None of our own politics in the play.

This last point was very important. Emily and I were committed to this play *not* being about us. It was about those we listened to and so we had to—at all costs—keep our own politics off the stage.

There were a few other rules of engagement that Emily and I created that guided our interview process. I included the following rules in an article I wrote for *American Theatre* in 2011[4]:

- When interviewing, tell all our subjects that this play is not about the politics of the war, but rather about what it's like to come home. This was a relief to many, since most defined themselves as apolitical, explaining to us that they must be able to serve as "the arm of the people" no matter who is commander-in-chief.
- Don't say things like, "I don't support the war, but I support the troops." Emily was the first to understand this, though I struggled with it for a long time, but I finally understood why this would shut them down: If someone wanted to start a relationship with me and one of their first comments was "I think theatre is irrelevant and a waste of time, but I think it's neat that you're a theatre director" that would certainly *not* encourage me to welcome them into my home and life.

- Take the time to learn a little of their language and a few key rules. Don't call a sailor or a marine a soldier (that's Army), or if you're talking to someone enlisted, i.e., not an officer, don't call them sir or ma'am, call them by their rank: Staff sergeant or sergeant major. It takes a little study to learn the rank and chain of command, but one afternoon of research went very far in establishing trust and respect.
- Thanking someone for their service may not be as welcome as you might think. Though most appreciate the sentiment, many shared with us their conflicted feelings about being thanked. Responses ranged from the benign, as a female Army officer told me, "I guess I feel guilty when people thank me. I didn't see the worst, and I feel guilty about that" to the more emotional, as a staff sergeant who was severely injured in an IED attack told us, "Thank you for what? For getting blown up? For being in the wrong place at the wrong time or for doing what you wouldn't go and do? Whatever, just buy me a beer and we'll call it even." (I break this rule all the time; I still thank them for their service. I just make sure that I know something about them as people before I thank the uniform.)
- Set aside our cultural cliches and assumptions about who "we" and "they" are. For example: We, as a collective of Americans, tend to assume America has a warrior culture. America does not have a warrior culture. We learned this from a commanding officer who was speaking to a room full of parents of young marines at a conference we attended. He told them:

> Believing America possesses a warrior culture reflects more wishful thinking than reality. Much has been said about Americans being desensitized to violence, via Hollywood and video games. But there is no correlation between watching two-dimensional, third-party violence and having the faculties to face and kill an armed opponent, while doing so inside the intensity of fear for one's own life. Our alleged comfort with interpersonal violence is an illusion. We have to shatter these illusions because there's a severe hazard when the expectations of combat are based on wishful thinking and dreaming of Rambo-esque achievements rather than harsh, cold reality and rigorous drill.

Hearing this coming from an infantry commander helped me understand the disconnect between my assumptions and his reality.

- Use audio recorders and transcribe. Use transcriptions directly as dialogue because we don't want to get any of this wrong.
- Have an advisory board made up of veterans and active-duty service members. Their job was not to tell us how to write the play or what to put in it, bad rather, to read drafts and tell us which experiences were missing and provide introductions to people who could share those experiences with us.

The final step was to find *ReEntry's* organizing question. The organizing question wants to be something open enough to allow for many branches of inquiry, and it must be a question not a statement. If I start with a statement, then the work can very easily fall into pedantic, obvious cliches. So, were we to start with "war is bad," then the interviews become fishing expeditions to find the interviews that support our thesis statement. Our organizing question became, "What is it like to go from combat to standing in line at the grocery store?" Then, our paths of inquiry were able to move in many directions and ultimately took us places we did not expect.

We interviewed people who had served in all the different branches of the military, at many different times, in many different wars and deployments. Then about half-way through the process Emily and I decided to go deep rather than wide and chose to focus on only a handful of individuals who we spent more time with over the course of two years, returning to interview them as they continued to serve multiple deployments. We chose to focus our lens even tighter by centering our play on members of the USMC because we were taken by the highly cultivated ethos of the Marine Corps and its tight-knit culture. As that USMC commander once jokingly told me, "We put the cult in culture." About 98% of the dialogue in *ReEntry* came directly from transcriptions with this small group of Marines. We didn't need to create any sort of fictional dramatic arc. All we needed to do was simply spend time with them, listen to them, and listen to how their lives were unfolding as they prepared for war, left to fight, and returned from war ... and then left *again* for redeployment. The drama was inherent in the circumstances. We just needed to listen. And we found that these Marines were telling Emily and I things that they could not say to anyone else because we were not stakeholders in their lives. We weren't their wives or girlfriends or children or parents; we weren't their peers; we weren't their commanding officers; we weren't their therapists. We were simply compassionate, non-judgmental listeners. They knew they could tell us *anything* and we would not judge them one way or another. And they did, in fact, speak quite candidly. One Marine explained to me why he was telling me things he would never say to a therapist (we put this in our play):

> Yes, when you get back you always get "the talk"—get your tempers under control. And you're given a form to fill out. Everyone lies on that form—of course you do. They ask, "What did you see?" And you give them the bare minimum. They ask you, "Did it effect you?" And you say, "No, absolutely not." Because it would be the end of my career, of course, at this level? No, you lie through your teeth. If I had seen a therapist, I wouldn't be where I am now. I know that.
>
> I never raised a hand to my wife, never raised my voice. I was full of self-loathing, and that's when the insomnia really kicked in, but I took care of it all myself. I'm very disciplined about my vitamin A ... Ambien? Oh yeah, time for bed, I take my Ambien, and I put myself to bed."

It was this very sentiment—that a career warfighter would never talk to a therapist—that set a whole new trajectory for *ReEntry:* After *ReEntry* ran Off-Broadway, I had a very interesting meeting with Dr. William P. Nash,[5] a retired Navy Captain and psychiatric researcher, educator, and author, who at the time was senior policy consultant in Combat and Operational Stress Control (COSC) for the Navy and Marine Corps. He had seen *ReEntry* in New York. I'll get back to Dr. Nash in a moment, but a quick tangent first ...

It was in New York at our first preview that I had one of the biggest revelations of my career. We invited some of the Marines we had interviewed to come see the show. They sat in that theatre next to "average" New York theatre-going audience members—that is to say, an audience of liberal New Yorkers, who had probably not served and likely didn't even know anyone serving in our wars. I sat in the back row, and as the performance began, I watched these combat veterans watching our play. I wasn't the only one who knew there were service members in the audience. It was likely most of the civilian audience knew as well—an Off-Broadway theatre is a rather tiny venue, and a Marine is hard to miss, even in street clothes. So as the performance proceeded, there were certain lines in the play that got robust laughter, the kind of laughter that only comes from firsthand experience. *ReEntry* has a lot of humor because Marines are often very funny. They work on being funny. In fact, that same colonel who led the US invasion of Iraq told me that they teach the value of humor to officers in training because a laugh interrupts one's breathing pattern, changing the breath, which can break up the body's panic cycle. If a Marine is in trouble, a well-placed joke can actually save someone's life. So, *ReEntry* has some jokes, and many of the jokes are dark and quite irreverent.

At that first preview, during the first 20 minutes of the performance, I could tell that the civilian audience was nervous and not sure if they should laugh, but when it became clear that the veterans in the room were laughing, they taught the rest of the audience that it was ok to laugh. And when scenes got emotional toward the end of the play, as the veterans in the room held their breath, the rest of the audience did so as well. It was really something to behold, and this memory (as I place it in a fragile state and reconsolidate the memory as I write and remember!) takes me right back to that moment when I realized that by sitting in a room *together*—civilians who had no connection to these wars and veterans who were literally giving *everything*—by listening to these stories together, the theatre was actually, tangibly, *viscerally*, building a bridge between people. And the play was saying to that tiny percentage of Americans serving, "We see you. We hear you. You matter."

After he saw the show, Dr. Nash and I met for coffee and he told me about a conference he was planning for military leaders to examine the effects of combat operational stress, moral injury, and PTSD. Dr. Nash and his colleagues knew that they were looking at protracted wars and that they needed to prepare for the effect that unprecedented numbers of multiple deployments would have on troops. They were also familiar with warfighters' reluctance to seek therapy, so were exploring progressive ways to encourage troops to get help. Dr. Nash wanted to present *ReEntry* as a keynote at his conference for military leaders.

A few weeks later, there we were, performing our play for hundreds of military brass. Right after our performance the first person to speak was USMC Major General Thomas S. Jones,[6] who talked about the difficulties in getting Marines to seek help. He said that they could use the play as an entry point for discussing the traumatic effects of war. The next to speak was USMC Base Quantico's Command SgtMaj Leon Thornton who hired us that very day to perform *ReEntry* at Quantico. After that first base performance, word traveled through military channels, and for about seven years my company, American Records, contracted with the Department of Defense and took *ReEntry* to military bases across the country and internationally, where it was used as post-deployment resiliency training for troops returning from combat.

We also performed at VA hospitals as sensitivity training for staff and at Camps Pedleton and Lejuene for recruits and drill instructors. Most often troops were not told that they were called to watch a play but were simply ordered to show up for resiliency training. I would introduce myself, note the intense content of the play, and let the troops know that they were welcome to get up and stand in the back, or leave and come back, or just leave, if they needed to. We had chaplains and mental health professionals at all the exits, and if they wanted to talk with one of them, they were there at their service. I would also note that the play was not meant to represent everyone's experiences and that however they responded was fine by us. After the performance, I would lead a town-hall discussion and would ask two simple questions:

1. Were there any characters in the play that you identified with, and if so, can you talk about that?
2. If we were to write *ReEntry* part two based on your experiences, what else should we put in the play?

These two questions were enough to start them talking about their own experiences, struggles, and needs. We found that individuals who had trouble speaking about themselves had a much easier time talking about the characters in the play. I suspect that a big part of what made *ReEntry* a helpful tool was that military leadership was not running the conversation. I was, and I was nobody. Leadership sat in the back and listened; they did not speak. And I think they heard an awful lot: They heard troops express their distrust and lack of faith in the mental health profession. They heard troops talk about all the other stresses in their life and their frustrations with leadership. Most importantly the service members got a chance to listen to each other, which helped them see that they were not alone in their struggles.

There is one section of the play that generated much discussion, which I include below. FYI, the characters speak directly to the audience as though they are being interviewed in the moment. Trigger warning: The material includes reference to acts of violence and suicide …

CHARLIE

Yeah, my sister doesn't like some of the shit I say. Well, they're thinking of sending me back, and I'm like, "If I fucking go back, shit's going to be different. Like, I'm going to fucking kill some people. I don't care. I'm not going to be doing shit the same way we did before if I go back. 'Cause there are people that need to be shot. And there's all these rules and shit, stuff that we can't do. So if I have to go back over there, and get fucking shot at and get blown up, I am going to get the job done." Liz doesn't like it when I say that stuff. And going fast on my motorcycle. She says that I am living like I'm already dead. Whatever. I need to get a weapon. I would feel better. Seriously, if I had a gun I would feel better. Like, I would be able to protect myself if something happened or something.

(CHARLIE recedes but doesn't exit.)

JOHN

Everything you people get so excited about is fucking pointless. Like, fucking recycling. Go anywhere else on Earth and there is so much shit burning in the streets. There's so much crap just burning everywhere. You look at, like, an old car just burning in the streets and the smoke it generates and you're like, "Yeah, I'm glad I recycled that motherfuckin' milk bottle!" You know? It's pointless. If you're so bored with yourself that you get excited about recycling, then you need to get a hobby. One person recycling some fuckin' soda cans makes about as much sense as a Tyrannosaurus Rex trying to take a shit on a napkin so as not to make a mess!

What should we do? You want my honest opinion? Everyone that is pissing us off, we should nuke the shit out of them and turn their country into glass and then build it in our own fashion!

Right now, I'm just happy that I'm not being shot at. But at the same time, I'm kinda upset that I don't have anyone to shoot. It's like, yeah, I do wish I had a relationship, a girlfriend. I do. But how do we marry these two extremes? Like, back in the day all the women wanted to be with a gladiator, right? Well, try to take a gladiator to god-damned dinner! Cause for the most part it's, like, you are trained to be a certain way—to do certain things—and then you are just supposed to turn that off and go back into society with the rest of you fuckin' pussies?!?

(JOHN slams and lays a locker down horizontal on the ground then recedes but doesn't exit. A small shift. LIZ and MOM have been in the background of this scene and now come forward).

LIZ

Have you seen their tattoos? I have some of them on my phone. Here, let me show you.

(PROJECTION: a black band tattoo wrapping around a bicep.)

This is John's. It's a mourning band. He said it hurt like hell to get it. And here, these are Charlie's ...

(PROJECTION: a tattoo across the shoulder is a skeleton Grim Reaper wrapped in the American flag.)

This is on one arm, and this is on the other ...

(PROJECTION: A tattoo across the other shoulder of boots, an upside-down rifle, and helmet with the words "BROTHERS IN ARMS, NEVER FORGOTTEN"—the memorial of a fallen Marine.)

LIZ

It says, "Brothers in arms, never forgotten."

(pauses, then decides to continue) A few weeks ago ... Charlie had a flashback. It started with him not feeling right. He said that he wasn't feeling like himself. He was angry and couldn't control his emotions. And he did go to someone in his command. I don't know who—probably like a lower-ranking guy. And the guy was like, "Suck it up, you're a Marine." And I'm sure Charlie was like, "It's not a big deal. I lived." I'm making that up, but I feel that that's probably what happened. So he was back on the base and in a training op and he—you know, big loud noises, explosions ...—and he had a flashback. He just froze. And that's a very big fucking deal when you're a Marine—when they're like "go, go, go" and you don't do anything—you just freeze.

MOM

He was out in the field, and he was just incapacitated. He was in the middle of the flashback, and he couldn't get himself out of it, so they took him out and took him to medical.

LIZ

Whoever it was, whatever douche told him to suck it up—it makes me furious, all this tough-guy, "PTSD is for pussies." I know, I know, it's not all like that—a lot of them do take it very seriously. Charlie's commanding officer did pull him out, and he's getting help. But Jesus, Charlie wouldn't even go to the doctor after the IED, when his eye was all fucked up ...

MOM

He was clearly having some problems with his vision. Symptoms of what I thought was a detached retina. But he wouldn't go. And I really thought it was because he was comparing what had happened to him to what had happened to his friends, and he just felt like a wuss even saying anything about himself at all. He would not go.

LIZ

The very same week Charlie gets taken out of the field? John fell apart ... He was home alone, and he said he had been drinking by himself. And he drinks ... he drinks a lot. And he was sitting out on his balcony, and he realized how exposed he was out there. You know, he saw all the positions where a sniper could be. He's sitting on his balcony in San Diego, California, and he's looking around for snipers. And he became absolutely convinced that someone was gonna come into his house and kill him. So he got his guns out. He had a shotgun pointed at the door. Thank God his roommate didn't come home. But he knew he was losing it. He knew it wasn't real. But it seemed and felt so real that he then knew that the only way to stop it ... was to kill himself.

MOM

John texted Charlie something to the effect of, "I'm having a hard time here. Can you come over?" And when Charlie got there, John was very drunk, had all of his guns out, and was talking about how he was going to blow his head off and how life wasn't worth living and all that. And Charlie just stayed with him until John fell asleep, finally, because he was so drunk. And that was when Charlie called me to tell me what was going on.

When I first saw John, when I first got there ... he was like a zombie. I don't think I even said anything to him. I just held him and patted him, and ... he really didn't talk about all of that. He really didn't talk, at all. I just said, "I'm here." And he said, "Thanks."

Yes, I was furious when it happened. I was furious that anybody would be in that position to become so emotionally harmed by what they have been through. I felt helpless as well because I didn't know what to do except let my mothering instincts take over. And that's what I did. That is what I had to offer them. There's no way I can be his psychiatrist, and I can't patronize him or tell him that things are going to be fine and get over it. All I could do was take care of him. I just wrapped my arms around him. I held him tight, let him know I was there, that I had him.

You know, if they want to talk about it? I'm here. But I'm—you know, how do they say, on a need-to-know basis? If they had something they thought I needed to know, they would tell me.

But I have to tell you, that weekend? I was more terrified for my sons' lives than any of the times that they were deployed.

LIZ

When they're deployed, you try not to think about it, but you do. You prepare yourself for the possibility—that they could get hurt, they could die. But you know ... if they get hurt or whatever over there, well, at least it's the bad guy's fault. But if something happens *here*? Who's fault is that? I don't know what to do. I mean, really, what am I supposed to do? *(gives up; can't talk anymore)*

MOM

You know, the thing about John, I know that he isn't just this big, bad Marine, but a sensitive, caring person. I think I told you, he did an internship at a funeral home before he became an officer. And he would be the one to go when they got a call to go pick up the body. And one of the calls he had was to a four-year-old boy who had been sick, and they had planned for this boy to die at home. And when he went to pick up the little guy, John—John wasn't going to put him in the back—in the back of the hearse. He held him in his arms. And that's a big, bad Marine. He didn't tell me any of this—the mother of the boy did.

Now that John and Charlie are facing difficult things, I just feel very grateful that they have each other. To keep each other going. And I know that Tommy—When I called Charlie the other day, you know, to see if he was taking his meds—basically, "I'm watching you!" – Tommy was there. Tommy was there to take care of Charlie. I was glad for that.

(LIZ and MOM exit. Lights. TOMMY enters.)

TOMMY

Yeah, I'm looking out for Charlie. But I can't do nothing about his *World of Warcraft* addiction. Can't do nothin' about that. I hate that game. He got help though. Yeah, I knew he had PTSD. He's like, "How do you know I've got it?" And I'm like, "I know you've got it." The scenario we were in, and after I talked to him a couple times, and he started drinking more, too. And I was like, "Dude ... you were in between Jay and I." We were in a little like triangle thing. He got shrapnel from the both of us—probably got shrapnel from my body parts and from Jay's body parts, too. All of a sudden you see your friend, like, blown up and your other friend, like, bleeding to death. We were in the middle of nowhere. I was like, "You saw two of your colleagues just get mutilated." Yeah, he freaked out.

Um, yeah, I'm getting out. I don't know what I'm going to do—something. No, I don't want to, but I don't have a choice. Well ... *(takes off glasses)* see how my eyes are all brown with blue in the center? Yeah, I'm blind for the rest of my life. It sucks ass, but it could be worse.[7]

When I began booking these performances, I couldn't believe that the Department of Defense would want to present such incendiary material *without any censorship.* We went to over fifty military bases and hospitals; all read the script beforehand and not a single chain of command asked for revisions. In fact, the only people to have ever asked Emily and I to change the content of the play were colleagues in theatre. Some of our artistic colleagues felt the play should take a stand against the war. One artistic director insisted that we change the ending to make a clear anti-war statement. This artistic director wanted us to tie the ending up in a neat bow. We never did, never gave in. We couldn't end the play in any definitive statement at all because the wars were ongoing and the reality was that John and Charlie—with as many challenges as they faced—were being redeployed. They were going back. And we were not going to pretend otherwise. There was nothing neat and tidy about these wars. No doubt that what Charlie says about "killing some people" and John talking about turning another country "into glass" and then rebuilding it in our own fashion is rather terrifying. But our military audiences made the connection between that fear and rage at others and how easily it can then turn inward toward self-harm. That's why our play was brought to bases, because commanders, chaplains, and mental health workers could see the rising rates of suicide and motorcycle accidents and needed to find any and all ways of addressing this crisis. And one of the strategies was to let warfighters speak. And to listen. And let them listen to each other.

As I ran these post-performance discussions, I listened to hundreds of service members tell their stories. We all sat and listened. As each warfighter told their story, they revisited the memory of a particular day, a particular experience, one moment of extreme trauma. And now I wonder: did that context affect how that person now remembers that experience? Did the act of telling listeners their story actually have an effect on the physical makeup of the memory itself?

When talking with Dr. Daniela Schiller, as she described how external influences like time and place can impact memory and how those memories can be reconsolidated when we recall them, I wondered about the role of narrative and storytelling in the process:

KJ: This discussion about memory makes me think of Homer. *The Iliad* and *The Odyssey*, there's a theory that the author Homer was never a person, but Homer was a group of people and the story was told and retold through oral storytellers. And so, each of those storytellers is remembering the story that they heard and then telling the story again, and so the story gets rewritten and rewritten and rewritten throughout time. It's just something that I thought of, of memories being so malleable and when you describe piecing them together like a puzzle, there's so much art in retrieval of memory.

Dr. Schiller: Yeah. Absolutely. I completely agree. I was actually also thinking about Homer. Because when one person retrieves the memory again and again, it's like it really was transferred between different people. Because you are a different person, in each time. Each timepoint you have changed and your life changed and your knowledge changed, your mood changed, everything changed. So, it's really like a story that is being transferred among, you know, different people. So, it's really like something that is constantly being created and changed.

Since the beginning of recorded time, we have told our stories, stories of struggle and danger and trauma. Why is it that in one form or another we have always had some sort of "you speak, I listen, and thru this exchange we heal" process? From stories around a campfire to talk therapy, speaking and listening has been a part of who we are as a species. I asked Dr. Christina Alberini about this instinct to heal through telling our story. Though she suggested that perhaps we place too much emphasis on talk therapy, she offered:

> I don't know of any scientific studies that have demonstrated why, but if you look at perhaps interpretations even by therapists, or psychoanalysts, what they would say is putting those experiences into words help contextualize them. Traumas often have a major component that is emotional. And often who is traumatized cannot talk about it—often those memories are very blurry because when there is too much stress or stress recognition, and that is known, the memories are less clear and there is a memory impairment that happens in those conditions. So, they are very scattered and have a lot of emotions attached.
>
> For someone who is traumatized, it is not that easy to get into recalling memory, but with help, especially with time, when they become able to talk about it, then they contextualize the memory.

Perhaps contextualizing our memories may play a role in helping us move traumatic memories from the PCC (where they are experienced in the moment over and over again) to the hippocampus (where they can be organized as an experience of the past, not present.)

Dr. Alberini helped me understand that memory is not just about the big moments or experiences in our lives, but is central to who we are, how we learn to function and live our lives:

> We are who we are because of our memories. And memories are not just what we remember consciously, it's also everything we do—coming home from the walk, finding the place where I live, grabbing a glass for drinking water, they're *all* memories. And you know, you take a newborn—they're born, they don't know anything; they cannot do anything, and the learning that we see in those developmental ages is extraordinary. You can think about the motor learning, when they learn how to walk, how much they practice. Because they're learning. It's the same for learning about relationships, and places, and communication, and of course language.

Learning to walk, to talk, to feed ourselves, these all become memories that help us survive. If I touch a skillet from out of the oven and burn myself, the memory of that pain teaches me—i.e., *reminds* me not to do that again. My memory keeps me from harming myself. Dr. Alberini responds:

> That's why biologically the memories of negative experiences are very strong, because we have to protect ourselves from danger. So, in a way trauma is a byproduct of protecting our existence.

Dr. Alberini went on to tell me that though traumatic experiences might sometimes be less likely to become vulnerable to reconsolidation, each time we recall them there is the opportunity to *recontextualize* them:

> The memory, it's now clear from many studies, it's not a stable representation, it's not a stable box that we have and that we open every time we want to retrieve the memory, that's clear. It becoming fragile and reconsolidated *every* time it's retrieved, that's not correct. Sometimes it reconsolidates and other times it doesn't. Sometimes we make *new* memories that are *linked* to what we retrieve. So, we recall a memory, and then we change it because in the present we have other experiences and then we link them to the recalled memory, and now the memory is linked to something new. And if you think about the many times that we do that, over a lifetime, you can imagine that when we recall memories and we recall the linked memories as well, they're not all accurate. And that's how we mix and match when we recall memories. And the memories may not be accurate because we may remember a person from a context, but we actually place it into another time or into another context, and then we link them all together. When we store them again, we make these links to the new experiences. The essence of the research says that memories are not stored in a fixed manner. They change, over time.

My takeaway from this conversation makes me wonder about our *ReEntry* sessions on military bases. I wonder how many of those memories that warfighters shared with us and with their fellow warfighters are now linked to the experience of seeing the play and then sharing their own experiences. How many are recontextualized with the experience of sharing their stories with peers and hearing peers share their own, and the *collective* understanding that what for them seemed to be a singular experience now comes with the knowledge that they are not alone?

I also wonder about being redeployed and the possibility of having old memories re-triggered while one is deployed again. How many of those memories and experiences are becoming linked? And what effect might that have on the individual? What effect does that have on the individual who is redeployed dozens of times during their career in the military?

And now, our troops are not only being redeployed to combat zones but are also being deployed and redeployed to serve as first responders to natural disasters. I worked with the US Navy on a version of *ReEntry* that would specifically address the challenges that sailors, Seabees (Naval Construction Battalions), and Navy SEALs are facing, given that they are the branch of the military most often deployed to provide aid after natural disasters. With climate change has come increased severe weather, which is leading to increased events such as droughts, floods, mudslides, and wildfires, and the US Navy is experiencing an uptick in deployments to natural disaster sites.

For this second script, I conducted new interviews, and one that sticks with me today was an interview with a Navy chaplain who told me (trigger warning: Discussion of extreme human injury):

> Something most civilians don't know is sailors serve on a lot of disaster relief deployments.
>
> With combat, it can be very intense for 20 minutes or two hours and then eight months of boredom. On disaster relief it's ... it's very stressful most of the time. You're doing things from picking up body parts, going to a blown-up plane and picking up bodies, or going to a flood zone and recovering people's lives and personal possessions knowing that that person's life is never going to be the same, and those images, they don't go away.

The first week back from a disaster relief deployment ... you have to adjust to the fact that you're in a different world. You're in a world where if gas prices go up ten cents, things are really bad. Not a world where people can't get water unless they walk ten miles.

I think it's natural to feel guilty and grateful at the same time. Some of the more difficult ones are when you go to a disaster site and you're not allowed to help as much as you can. And so, what you've got to understand when you're young and when you're new is that you're not the one making the decisions. There's a lot of political choices you can't control. It's following orders and doing the best you can.

You know, a lot of expeditionary sailors were deployed helping other people on the planet while their own families were suffering during Katrina. So just the, uh, the absolute paradox and the absolute irony of being out there and handing out food to people that are having a hard time in life and knowing that your family may be in trouble is something that takes a long time to get over.

And coming home, it takes a little while. It's not uncommon to come back and look at everyone as though they have an agenda because when you see the worst in people—sometimes you project that onto humanity itself. So that's part of it ... learning to trust society again after seeing the worst of the world.

You know, my wife, my kids ... I want them to understand some of the things that I've done, but I don't want them to experience the hardships. But ... to step off onto the bridge wing and look up on a cloudless night, and you see the stars and not one or two here or there, but thousands. You see the Milky Way and it's bright! Like someone took a piece of gold lace and stretched it from horizon to horizon. I share that with my kids. The fact that I'm out there and looking a dolphin in the eyes and it's playing in front of you. I share that.

You asked earlier "Are there times when you don't know what to do?" Well, there are moments when you need to know yourself and the situation well enough to say 'This is something bigger than I can handle.' And that's a scary thought. Cause at that point you recognize what fragileness you have ... that you're handling. When a sailor or marine comes to me and I give him some guidance, they have every right to say 'you're full of it and I'm gonna keep on doing what I'm doing.' And I'd love to go out and grab 'em from out in front of the train that they seem fixed to run right in front of but ya can't. When you're in a tunnel, there's this big light. "So, ya see that?" "Yeah." "That's not the end. That's a big engine that's fixin' to run you down."

As the chaplain said so beautifully, returning from traumatic experiences is a difficult process. Just like that of a spacecraft, the warfighter's trajectory of return has an immense impact on how, or even if, they make it back whole. All of our past experiences—the good and the terrible—live in our memories. And we now understand that those memories might be accurate sometimes and might be completely unreliable at other times. Our memories get reconsolidated sometimes, and other times they get recontextualized or linked. Our memories are networks that live in different parts of our brain, in different parts of our bodies. Each time we ask someone to tell us their story, we are asking them to retrieve a memory and thereby offering an opportunity for reconsolidation or recontextualization. If we are what we think and what we think is tied to what we remember, then the act of listening becomes an active part of changing who we are.

NOTES

[1] Loftus, Elizabeth, & Guido Zanni. "Eyewitness Testimony: The Influence of the Wording of a Question." *Bulletin of the Psychonomic Society* 5 (1975): 86–88.
[2] Barry, Ellen. "Brain Study Suggests Traumatic Memories Are Processed as Present Experience." *New York Times*, November 30, 2023.
[3] Emily Ackerman is a member of the Civilians where she originated roles in seminal Civilian productions including *This Beautiful World* and *Gone Missing*.
[4] From "Joining Forces" by K.J. Sanchez. Originally appeared in *American Theatre* Magazine, 28, no. 6 (July/August 2011). Used with permission from Theater Communications Group.
[5] William P. Nash, MD, was Director of Psychological Health for the US Marine Corps. While on active duty in the Navy, Dr. Nash was deployed to Iraq with Marines of the 1st Marine Division during the Second Battle of Fallujah. He is the coeditor of *Combat Stress Injuries: Theory, Research, and Management* published by Routledge, an imprint of Taylor and Francis Group, New York, and coauthor of *Adaptive Disclosure: A New Treatment for Military Trauma, Loss, and Moral Injury* published by The Guilford Press, New York.

[6] General Jones is now retired and is the founder and Executive Director of Outdoor Odyssey: https://www.outdoorodyssey.org/our-team.

[7] Sanchez, K. J., and Emily Ackerman. *ReEntry*. Playscripts Inc., 2010. To purchase the full script of *ReEntry* please visit www.playscripts.com.

BIBLIOGRAPHY

Alberini, Cristina M. Alberini Lab: NYU Center for Neural Science. 16 February, 2017.

Alberini, Cristina M. *Dana Alliance for Brain Initiatives Elects Fifteen New Members*. Dana Foundation. 4 February, 2020.

Alberini, Cristina. *Telephone Interview*. September 13, 2022.

American Psychiatric Association. Diagnostic and Statistical Manual of Mental Disorders: DSM-5-TR. 5th ed., text revision. Washington, DC: American Psychiatric Association Publishing, 2022.

Levin, Aaron "From Theater of War to Theater Stage, Soldiers Reveal Their Thoughts." *Psychiatric News* 46, no. 3 (2011): 1.

Perl, O., O. Duek, K. R. Kulkarni, et al. "Neural Patterns Differentiate Traumatic from Sad Autobiographical Memories in PTSD." *Nature Neuroscience* 26 (2023): 2226–236.

Sanchez, K. J. *Scaling a Project: As Easy as Alpha, Bravo, Charlie*. Artsblog, Americans For the Arts, December 11, 2012.

Sanchez, K. J. Lessons from the Road: 7 Theaters, 17 Military Bases, 8 Hospitals, and 4 Conferences Later, How a Girl Fell in Love with Touring, *Howlround*. October 14, 2012.

Schiller, Daniela. *Telephone Interview*. July 24, 2022.

Schiller, D., M. H. Monfils, C. Raio, et al. "Preventing the Return of Fear in Humans Using Reconsolidation Update Mechanisms." *Nature* 463 (2010): 49–53.

3

LISTENING AND RECONCILIATION

I'm curious about the connection between our ability to listen to others and how we listen to our own instincts and intuition. Where does the impulse for inquiry come from? Sometimes it comes from external sources: We are hired to investigate, or we see something remarkable (beautiful or terrible) that we *must* share with others; other times it comes from within us: There is something we need to figure out for ourselves and the work becomes a kind of seeking-out, and what we're searching for are answers to questions:

What happened?

Why did what happened happen?

How do I make sense of it?

My own work began with a need to make sense of a personal and painful experience. I needed to understand what I was feeling, and I needed to create intellectual and emotional systems for organizing this difficult experience, not to find closure or resolution, because I'm not sure I believe closure or resolution really exists, but rather, what I was seeking was *comprehension*.

In my young adulthood, I experienced what many people have, unfortunately, experienced: The loss of a loved one to mental illness. One of my brothers, who was diagnosed schizophrenic, took his life. Many know this pain—the heartbreak we and our siblings feel, the crushing sadness for their spouse and children, and the unbearable reality of witnessing a parent mourn the loss of a child. I didn't know where to put all this sadness; I didn't know how to make sense of the senseless.

Over time, the sadness did not dissipate, but I found scraps of solace in research. I started seeking out studies on schizophrenia, which were helping me see mental illness as an *illness* like any other physical illness; I read about the history and relationship of suicide and the Catholic Church (which did not make suicide a sin until Thomas Aquinas condemned it in the 13th century), which helped me unmask the shame and guilt and see the complicated ways politics has informed church teachings on what is good or evil; I read about others' experiences with this kind of loss, which helped me understand that I was not alone. To this day, I still seek comfort in stories shared by others, such as Miriam Toews's 2015 novel, *All My Puny Sorrows,* which is about her sister's mental illness and their family's history with suicide. Toews, whose eight novels include *A Complicated Sadness* and *Women Talking*,[1] begins her process with her own lived experiences or someone else's real story that she has personal knowledge or familiarity with. She then builds fiction from or around the real. In an interview with Katrina Onstad for *The Guardian* August 18, 2018, Toews describes *Women Talking* as an "imagined response" to a real crime.

I've also taken comfort and inspiration from other artists who take the real and difficult things of the world and use art to process and comprehend, such as the actor, writer, and monologist Spalding Gray. Gray began his career in theatre in the late 1960s as part of Richard Schechner's seminal experimental theatre company, The Performance Group. Then, in the early 1970s, Gray co-founded The Wooster Group with Elizabeth

LeCompte and Willem Dafoe. In addition to performing other writers' work, Gray began performing monologues that he wrote himself. Gray's 1983 *Swimming to Cambodia*[2] is, for me, a shining example of what theatre can do when it begins with the self and then expands into societal inquiry. In his 1986 review of Gray's *Terrors of Pleasure*, New York Times Theatre critic Mel Gussow wrote that Gray "invented a new performance art form," and I agree. Gray, with *Swimming to Cambodia* and with all of his subsequent monologues, kept his *mise en scene* rigorously simple: He sat at a desk, and on this desk was a microphone, a few loose-leaf pages with an outline (which he rarely referenced) and a glass of water. Behind him hung a world map. That was it—no theatrical bells and whistles, just a man sitting at a desk. And this man was *just* talking. He was free-associatively talking about his experiences and life, telling a story that was four hours long, told over two evenings.

Swimming to Cambodia was set in motion by Gray's experience acting in a small role in the 1984 film *The Killing Fields*,[3] which was based on the real experiences of New York Times correspondent Sydney Schanberg and Cambodian journalist Dith Pran. The film covers the 1973 civil war between the Cambodian National Army and the Khmer Rouge, the US involvement in this war, the 1975 arrival of the Khmer Rouge in Phnom Penh, the closing of US embassies, the forced evacuation of all US journalists, and Dith Pran's struggle to stay alive under the Khmer Rouge's reign of terror. Gray played a US Consul in this film, and though his role was rather small, his time on location (shot in Thailand) was unusually long. Gray described himself as a "collage artist"[4] and in this, his first work in monologue form, he collaged experiences that ran the gamut from the geopolitical quagmire of the US involvement in the wars in Vietnam and Cambodia to rambling stories of tourism in Thailand, to his life back in New York City, where he and his partner had an ongoing battle with noisy neighbors. Moving seamlessly from the profound to the banal, Gray was fueled only by his insatiable curiosity and need for comprehension. When I watch video recordings of Spalding Gray's performances, I see a man starved for understanding, recreating a moment using nothing but his own mastery of language, desperately trying to figure something out. In his own words, he was "using the public to figure it out."[5]

In the years after my brother's death, I turned to art making as a way of helping me figure out how to live with my loss. But I had no idea how to do so. I had never written my own play.

However, I did have a pile of research and some technique to start with. That technique was rooted in the art of sampling. At the beginning of my career, when I was an actor living in New York, I had the good fortune to work with the theatre maker and artistic pioneer, Anne Bogart. I was in her SITI Company[6] for the first few years of the company's life. With the SITI Company, I performed and collaborated in the creation of three original works: *Going, Going, Gone*; *Small Lives Big Dreams*; and *Culture of Desire*. All three works were built in relatively the same fashion: Anne would first offer an organizing question to the ensemble comprised of actors, designers, dramaturgs, stage managers, and (what I loved about working with Anne) anyone else who was in the room and truly listening. Anne's organizing question would generate a pile of research. Then, in a relatively short workshop or rehearsal process, a time frame that offered what Anne might call "the exquisite pressure of time," we would get on our feet and explore physical sequences; later the same day we'd sit around a table and collectively write the script—with all the dialogue directly sampled from our research. Similar to how a DJ samples someone else's "hooks" into their own new tune, we sampled words from a wide variety of sources into a collage of moments, words, sounds, repetitions, dances, and compositions that put Bogart's organizing question through a kind of creative prism, and the result was a performance of those many refractions. Our goal, at least as I understood it as an actor/writer working from the inside, was to multiply the potential ways our audience might find their own kinesthetic, emotional, and intellectual responses to the subject. I saw my work with SITI as a call *not* to answer the question, but to be the catalyst for multiplying it.

In 1999, when I was ready to make my own work, I relied on these techniques of dance theatre and sampling extant text as my first steps toward making a theatre piece about what happened to my brother. My intention was not to make a work that was

LISTENING AND RECONCILIATION 51

literally about him—that story wasn't mine alone to tell, as it belonged to his wife, children, my siblings, and my mother. I needed to find an avatar for my inquiry, which I found in Shakespeare's Ophelia, a character I had played in Jon Jory's production of *Hamlet* at Actors Theatre of Louisville. Performing Ophelia is a very lonely experience. The play is about a man who might be mad or might just be acting mad, and everyone is worried about him. Yet right in the middle of it all is a young woman actually, truly going mad ... and no one even notices. She's the perfect good girl who does everything that is asked of her, and no one sees her fall between the cracks.

And so, I used Ophelia's character arc in Shakespeare's *Hamlet* as a skeleton narrative structure for my own play, which I titled *Too Much Water*. My organizing question was: At the end of Ophelia's life, if she had one more dream before moving on to the afterlife, what would Ophelia dream? Collaborating with students at the University of Washington, our production started with Ophelia's burial. She then crawled out of her grave and revisited her scenes in *Hamlet*. Between those scenes, I collaged dances and found text that explored the themes of mental illness, suicide, and being unseen. I hadn't found my interview process[7] yet so relied on sampling others' writing. (A few decades later, I now use sampling much more judiciously, and properly cite and get permissions.)

Once I was introduced to and fell in love with making plays from interviews, my method of playwriting changed, but my modus of inquiry did not. I was still using the work to understand, and once I started listening to others, my circle of inquiry expanded beyond trying to understand my own experiences to trying to understand the experiences of others.

One afternoon in May 2006, I sat on a metal folding chair in a small room used for storing props and supplies. Sitting across from me and so close our knees nearly touched was a man I will call Henry. Henry's not his real name. I promised Henry that I would never use his real name. Henry had recently gotten out of prison after serving many years in a maximum-security prison facility in California. Henry leaned forward, resting his forearms on his thighs. He looked at the floor and every few minutes would wring his hands. As we talked, little by little, Henry began to look up. We talked about his parole and the rehabilitation program he was in. We talked about living in Los Angeles and how much had changed since he was sent to prison. We talked about the weather and traffic and the best place to get tacos downtown. Eventually, we talked about Henry's wife. And he told me about the day he killed her.

He didn't mean to kill her. He meant to shoot the car driven by his wife's new boyfriend. Henry shot at the car, attempting to scare them, but the bullet ricocheted and hit his wife, killing her. Henry pleaded guilty and went to prison. And every night of every day since that day, his wife comes to him in his dreams. He throws himself at her feet, weeping, and begs her for forgiveness.

Henry agreed to talk with me because I was writing a play for the Los Angeles-based Cornerstone Theater Company. For over 30 years, Cornerstone's mission has been to make plays "with and about communities," and the company is dedicated to the precept that "artistic expression is civic engagement and that access to a creative forum is essential to the wellness and health of every individual and community."[8] Cornerstone commissioned me to make a play that would be produced as part of their Justice Cycle[9]—a series of plays centered on questions of justice in America. My offering was a play titled *For All Time*.

For All Time was a meditation on one question: How do people, both victims *and* perpetrators of violent crime, move forward after an act of violence? As part of this project, I wanted to listen to people who had served prison sentences for violent crimes. I wasn't trying to write a play about wrongfully accused individuals—that play has already been made and is titled *The Exonerated*, written in 2002 by Jessica Blank and Eric Jensen. *The Exonerated* was based on legal records and interviews with death row inmates who had been freed after exoneration. It ran for over 600 performances Off-Broadway and has been produced across the country and internationally. The work has even had an influence on public policy. In 2002, just before leaving office, Republican Governor George Ryan commuted all 167 death row inmates sentenced to life in prison. Though Ryan had already shown opposition to capital punishment and had commissioned an extensive investigation into wrongful conviction cases, he noted that being in the audience and seeing a performance of *The Exonerated* did indeed have an impact on his decision. The playwright/directors Blank and Jensen have since become advocates for documentary theatre as a catalyst for empathy and change. In 2005, in a keynote speech to the Mid-America Theatre Conference (MATC), they laid out their faith in theatre for social change via empathy:

> When we empathize, the wall between self and other, between us and them, begins to disintegrate. We can no longer view the other as an abstraction or an object—we have to experience the other as human; as human as ourselves. And then the questions that their stories raise—because all stories raise questions—become our questions too.
>
> This, we believe, is why documentary theater can bring about social change. Not because it pumps its fist and warns us all of the grave dangers our society is facing. But because if you tell a story in the theater, and tell it well and clearly, the audience will empathize; and if the audience empathizes, they are implicated and involved. Documentary theater can, done right, involve us all, on an immediate, human level, in stories that are happening all around us, in reality, every day; stories we might think are not our responsibility, but which in fact affect all of us. Documentary theater can show us—as long as it refrains from *telling* us—that this is true, and in so doing can help raise all kinds of questions that we desperately need to be asking as a society.

The Exonerated had a hyper-specific focus, and Blank and Jessen were rigorous in limiting scope and content. Just as a photographer makes specific decisions about what is in the frame and what is not included, so too does the Documentary Theatre writer make editorial choices about what goes into the play and what does not. Editorial decisions will always be part of conversations on the ethics of documentary and investigative art forms, and *The Exonerated* generated valid considerations about what information was left out of the play, which I discuss with Christine Simonian Bean, in Chapter 13, Dramaturging the "Truth."

It's an extremely difficult task, to decide what goes in the play and what does not. Especially when trying to tackle a difficult question. With Cornerstone, I was trying to tackle a huge question—how do people, victims *and* perpetrators alike, move forward after an act of violence? Instead of writing about people serving time for crimes they did not commit, I was interested in writing about individuals who had acknowledged that they *did* indeed commit an act of violence, and I was interested in finding out who they were after that act.

My inspiration was *The Oresteia,* written by the Greek tragedian Aeschylus in the 5th century BCE. Aeschylus was not only one of the most celebrated playwrights of his time but also a combat veteran who fought in the war between Persia and Greece. And his gravestone, which he wrote himself, makes no mention of his playwriting. Instead, it reads:

> Beneath this stone lies Aeschylus, son of Euphorion, the Athenian,
> who perished in the wheat-bearing land of Gela;
> of his noble prowess the grove of Marathon can speak,
> and the long-haired Persian knows it well.

He was a combat veteran who wrote about war and trauma, and his audience was filled with citizen-soldiers, combat veterans like Aeschylus, who came together to listen to this former general's plays about war and the ramifications of violence. *The Oresteia* is a trilogy that begins at the end of the Trojan War and culminates with the creation of the first modern murder trial. The story is wonderfully dense and complicated, but the gist is this: Agamemnon kills his daughter Iphigenia as a sacrifice to the gods so that the wind will blow the Greek army's ships across the sea to Troy, where the Trojan prince, Paris, had absconded with Helen, Agamemnon's brother's wife. After years and years of protracted warfare, when Agamemnon finally returns victorious, his wife, Clytemnestra, kills him as retribution for killing their daughter. The god Apollo tells Orestes—Clytemnestra and Agamemnon's son—that he must kill Clytemnestra as retribution for her killing Agamemnon. Orestes does. Then the Furies, who are more ancient than the gods and who prosecute those who commit matricide, arise to torment Orestes. He flees to Athena's temple and pleads for refuge. Athena holds a trial—the Furies are the prosecution, Apollo the defense—and she calls twelve citizens to serve as jury.

I'm obsessed with this trilogy because I think what Aesculus was doing was *warning* us that our modern judicial system has a real problem: Human justice is inevitably corrupt. It is corrupt because we, the judges and jury, weigh our judgments based on our own personal experiences. In the trial of Orestes, the jury is deadlocked—six cast votes to acquit and six vote to condemn. So, Athena casts the tie-breaking vote. She votes in favor of acquittal. She says that when weighing which is the greater transgression, the murder of a father or the murder of a mother, she believes patricide is the greater crime because she was not born of a woman, but rather sprouted from her father's brow in battle and therefore, for her, the greater sin is to kill the father. Orestes is set free. Athena bases her judgment *on her own experiences*. And that is what we all do, to lesser and greater extents. If I am a jurist and am listening to testimony, I am asking myself, "Is this believable? Are these actions reasonable?" And what defines believability and reason for me? I base my opinions on what *I* would have done in that situation, and how *I* would have behaved in those given circumstances.

When they hear Athena's ruling, the Furies threaten a scorched-earth response. What does Athena do? She buys them off. She promises the Furies their own temple with hordes of worshippers; she promises to lift them out of the dark and bring them into the glory of the light ... so long as they calm down and act nice. And they do! All those many years ago, Aeschylus was warning us that justice is intrinsically corrupt.

Assuming that justice will help us recover from an act of violence is problematic. So how *do* we move forward after a moment of terrible violence? How are we changed, where do we find solace or rest or redemption? Can we? Is it even possible? That's what I wanted to find out with my Cornerstone collaborators. Our process was rooted in two methodologies: (1) Interviews and (2) Story Circles.

A Story Circle is a process in which people are brought together in a group to discuss a particular subject or experience. The mission is to let the members of the group prompt each other and lead the conversation, which is essential in order to move away from group interviews being transactional. It's a conversation not a harvesting of information. The group facilitator starts with exercises such as culture mapping. Culture mapping, or at least how I experienced it with Cornerstone at that time, starts with everyone up on their feet, chairs pushed to the side. Participants are invited to imagine a map on the floor and different parts of the map relate to different themes, experiences, opinions, or identity markers. Some maps can be literal: For example, the facilitator might say, "Imagine the floor is a map of age groups—on the left side of the room are the very young, on the right the very old. Please place yourself where you belong on the map." Then everyone moves to their place on the map. Other themes are less literal: For example, the facilitator might then say, "Now the map represents not your literal age but how young or old you *feel*. Please place yourself on the map—left side you feel young, right side you feel old." The themes used in culture mapping can, well ... be all over the map (apologies for the pun) such as personal ethics, lived experiences, ambitions, opinions, desires, and personal data such as where someone grew up or how many members were in one's family or one's profession or education, etc. Once everyone has moved to a certain place on the map, they're then asked to talk to those nearest and find three other things they have in common. It's a wonderful way to break the ice, encourage trust, and invite vulnerability because it shows us over and over again the many ways we are not alone.

After my Cornerstone colleagues facilitated culture mapping, we would then grab our chairs and sit in a circle to continue the conversation. The facilitator then led the group in a discussion around our topic: Justice and personal experiences with violence. All participants knew what the subject would be beforehand, so therefore they self-selected. The facilitator started us off with one or two questions, but after that, one participant's answer would naturally prompt another person's share; and at this point, the facilitator's job became one of just making sure that everyone got a chance to share and that the group maintained an open-hearted approach, with all opinions and experiences respected and honored. My job was to simply lean forward and listen.

We listened to groups of individuals who had formerly served prison time for violent crimes, and we also listened to victims and the families of victims of violent crimes. I should tell you why my writing process includes "we" rather than "I": I have written many plays alone, but sometimes I can't. I need collaborators to bounce ideas off of; I need collaborators to offer perspectives that I am blind to; I need collaborators to keep me honest and on mission. I need collaborators to pull me off track, because tangents are generally where the best material lies. I need collaborators because I want to hear from as many people as possible, and I can't do it all alone. Working with Cornerstone made this need for collaborators even more vital, as it was important to have community participants involved in the play-making process. And that is what Cornerstone does so well. In addition to the Story Circles, we gathered a group of professional theatre makers *and* community participants, and I shared with them the interview techniques I use. We then went out into various communities in the Los Angeles area and began asking questions and, more importantly, listening. We listened to groups; we listened in one-on-one interviews. We visited support groups, people living in recovery residences; we went to parole offices and public defender's offices, and we went into the California Institution for Women, a women's state prison located in Chino, California. We also spent time with victims' support groups, advocacy groups, therapists, and lobbyists.

What is a community participant? Community can be a tricky word. I think it's a catch-all term frequently used as code for poor people or people of color. It's like the word ethnic, which far too often is misused when referring to people of color: "Do you know that girl, Sally? The ethnic one?" We hear the word ethnic misused *all* the time. The actual word simply means relating to a population subgroup. Everyone has an ethnic background. No one can *be* ethnic, but rather, we can all be informed by our ethnic heritage, our ethnic interests, or our ethnic identity, no matter who we are or where we come from. So too, any group of people defined by a common trait can be a community. Football fans are a community; neuroscientists are a community; plumbers are a community. There is no such thing as *the* community.

Only *a* community. In writing *For All Time,* I was interested in working with communities brought together via an act of violence: A community of perpetrators *and* victims. What makes Cornerstone so special is that they not only base their work on and for specific communities, but they invite members of those communities into the creative process as actors, dramaturgs, designers, etc. And so, in addition to my primary collaborator (and the director of the production of *For All Time*) Laurie Woolery[10] and Cornerstone ensemble members, who are professional theatre artists, I also collaborated with a team of community participants.[11] Out of our cast of 21 actors, nearly half had served time in prison; other members of the cast had been victims of violent crime (and some were from *both* categories at once). A handful of Cornerstone facilitators knew who was from which subgroup, but they kept this information confidential and did not share it with any of us. When we were together in Story Circles, script development meetings, or rehearsal, our rule of engagement was that no one would be outed, but if anyone wanted to share their personal experiences, they were welcome to do so.

Giving everyone in the room—professional artists and community members alike—agency over their own personal narrative not only created a brave space, but it equalized how we served the mission of making a play together. When we worked, we became one larger community of artists, and that's it. I shared my interview process with all, and together we went out into the world to listen, in groups and one-on-one interviews.

One of the earliest interviews that I was granted for this project was Emily (not her real name) who was a parole officer in San Diego (not where she works). We chatted for a while about her job, and as she told me about the offenders she worked with, she said that many of them are both perpetrators *and* victims of violence (trigger warning, discussion of extreme violence):

> Hurt people hurt people is the way I put it. And the offender needs to heal, needs to fix what is broken.
>
> I was working with this guy—Tai was his name. His time was for murder. He was a murderer. To say this man had a broken childhood

would be an understatement. His father had murdered his mother, right in front of his eyes. Then as a teenager, Tai committed murder.

We met after he got out, I was his parole agent. And we had done a lot of work. He had come such a long way.

Well, I had been invited to speak to a group of mothers, mothers who'd lost their children to violent crimes. And I asked Tai to join, I had learned so much from him about the power of redemption, and he had already spoken to lots of other groups. But we get there, and I went first, I did my presentation, all is going well, and then Tai gets up. And he looks around the room and, uh, and he sees all these faces, the faces of all these mothers, and maybe he's suddenly reminded of his own mother, or maybe the mother of his victim, whatever it was, he starts to lose it. And he's pacing up and down, and the tears, the tears are just pouring down his face, uh, no expression, just tears gushing. And the women, everyone's getting really scared. Something is about to happen. So, I turn out the lights. And I say "Tai. Look at me" and he won't, "Tai, look me in the eyes. Right here, right here. Right here." And he looks at me. And I say, "Tai, what's going on?" "I want ..." "What is it, what do you want?" "To kill someone! I wanna kill and I can't!" "Why can't you?" "Cuz it's you! It's you keeping me from killing someone! It's you!" "No Tai. It's not me. You want to kill someone, I can't keep you from doing that. It's not me that keeps you from killing" "It's YOU!" You keep yourself from killing. Every day you keep yourself from hurting someone. You do that. YOU" ... and finally ... he starts to breathe. His shoulders start to relax. His fists open. And it's over.

No, the men I work with? Most certainly I would never tell them about my brother.

People, my friends have asked me, with DNA and all the technology now, don't you want them to find your brother's killer? No, I don't. I have no need to find out what happened to the killer. How could that help me? If they've found redemption, if they have kids, a home, a positive life now, then yeah, that would be good, but if they're still living in violence? How on earth could that be good for me?

> No, very few people know about my brother. And I never bring it into a professional situation. Yes, there are times when I think about him, and the feelings start to well up. And what I have to do is compartmentalize. I actually visualize compartments. I close my eyes and I see these compartments and I see one here, and I take what I'm feeling and I put my emotions in that box, and I close the lid, and I say to it, "You wait there. Such and such a time, I'll come right back to you, I'll be able to feel pain then." And I visualize moving that compartment to the side and then I look at this compartment and say, "Okay. This is my job, and this is where I have to put myself right now. This is where I have to put my mind, my heart."

When Emily replied to our project description and agreed to be interviewed, all I knew was that she was a parole officer who worked with men and that most were convicted of violent crimes. I had no idea that her own brother had been killed by someone else. Had I not earned Emily's trust, I highly doubt that she would have told me about her personal loss. How did I earn her trust? I simply listened without an agenda. I was not fishing for quotes I could use in my play. I doubt she would have shared much of anything with me if I had gone fishing. Emily has devoted her life's work to helping others find redemption for their transgressions. That is so far from the assumed stereotype of a parole officer. Listening shatters assumptions.

This need of Emily's to file her emotions away in a compartment ... I wonder if this is a common need in all of us, in one way or another. Emily needed to put her feelings aside so she could focus on the task at hand. It's likely that you who are reading this might have a different response to Emily's actions than I did (and that is what I love about this art form—we are allowed to have our multitude of responses), but perhaps we all have compartments in one way or another. Some of us fill a compartment marked "revenge," others "retribution," others "reconciliation." It's curious that so many words in the universe of justice start with the letter "R": Revenge, retribution, repentance, regret, remorse, restitution, rehabilitation, recidivism, reconciliation, redemption, and restorative justice.

Not everyone responded to violence like Emily. In fact, and no surprise, each person was at a different point on a spectrum of reactions. Our director, Laurie Woolery, and I spent a Sunday afternoon visiting a group of mothers who had all lost a child to violence. They had formed this group themselves.

Laurie and I witnessed these women, who turned to each other because they felt that no one else in their life could hear their pain anymore. They talked about their rage; one woman talked about her rage taking over her life and how it had made her fearless. She told the group about a recent incident when someone cut her off at a gas station and she was ready to pull out a crowbar from her trunk and fight them because she was so mad and no longer cared who she took it out on. Others talked about the failed judicial system and the fact that their child's killer was never found. They talked about feeling isolated. One woman told the group:

> No one wants to hear you cry any more—my therapist, she says to me, "you've got to move on!" Move on? My son was taken from me, my only boy, I carried this child in my womb, I raised this boy to be a man. Move on? To where?

Another responded:

> When I go to a repast, I push my way through all those people, I go right up to that grieving mother and I tell her, "*I* know what you're going through. I know all about it. And a month from now, all these people'll be gone, but *I'll* be here. I'll be right here with you, I ain't going nowhere." No, we don't move on. Somebody's got to carry the torch.

Toward the end of the session the group leader handed out blown-up balloons and sharpies. She invited the women to take the sharpie and write on the balloon all their fantasies of punishments they would want enacted upon those who harmed their children. After writing all the things they would do to the killer, they were then instructed to squeeze that balloon until it popped. After they had done so, the group leader then asked everyone to take a piece of paper and write "I forgive." The room erupted.

Some rejected the gesture and said they could never forgive. Then one woman spoke:

> I'm sorry, I'm sorry but I've got to speak, I've been sitting here quite long enough, I've got to speak. I'm sorry but I already forgave my son's killer. I don't want to see him suffer. You know what I want from him? I want him at the foot of my bed. I want him to come home and tell me about his day, I want him to rub my feet, I want him to take out the trash, I want him to *be* my child, I want him to *replace* the child he took away."

Laurie and I got just a tiny glimpse into the pain that is an everyday reality for these mothers. The repercussions and reverberations (there are those "R" words again) become an everyday reality for the victims … and for the perpetrators alike. I chose the title *For All Time* after hearing a public defender explain to me how for his client, "the rest of his life is forever defined by those three minutes of violence."

When we got to the point of staging the play, Cornerstone's values and process once again had a huge impact on all of us: A core casting principle of Cornerstone's was to—as often as possible—cast participants in roles that were uniquely *different* from their own lived experiences. What they did was the *opposite* of type-casting. Michael John Garcés, who served as Cornerstone's artistic director from 2006 to 2023, explained to me the thinking behind this approach:

> When people are not playing their perspective, and in fact if they're playing something that is either counter to, or at least quite different than their perspective, it really opens up the potential and possibility for empathy to become something more, right? Because once they're playing a point of view that they're not sympathizing with and they can't easily empathize with, they start to feel compassion for the other point of view, because you have to in order to play it, and the more you play it, and when people see a person who's going through that process, I think they intuit it—and a lot of times in the community, they know it—it creates a lot more richness in the dialogue, and the possibility for change, the dialogue that comes *out* of the piece that is made is important.

And I think it changes the person performing. It makes them vulnerable because they're saying things they don't agree with and they're trying to find ways to believe it. And that's a vulnerable place to be.

There have been exceptional times when we've done the opposite. And, in fact, I can think of one on the show you did with us, *For All Time*, where we had to give a community member who was a prison abolitionist her moment to be a prison abolitionist. Crucially she also played a parent mourning her daughter, which she really didn't want to do because her life's work, her personal, passionate mission, is as an activist and advocate for perpetrators not for victims; she wound up being extremely good as the parent and learned a lot, I think, through that process, as did we all. But to get her to the finish line, to make it possible for her to inhabit the character of that hurting woman, she needed a platform where she could be herself, saying what she believed, advocating for her own position. Freed to do that, she then allowed herself the space and vulnerably to empathize and find compassion for her character.[12]

I remember this moment quite clearly. The community member Michael mentions was a prison abolitionist who was cast to play the mother of a murdered child. This character, based on a real person we interviewed, wanted revenge. She wanted her daughter's killer in prison. It was clear how hard it was for this community member to play a role in such opposition to her own beliefs. And she asked me to re-write the scene, to make the mother of the murdered daughter have a change of heart and talk about restorative justice[13] as a solution to imprisonment. I couldn't do that because I felt I would be dishonoring my agreement with the mother we interviewed and it would be unethical to misrepresent her. This tension raised a very difficult question for me: Do I represent the world as I see it, or should I represent a world that I would *want* to see? It was the director, Laurie Woolery, that offered the way out: Laurie used lights, sound, and staging to create a moment of suspended animation when the performer/community member could step out of the role, say what she needed to say, and then step back into the person she was portraying. And as Michael notes, once the prison abolitionist was able to say her peace, it became much easier for her to *also* empathize and honor the mother's point of view. What we, the audience, saw on stage was one person, one body, containing two conflicting personal truths. We didn't have to erase one to make room for the other. It took a lot of work to find this solution, and we couldn't have gotten there without listening to ourselves while also listening to others.

For All Time was only one of several plays commissioned by Cornerstone for their *Justice Cycle*. The other plays were:

- *Los Illegals* by Michael John Garcés, directed by Shashir Kurup, in collaboration with undocumented day laborers and domestic workers.
- *Someday* by Julie Marie Myatt, directed by Michael John Garcés, which examines points of view regarding reproductive justice.
- *Touch of Water* by Julie Hébert, directed by Juliette Carillo and centered on water rights.
- And the final play in the cycle was written by Naomi Iizuka and was what Cornerstone called the "Bridge Show." Iizuka spent time getting to know all three preceding plays and then wrote *Three Truths*, which asked, "What is truth?"

Michael discussed the impact that the Justice Cycle had on him:

> You know, I was really affected when we did the Justice Cycle. The final play was by Naomi Izuka, *Three Truths*, and at the end of each performance we put disparate groups together on stage for public conversations. And there was this one extremely powerful evening, we had Pablo Alvarado, who was the head of the National Day Laborers Organizing Network, and we had Father Greg Boyle, the founder of Homeboy Industries, and then we had a former Los Angeles Police Commissioner.
>
> And each one of them had a very profound perspective on things, but there was this unexpected commonality that came out the conversation, with these three guys who are pretty different in their manner and in their presentation, and, and in the kind of things that

they do and believe. And that commonality had to do with compassion, with love. Pablo talked about how he had just come from Arizona—he'd been on the front lines of a very hot time in Arizona, working for the rights of immigrants. And working with undocumented workers. Arizona was on fire at that particular moment in time; the anti-immigrant sentiment was really hot, and there were a lot of demonstrations, a lot of arrests. And he talked about how he coped with all the anger and despair he witnessed and experienced in doing the work was learning how not to hate the other side, not to be angry at them and not to hate.

And an audience member responded, "How do you not hate them?" and he said, "I *have to* not hate them for *me*. Hatred was just killing me. I had to learn how to love those people." And people were, like, "You love them?!" and he said, "Yeah, I have to see the other human being in front of me and understand that they're fearful. Understand that they have something to protect. And however wrong I think they are, in how they're going about it, I have to learn how to see the human being there and say, 'That's another human being just like me, who loves things just like I do.' And I'm gonna work hard not to hate that person, to just keep trying to see the human. To save myself. Otherwise, I'm going to eat myself alive. I love those people. They are my fellow humans. They are my fellow citizens in this country. I'm an American citizen. I grew up in El Salvador, and I came here. Undocumented. And now I'm a citizen, and I'm gonna love those other citizens, and I'm gonna do my best to convince them of my perspective, and to see the humanity in me, so they can be relieved of their fear and pain. But I can't do it through hate. I just can't do it."

The play I had in mind when I began working with Cornerstone and the play I had when *For All Time* opened looked nothing like each other. I began with a fascination with *The Oresteia*, and I ended up meeting modern-day versions of all the characters in Aeschylus' plays: I met various Orestes, who took actions that they felt they had no choice but to take, I met Athenas, judging others based on their own experiences; Apollos, who were certain they knew what justice really was; and furies ... souls that cannot rest until their definition of justice is served.

I began with one question: How do humans move forward after an act of violence? And when all was done, I had more questions than I had answers, and that's right where I hoped to be. I'm most interested in the conversations after audiences see the play, what resonates and triggers even more questions. For me, in all of this, the "R" word that stuck with me the most was: Reconciliation. Every day, and in so many ways, we try our level best to reconcile actions—our own and others.

When I made my very first play, *Too Much Water,* the genesis of which came from my own struggle to reconcile the many shards of grief, guilt, and confusion I felt about my brother taking his own life, I found an avatar that helped me work through my pain without putting myself on stage. Watching the audience listen to my play helped me feel less alone. And when I made *For All Time* with Cornerstone, my personal inquiry was only the smallest start—it was the tiniest pebble dropped into the well that is the human experience of violence. We spent a good long while listening to others talk about their lives after a life-changing moment of violence. We listened to the many ways humans try to reconcile the irreconcilable truths of living in a violent world.

The act of listening is crucial. Our words of pain, rage, regret, suffering … they must fall on someone's ears. They must be heard by someone else. Perhaps the act of listening is, in and of itself, an act of reconciliation.

NOTES

[1] 2022 film based on this novel adapted and directed by Sarah Polley.
[2] 1987 film version directed by Jonathan Demme.
[3] 1984 film directed by Roland Joffé, produced by David Puttnam.
[4] Rose, Charlie. "Spalding Gray." *Charlie Rose* September 25, 1997. https://charlierose.com/videos/12417.
[5] Rose, Charlie. "Spalding Gray." September 25, 1997.
[6] Founded by Anne Bogart, Tadashi Suzuki and company members in 1992 as an ensemble dedicated to new work and the training of theatre artists.
[7] I was first introduced to interview techniques by Steve Cosson, founder and Artistic Director of The Civilians, who first practiced interviewing with Les Waters. More information on both in Chapters 9 and 10.

[8] "Mission and Vision." Cornerstone Theater Company. Accessed February 20, 2024. https://cornerstonetheater.org/mission/.

[9] "2007–2010: Justice Cycle." Past Work, Cornerstone Theater Company. Accessed February 20, 2024. https://cornerstonetheater.org/work/2007-2010-justice-cycle/.

[10] At the time, Laurie Woolery was the associate artistic director of Cornerstone. Currently, she is the Director of Public Works at The Public Theater in New York. In addition to being a director and producer, she is also an educator and playwright.

[11] Cornerstone has a long history of producing plays with casts that are a mix of professional union actors with extensive professional experience and community participants who might be performing on stage for the very first time.

[12] Interview with the author, 2023.

[13] In restorative justice processes, the perpetrator and victim have a guided discussion about their own definitions of justice and forgiveness that are outside and/or beyond conventional punishment.

BIBLIOGRAPHY

Aeschylus. *Oresteia*. Translated by Christopher Collard. Oxford: Oxford University Press, 2002.

Barry, Robert. "The Development of the Roman Catholic Teachings on Suicide." *Notre Dame Journal of Law, Ethics and Public Policy* 9, no. 2 (1995): 449–501.

Blank, Jessica, and Erik Jensen. "The Uses of Empathy: Theater and the Real World." *Theatre History Studies* 25 (2005): 15–19.

Gray, Spalding. *Swimming to Cambodia*. New York: Theatre Communications Group, 2005.

Sanchez, KJ. *For All Time*. Directed by Laurie Woolery. Los Angeles, CA: Cornerstone Theatre Company, October, 2008.

4

TELL THEM I WAS HERE

Krista Tippett and her Peabody Award-winning podcast and former radio program *On Being with Krista Tippet*[1] offer a compelling model for radical listening. As noted in previous chapters, when I interview someone, I find value in keeping my beliefs and opinions at the door and outside the conversation. However, for Tippett, her personal beliefs are part of the equation. *On Being with Krista Tippett* is an examination of belief systems and their impact on our lives and society. Though Tippett's faith is rooted in Christian tradition, she interviews people from an expansive and wide variety of faiths and beliefs. She interviews humanists, agnostics, and atheists as often as she interviews priests, rabbis, and monks; and all these conversations fit wonderfully under a big umbrella that I would describe as an investigation into what we believe and how those beliefs help us live our lives. It's about being human—mind, body, and spirit.

I offer her work as an alternative approach to listening because her style and technique have provided decades worth of fruitful investigation. I offer the option to choose an objective or subjective approach, depending on the needs of one's project. Here are a few key elements of Tippett's work that I admire:

- She's lead by an insatiable curiosity, an approach she calls Generous Listening. This is defined in *On Being's Better Conversation Guide*:

   > Real listening is powered by curiosity. It involves vulnerability—a willingness to be surprised, to let go of assumptions and take in ambiguity. It is never in "gotcha" mode. The generous listener wants to understand the humanity behind the words of the other and patiently summons one's own best self and one's own most generous words and questions.[2]

What an incredible gift to give another human being! To ask them questions that are not designed to catch a person in a compromising position but rather to ask someone questions that bring out their best self. Let's say I am interviewing someone who had recently been in a fist fight in a bar: If I ask them, "Why did you punch that guy?" this question puts the person in a defensive position, needing to defend their actions. But if I ask, "What do you think were the factors that lead to the fight?" this simple adjustment invites the person to bring their best self to the discussion and acknowledges that any given moment is likely more complex than, "Why did you do it?" It invites the person to bring their humanity into the solving of the problem—the problem that is framed as a confluence of circumstances, rather than one single act to be defended.

- Because there are no easy answers, the investigation becomes the point in and of itself and not a means to an end. Tippett embraces the investigation, filling every conversation with "what if" prompts. So, going back to that same hypothetical interview with the person in the bar fight, our Tippett-inspired prompts might include: "What if you saw that person today? What might you say to them?" "What if it had been earlier in the day—do you think things would have unfolded as they did?" Etc.

- Tippett's guests are encouraged to speak only for themselves. They are never expected to speak on behalf of their community or religious group or any other association. Lifting the weight of representing a group allows the conversation to be much freer. If I am invited to speak only for myself and my own life, then I am much more free to be inquisitive rather than didactic, to speak in draft, to let the conversation take us where it will.
- Tippett often began her *On Being* interviews with one common question: "was there a spiritual or religious background to your childhood?" This common question serves as a touchtone for the listener, and it's a terrific opening question, as it immediately sets the foundation of the conversation in memory, personal experience, and given circumstances. The Investigative Theatre company The Civilians have used this same tactic—asking all interviewees one common question, and for them, the question became a sort of Rorschach test. Either way, it's a helpful grounding question. (More on The Civilians in Chapters 7 and 10.)
- Tippett leans into complexity. She leans into, as she says, "the quiet, the good." In a 2022 interview in GQ magazine, she talked about her passion for the positive, for quiet complexity, and suggested that we all have a bias toward focusing on the bad things in our lives, rather than the good. Perhaps this is a needed part of our function and survival as a species, meaning that when we focus on the calamitous, ruinous, and tragic, we can then fix the problem, or perhaps prepare ourselves to help others through the post-negative event fallout, or at the very least learn to avoid areas, people, and things that bring destruction. However, Tippett suggested that we—the listeners and the story-tellers of the world—are fixated on the negative aspects of life to the point of distraction, not allowing reflection and representation of a whole spectrum of other positive and healthy human experiences. In this article, she asked: "How can we make goodness as riveting as evil and destruction?"[3]
- Last, Tippett lets herself off the hook to be a perfect interviewer, and she resists asking perfect questions. Sometimes she

does not know how to ask a question, and I have heard her say something to the effect of, "I'm not sure how to ask this but …" It takes a great listener to acknowledge the imperfection of the question. Sometimes when we are interviewing people, we get that "spidey-sense" that there is something just under the surface, some idea or anecdote or feeling about to reveal itself … we just aren't sure exactly how to get there. Tippett leans into this moment and gives herself permission to also speak in draft; she'll talk around the question, and explain the context around her inquisition, this way Tippett and her guest can find the question together. And this is one of the things that makes *On Being* so interesting to me: The interview is actually a collaboration between interviewee and interviewer. Tippett sets the stage so that together the two of them can, through dialectical thinking, find themselves in places that neither of them expected.

Tippett has interviewed thought leaders, philosophers, spiritual guides, activists, and authors. One such author is Luis Alberto Urrea, who has written both fiction and non-fiction. His work includes *Into the Beautiful North*, *The Devil's Highway*, *The Hummingbird's Daughter*, *The Tijuana Book of the Dead*, and *The House of Broken Angel*, and it often focuses on people living on borders or, as some might describe, "living on the margins" of society. Urrea was born in Tijuana, Mexico, where his parents had moved from Mexico City. At the age of five Urrea and his family relocated to Logan Heights, a southern suburb of San Diego, California. Urrea attended the University of California, San Diego where he wrote poetry and plays and lyrics for local rock bands. Through a roommate, he ended up meeting a pastor with the Clairemont Emmanuel Baptist Church—Pastor Vaughn—who invited Urrea to travel to Tijuana with him to minister to the poor. Urrea thought, "Well, what are these gringo Baptists going to show *me* about Tijuana?" But he went, and "it blew my mind."[4] Urrea became Pastor Vaughn's translator, which—as Urrea tells it—honed his skills as a listener because when one translates, one has to listen as fully, as deeply as possible, so as to not get anything wrong. (I'm curious how our artmaking process might be informed by approaching an interview as though we were about to immediately translate what we hear. I wonder if pretending to be a translator might improve our listening.)

Urrea worked with Pastor Vaughn for years. Even when he began teaching at Harvard University, he would return on breaks to keep working with Vaughn. They would cross Tijuana, working in the poorest, most strife-ridden areas, including the garbage dumps where the poorest of the poor lived and lived off of what others threw away. On one such mission, Urrea had taken a pause in the work, found a place to sit, and was writing notes in a journal that he always kept with him. A man covered in soot and mud who lived in the dump approached Urrea and asked him what he was doing. Urrea explained to the man that he was writing down his experiences, writing down what he saw and heard. In his interview with Kristen Tippett, Urrea tells her:

> Then he looked at me—I've described it elsewhere as that moment when you're around somebody and you don't know if they're going to hug you or hit you, perhaps if you're out drinking or something, and that person smiles a little and leans back. And I thought, "Uh-oh, what's ..."
>
> And he came back, and he said, "You know, that's good. That's good. Write it down. Write about me," he said, "because I was born in the trash. I spent my life picking trash. When I die, they're going to bury me in the trash." He said, "You tell them I was here."

Urrea was charged by this gentleman to remember him, to tell others that he walked this earth, that he *existed.* Being charged to memorialize another person's existence is no easy task. It's a weight to own that kind of responsibility, and I am in awe of Urrea's nonfiction and the care, artistry, and sophistication of his representations of the truly extraordinary. Or perhaps I should strike my use of the word extraordinary when talking about the marginalized lives that Urrea writes about; they are people living in *extreme* circumstances, under remarkable duress with each day a struggle to simply survive ... and yet their experiences are far too *ordinary*, far too common today. So, what do we call lives like these? To get up each day and fight to keep yourself and your loved ones alive, when the world has given you nothing but calamity is—in my opinion—nothing short of heroic.

Not everyone living on the margins and/or in crisis *wants* their life chronicled by someone else. There are plenty of reasons some people want to remain anonymous, and when chronicling another's life, I think it's essential to understand the difference between honoring a life and placing that life in more danger. I don't dare to presume to have all—or *any*—of the answers, but here are some things I focus on when striving to chronicle the lives of those in strife:

- To start with, *how* we document the interview/interaction/conversation matters. A quick tip when using an audio recorder: Use the smallest, simplest one you can find. I found out the hard way that using a big fancy field recorder—the kind used by podcasters—is the opposite of helpful. It looks like a taser. Not the best way to help someone feel safe. And better to use a small audio recorder rather than the recording app on a cell phone. Pulling out one's iPhone reminds both the listener and the speaker of the wealth it took to buy it, not to mention its connection to the outside world, the ability to track one's location, or even the simple fact that it might ring or have a text light up, breaking the singular focus needed and deserved. Video recorders, for me, are out of the question as they feel far too dangerous—who might end up with that footage someday? Sometimes the only way to help someone feel safe is to put the audio recorder away and just listen. (Then, as soon as possible after the interview, you can get to a quiet spot and write down everything you remember. This is a muscle like any other muscle, and you will be surprised how much can be retained if you practice and note it as soon as possible.)
- Situational awareness is key. Pay attention to everything around you: Are you in a location that is safe and helps the person you are listening to be and feel safe? For example, when I was interviewing combat veterans, I learned that

some of them felt uncomfortable sitting with their back to a door. And so, if I was meeting them in a public place, like a café, I would wait for them out front, let them walk in first, and that way they could choose which seat they would take—the one with their back against the wall or to the door. I would never articulate any of this to them; I would simply and casually find a way to be the follower, not the leader in determining our relationship to the space. This allowed for the consideration that some people who have just returned from combat deployment feel uncomfortable with their back to a door without making a general assumption that *all* combat veterans who have just returned from deployment want or feel the same things.

- Find natural, organic ways to check in and give the person the opportunity to tap out, without making them self-conscious. Pay attention to their body language: Are they looking over their shoulder? Are their arms folded in front of them? Is there tension in their shoulders, arms, and hands? These can be signs that even though they have agreed to be interviewed, they may have felt pressure to say "yes," and their physical presence might be giving signals that they really don't want to be there or don't want to talk to you. It's helpful to give them the option to pause, tap-out, or "do this some other time" if they are exhibiting discomfort.
- Trust your instincts and pay close attention when it comes to how you archive. Sometimes the person you are listening to might want you to pull out your notebook and write it all down, just as Urrea's gentleman did; other times they might want you to use a recording device in order to ensure you don't get anything wrong. It all depends on the person's needs and level of comfort, and it is up to us to assess that quickly with care and sensitivity. There is no one rule that can fit all, be ready to follow their lead and need. There is also no rule about how people want to be cited in the final product. For example, I work with many people who want and/or need to be anonymous for their own safety and comfort. I usually offer anonymity first, but it's helpful to offer other options so that the person you interviewed remains in control

of their words and representation. Even though I've been doing this work for a while now, just recently I made the rookie mistake of assuming someone's preference and made the interview anonymous. When I sent them the work for approval before publication, they responded in no uncertain terms that I needed to revise the material and use their real name because it was important they get credit for their work and experiences, as opposed to being "merely a character in your play." And they were absolutely right.

- When a person prefers that the interview remain anonymous, it is our job to protect their anonymity *at all costs*. I find it helpful to create a pseudonym for the person I am interviewing right away. I keep a spreadsheet of real names and their pseudonyms, in case I need to reach them later for follow-up, but once that pseudonym is created, that is the name I use from there on out. These documents I keep in a password-protected folder that I do not share with anyone else. If I am collaborating with others who also conduct interviews, I have all collaborators sign confidentiality agreements to ensure that they understand the gravity and responsibility we have to protect identities. Any dialogue that could identify the person is changed as well.

- Everyone who talks to me does so voluntarily. They agree to be interviewed because, like Urrea's gentleman, they *want* others to know their story. If someone becomes hesitant to tell their story, I must immediately back off and stop asking questions. When a person has experienced a traumatic event, the re-telling of that story can be triggering, and so we must develop and rely on strong situational awareness skills to sense if the listening is helping or hurting. That's the deeper level of radical listening.

- In my opinion, it's unethical to write about someone's real lived experience without their knowledge—no eavesdropping or recording in secret. There are plenty of wonderful stories to be heard by willing participants. Being less than transparent about what I am doing and why holds no water for me. (Further discussion of the ethics of listening will be found in Chapter 6.)

When we then begin the process of transposing these interviews into an art form—a play, book, film, or article—the binary of objective vs. subjective tends to disappear. What I mean by that is that our artistic process will ask us to simultaneously hold varying points of view that are at times objective and at others quite subjective. When I am compiling source material into a play, the mantra I rely on is "It ain't about me." In order to authentically represent someone else's experience, I must try my best to remove my own agenda from the story. However, the *why* behind the making of the work, the reason I want to investigate a moment in time or an event or life, *must* be personal. I must have a personal investment, a very personal reason that compels me to listen. A student of mine recently told me that during her attempts at documentary playmaking, she had trouble remaining objective; and I realized, "Oh no. I failed as a teacher because I left out an essential ingredient!" As an artist, I don't think it's possible to *not* have a point of view. We most certainly should have subjective reasons for embarking on our inquiry. We should definitely have a point of view. There's a difference between letting our personal interests fuel our investigation and letting it write our play. Our point of view is the reason we *must* tell someone else's story—it should matter to the depths of our core. If we are going to spend years working on making one play (because it does indeed take years) then we must absolutely care about the subject. To be a non-judgmental listener does not mean we do not care. It just means we set aside our own agenda and ego; we set aside the need to make blanket statements or declarations or judgments and let the speaker, the life, the experience, and the story lead the way. In doing so, we must also let what we hear change us. We must let what we hear complicate how we feel. Our personal investment can help us lean into asking questions, not decreeing judgments; it will help us let go of the need to find simple answers and give us the courage to live in questions, uncertainty, and complexity. Our personal point of view will help us frame what we have heard and will help us take very complicated information and shape it into a consumable art form.

In 2016, I received a commission from the Guthrie Theater in Minneapolis to make a play based on interviews with people who were from various Minneapolis/St. Paul communities who were either new Americans, undocumented immigrants, asylum seekers, or displaced people in the federal Refugee Resettlement Program. Some were new to the United States and some had immigrated or resettled years ago and were long-standing US Citizens. This project came from my interest in the relationship between the Twin Cities and the migrant, immigrant, and refugee communities who call Minneapolis/St. Paul their home. On a very late night in September of 2015, I went down a rabbit hole after reading about Minneapolis' Mayor Betsy Hodges, who was one of 18 US mayors to sign a letter to President Obama encouraging the settlement of Syrian Refugees in their cities. Although, according to the Minnesota Department of Human Services, only seven Syrian refugees had been settled in Minnesota since October 1, 2014, this letter set off a maelstrom of opinions in both the local and national media, with individuals on the left praising the compassion and humanity of taking in refugees, while those on the right raised alarms about terrorism (citing an April 21 *Star Tribune* report that six men from Minnesota were arrested and charged attempting to fight alongside ISIS.)[5]

At that time, according to the *Washington Post*, Minnesota was in the top 20% nationally in refugee resettlement. A large majority of those refugees were from Vietnam, Laos, Cambodia, Burma, and Somalia.[6] Like Syrian refugees, the Somali community in Minneapolis is a topic that ignites passionate responses from all across the spectrum: From the many ministries and not-for-profit organizations that appeal to the humanity in all of us to help those fleeing war to the city planning commissions that note the consistent decline in birth rates of Minneapolis long-time residents and the income growth from immigrant communities, to those that spin the influx of Muslim refugees as a threat to national security and the local economy.

In the middle of this maelstrom are very real people forced to leave their homes and make their way in a climate, city, and country that is nothing like their own. I wanted to make a play about all of this because I was curious about what it says about who are we as Americans, as defined by how we offer or refuse refuge to those in need.

I became obsessed with the Twin Cities not only because the area has larger numbers of immigrants and charitable services for those immigrants than most of the country, but because of the area's history of German, Norwegian, and Swedish immigration at the turn of the century. I was curious to find out how immigration was different today and how it was the same. I wanted this play to have no easy answers but rather to create a platform for a multitude of unheard voices so that the audiences could make up their minds for themselves.

This commission began while President Barack Obama was in office. I went to Minneapolis and, along with fellow interviewer and collaborator Hannah Sobol, began interviews. I met incredible people running incredible resettlement programs. FYI: The Federal Refugee Resettlement Program had historically been a bi-partisan-supported program and both Democrats *and* Republicans supported resettlement of refugees. This program has only become decidedly partisan in the last few decades. I was overwhelmed and inspired by seeing the dedicated work and resources going toward supporting refugees. It wasn't perfect, but the support services were robust. And then after the 2016 election ... all that support came to a grinding halt. That was a challenge, to say the least, to try to reflect on a field of work that had a giant target on its back.

US politics aside, the interviews we were conducting were raising many other flags for me as well. We interviewed so many truly remarkable people who suffered extraordinary trauma. They told us their stories of loss and hardship, the extraordinary measures taken to flee their homes with nothing more than the clothes on their backs; the terrible things they witnessed, the terrible things they had to do to survive.

As I listened to these stories, I panicked. It seemed impossible to fit so much life, so much loss into one play. I also became extremely concerned with whether my work would help or create further pain—it felt pornographic to put one story of suffering after another on stage. My play started to feel like what I call "torture porn"—satisfying some deep and troubling part of human nature that is compelled by the suffering of others.

When we watch a documentary play or when we read biographies or memoirs, when we pick up the newspaper, visit our usual online sources, watch a documentary film, I can't help but wonder about how and why we are consuming these stories. Are we watching/following to understand the plight of others so that we can better help them? Or are there subconscious attractions at play? Is the part of us that slows down on the highway to rubberneck a car crash getting a little fix by watching stories of suffering? Or are we acknowledging someone's humanity by listening to their story? Where is that line in each of us? And, by hearing someone's story of pain and then sharing it with others, are we re-traumatizing the person or people who experienced that pain? I had to ask myself, was I writing this play because I felt *sorry* for those I interviewed? Did they need or want my pity? No, of course not. I was so overwhelmed by how many stories of suffering I heard that I became paralyzed. Trapped. Stuck.

And then Salman Rushdie showed me the way. I was deep in artistic paralysis when I read his collection, *Home.* Rushdie invited me to see the beauty in belonging, wherever one finds themselves. Birds fly away and people travel, it is a natural part of the world and though it can contain hardship, the flight also contains great beauty. And flight can be so common that perhaps it can also be *banal.* Perhaps flight is so common that really, it is no more unique than bird flight. Rushdie writes:

> Look under your feet. You will not find gnarled growth sprouting through the soles. Roots, I sometimes think, are a conservative myth designed to keep us in our places.

Rushdie writes without pathos; he doesn't want to invoke sadness or pity. I as the reader sense the pain of being an emigrant but it is not pathetic because he frames it in beauty, in metaphor, in *life.* Tree roots that are not really there, birds that take flight … his imagery and poetic framing lifts the experience to its rightful place, full of tenderness met with beautiful *banality.* He taught me that the only way to serve these stories and do justice to those I met was to do so with a nice healthy serving of theatrical poetry.

For my play about Minneapolis/St. Paul, one of the first people I interviewed was Saengmany Ratsabout. (He gave me permission to use his real name.) At that time Saengmany was the program coordinator at the University of Minnesota's Immigration History Research Center. His research included the Southeast Asian American experience, refugee resettlement, and return migration. I met him in his office. I brought an audio recorder and later transcribed our conversation. I parceled out the transcription, peppering sections of his interview throughout the play. I generally direct most of my own work and the staging is one-part direct address, one-part theatrical spectacle. In this production, the actor playing Saengmany sat at a desk, talking directly to the audience as though they were interviewing him in the moment, while over his shoulder another actor carried a live-feed video camera and shot close-ups of his desk. These shots were projected onto the scenery behind the actor playing Saengmany. These simulcast shots revealed an entire tiny imaginary world on his desk: A tiny stress-relief desktop Zen Garden became the banks of the Mekong River, post-its and file clips became a boat on which there were tiny little people floating across. (Much theatrical magic can be made with office supplies, model railroad figurines, and a great projection designer named Sven Ortell.) Here's an excerpt from the play:

SAENGMANY

Sure! You can turn your recorder on.

I've never been interviewed for a play before, so this is interesting.

You're to interview me and then use my words in the play?

Do you need me to sign anything?

(A desk magically appears.)

OK. So. We just start talking?

Would you like to see photos?

(He takes out a key and unlocks a drawer.)

I keep them here because always I know if my house burns down, this building is safest *(laughs)* that my files will be here.

(He pulls out a big padded envelope.)

All these documents. We were part of the second wave of refugees to come to the United States from Southeast Asia. Mid-eighties.

(He takes out perfectly preserved plane tickets.)

We have plane tickets over here ...

Yup! July 31st. Arrive in—port of entry was Seattle. Flight zero two zero. Actually, I had a dream about 2080 the other night. The future 2080. It was horrible. A nightmare. Jim Carry was running for President. *(he laughs)* Um. Speaking of 2080 ... the first flight, the flight from Manila to Seattle was zero two zero and the flight from Seattle to Minneapolis zero zero eight! So, that's close to twenty eighty!!!

And from Minneapolis, St. Paul we finally arrive in Atlanta Georgia where my Aunt live at that time.

Here is a memorandum of understanding that our family have to pay back the cost of the plane ticket. Yes. All refugees pay back costs. There were six of us. Close to two thousand dollars, I think?

I'm Lao. Not Laotian. Laotian is a term for people who are nationals of the country of Laos? Folks who left Laos without permission automatically lost citizenship to the country. And so, as refugees we are no longer national of Laos. And so based on that as well as my awareness of different terms—I choose to be identified as Lao or Lao-American. If that makes sense.

During the war in Southeast Asia, visive the Vietnam war, and civil war in Laos itself, my dad was part of a group that supported the American fighting covert operation war in Laos.

Our village, as well as our province was very close to the Ho Chi Min Trail, and much of the bombings by the US government, visa vie an airbase in Thailand, would fly to Vietnam, across Laos, would bomb the Ho Chi Min Trail as well and if there was any left-over bombs they would be just dropped. In Laos, right?

And officially we, the US, weren't even there.

My dad was not in high command, he was a simple soldier—which I feel very proud of that. That he did his part to protect us, to fight for what he felt was right for his country.

And so in the eighties, he was told that the government in power was investigating him. I believe early winter of 84.

The escape ... for me, it seems like a state of dream ...

Being two years old escaping.

My dad devised a plan. This was really an overnight plan.

They had to contact someone who had a boat, that could get us over the Mekong river across to Thailand. And so, in the morning my dad took me to a different route, so there would be no suspicion. My dad operated a bike tire repair shop and so he had asked his brother to open the shop, so they wouldn't be able to suspect anything. And my mother took my younger sister toward the river, on the other route. And then my older brother was tending the field with his favorite buffalo. Apparently *(he laughs)*

So we all got to the river.

Three of my cousins who went to send us off decided to escape with us.

That day, that my parents put us in a boat to cross the Mekong river, you know, bodies were washed up on shore all the time, my parents, they didn't know if we would make it across to safety.

But we made it to the other side.

From the Thai perspective, we were undocumented. From our perspective, we were taking refuge.

Once we got to Thailand my parents reported themselves to the authorities. My father was put in prison—put in detention. And we were within the compound of the detention center.

I think we were there for close to two weeks. Then we were resettled in a refugee camp. We were there close to two years?

An individual where my dad was under his command, was able to vouch for my dad and prove that my father actually served, in the war, under the direction of an American CIA operative. So that was one process. Proving you can't go back.

Then there was a series of other things: orientation, interviews, identifying sponsorships in the US. Um. Series of medical exams. Yup. I have my x-rays.

They were looking for tuberculosis. If I had been sick, they would postpone our application. But see, it says here that I am ok.

This picture is January of 86. I weighed twenty-four and a half pounds. I was four years old. Yup, malnourished—right here *(referring to document)* says right here, malnourished child, eleven point one kilograms *(laughs)*.

You know, right before we left, my cousin, he wrote all our names in the sand. On the bank of the river. Maybe at least to say, we were here. We existed and if we die, maybe someone find those names. I went back as an adult, to Laos. I went to that river and I brought home with me a little bit of that sand. To forever remember that moment ... when we escaped.

No, we didn't come straight here. We were first in Atlanta. We arrive at night. We went home—to my aunt's apartment. She and her church were able to set up an apartment for us later on. And um, that first night ... we had Kentucky Fried Chicken. *(laughs)* A bucket of KFC! And it snowed! A lot! My first time in the snow!

(Music.

Falling paperwork becomes snow.

The actor who was playing Saengmany *makes snow angels in the paperwork/snow.)*

Elements of theatrical magic, of dance, poetry, and interactive projection design became the key to staging these interviews. I finally found my north star. But even with a north star, I still struggled. The next challenge I faced was that when compiling, I felt the need to include *everything* I heard. I wanted to include every person's story because editing out just one sentence was heartbreaking for me. I was also overwhelmed with what I learned about the baroque systems asylum-seekers, immigrants and refugees must navigate and I felt the urge to put all of it in the play. By the time I had my first draft, the overall effect was of an artist trying to boil the ocean. It was just too much. It's painful but important to come to terms with how much an audience can consume in one sitting and so we artists must make very difficult choices about what goes in and what gets edited out. I make little deals with myself when I am making a painful edit: I tell myself, "that's for the book" I promise myself that the interview I am not using will someday go into a collection of stories.

Once I understood that I was trying to boil the ocean, that I couldn't put everything into one play, I had another question: How do I simplify without over-simplifying, without turning these extraordinary lives into caricatures, cardboard cut-outs, props? The only solution was to go deeper with fewer people. Instead of telling 20 stories (we had far more than that—more like 50) tell eight or nine but take the time to *really* tell that story. Then rely on poetic staging to speak to the complexities. If I can't tell everyone's story, I can at least put on stage a vignette in which we see an airport arrivals zone, the actors are walking through scansions, cuing up in various lines based on nationality and showing their paperwork and/or IDs to immigrations and customs officials. Live-feed cameras capture and project close-up shots of these exchanges, which are accompanied by the sounds of airports and debarkation. This one brief gesture dance can reference the many other people who we are not hearing from.

The name of this play (chosen a few years before I heard Luis Alberto Urrea talk to Krista Tippett, believe it or not) is *You Are Here*. Theatrical gesture and imagery not only helped me say what I could not put in words, they also helped me take the next step in the play's point of view. The only way around—or rather, through—the issue of what I call torture-porn was to turn to my own opinion. To me, the people that I listened to are *super heroes*. A woman who walks across a country, carrying her two children, who rides atop a speeding train, tying her children to herself and holding on to whatever she can, who has the strength and resiliency, the tenacity and courage and fortitude to go without food, face wild animals and freezing temperatures so that her children can be safe someday ... that woman is a super hero to me. Hers is the DNA that I want to populate my future country. She is who I want as a neighbor, as a fellow citizen, as my role model, and as a leader. She is a real-life super hero. So, I decided to use that opinion, *my* opinion as the engine the play. Interstitial moments of theatrical magic using projections, music, lights, costume and props transformed a woman sitting on a stool telling us her story into a super hero flying through the sky.

I finally found a way through my paralysis and made a play that I was proud of. My only regret is that *You Are Here* only received a workshop production and never had a full run. The reality was that in order for *You Are Here* to really work, it had to be beautiful which meant it had to be expensive. I suspect that the theater thought I would make a play that would be fairly simple in terms of production values, something that could be presented as a stage reading, something that could be taken and performed in "the community." But no, that's not what I built. Why take this play to the people who experienced these things? Yes, by doing so we could say, we see you, we hear you, you matter ... sort of. What would *really* say this? If the play were produced at the big, fancy theater, with all the bells and whistles. The audience that should see the show, in my opinion, are the regular subscribers who buy tickets to *Guys and Dolls* and *Christmas Carol*. That was my intended audience. And that was just not viable at that moment. Perhaps at some point, we can figure out a way to do it as I envision. But until then ... I wait and hope.

Art can break your heart. Disappointments abound. Listening hurts sometimes, when you can't share what you hear in the only way you know how. I suppose the biggest take-away for me was that there is another kind of listening at play here: Listening to one's own moral compass. Even if that means the work will struggle to see the light of day. There have been plenty of times when I have done whatever was necessary to ensure the work gets produced. I can rewrite like nobody's business. This time I couldn't.

When I heard Luis Alberto Urrea tell Krista Tippett about the man who said, "Tell them I was here." It broke my heart all over again. By not getting this play to large audiences I feel I failed the people who trusted me enough to tell me their stories. It haunts me. But this kind of art-making is a long-term venture. I still have these stories. I still have this play. If I'm patient and if I keep listening, perhaps I'll find the right place, the right moment, and the right audience. In the meantime, once again, it ain't about me. It's about these super hero people who face the unimaginable and carry forward with humanity, grace, and hope. And joy! I'll conclude this chapter with one last excerpt from *You Are Here.* This is Nawar Bulbul, his real name. Nawar is a Syrian actor, director, and playwright and he gave me permission to use his real name because it's important for others to know the work he is doing …

NAWAR

Hello!!!! Hello! Can you hear me?

(Nawar enters. We see him live, as he is addressing the audience directly, but we also see him simulcast in projections via his cell phone's skype video.)

Hello! My Friend!

How are things in Minnesota? Are you freezing?!

I look at the pictures, of where you are at in the winter and think, my god. And why all these people who wear sandals are coming to Minnesota to live?

(he laughs)

(He listens to our question.)

Yes. Right now I am in France.

Hello from France!

Go back to Syria?

Well of course, that is all I think, forever. All we want is to go home.

But the Assad regime is ...

There is no way.

There is no more home. For me.

　(Again he listens.)

Go to you? To the United States? *(he laughs)*

Noooooo. The US is ... I do not think I will be visiting you in Minneapolis any time soon.

(laughs)

　(Listens.)

Being a displaced ...

It is ... like a tear.

Like a tear in your heart.

Your heart, it is teared in two.

You understand, there is no going home, it will *never* be same and it ... it tears.

It breaks your heart forever.

OK. What else do you want to know?

You mean after the revolution?

So.

I'm working in TV, in theatre, in cinema, in radio, all these stuff before the revolution of course.

Like all the actors in the worlds.

In 2011 when the revolution coming, of course, I participate ... the people ... this revolution, become the most important thing in my life, I do it.

So after that, the Assad regime, or the Syrian regime of Assad, so ugly, so violent, uh ... so after the first manifestation, with the people in the street, in May 2011 the regime of Assad follow me and put me—not me specially—but us, five or six actors or actress, regime of Assad put us on the black list.

And we, let me say ... under siege in our home.

All of us.

After that, there's nothing to do, I can't to do anything because I am in my home, I'm trying to say something, to do something.

But one of us, a friend, she's working with the displaced in Damascus—she gave them some food and some milk and some and suddenly this ugly regime catch her and put her in the prison for five years.

So we know exactly who's this regime.

So, um, I shut up *(makes a zipping of his lips gesture)* and I'm staying in my home all the time.

I decide to go out Syria.

Because my wife, French, from France—of course, she went with children to France before and I am lonely in Damascus.

After that there's no solution and every day I say, "OK, maybe tomorrow, maybe after tomorrow, maybe ..." you know?

So finally, I went out, to France.

So.

After nine months in France, my wife, she has a post? In Jordan?

So we went to Jordan, all of us together.

So when I reach to Jordon in two thousand and thirteen, I decide to go to Zaatari, because I visited Zaatari before, just one day, to ...

To hand out supplies.

Zaatari is the refugee camp, for displaced Syrians in Jordan.

About 80,000 refugees living in camp. And uh, three? One of three?

A *third* of the camp, under 18.

The first time I saw Zaatari, this ... very shock for me.

I'm shocked because it's horrible.

So I decide to return to work in Zaatari, to work with the children in December?

Two thousand thirteen.

I started with them, and the first boy, my boy, was born in Zaatari!!

So I have two babies in Zaatari—my boy and "Shakespeare in Zaatari!"

I create a program called Shakespeare in Zaatari.

We did a production of King Lear.

With kids.

In the refugee camp.

But you added some Hamlet to this production.

"To Be or Not To be" speech.

To be or not to be, it's very important at this time.

To be or not to be, that is the sentence, for every day, not just from the time of Shakespeare.

This is the question we ask every day, to be or not to be.

That is everything.

Especially in Zaatari.

And then we do Romeo and Juliet.

You know our story?

OK.

Romeo in Amman, Romeo was injured boy, injured in Syria, Refugee—Romeo.

And Juliet, in Homs, under siege.

They are talking together via skype.

So the screen of skype exactly like balcony of Romeo and Juliet.

This is the story of love.

BUT, we change the end.

When Juliet sleeping, Romeo take poison and throws it down and says, "No! This is *our* scene!"

They decide—Romeos and Juliets—they decide they don't want to take this poison!

"We want to live! We need a life! We want to live like everyone in the world!"

And at the end of this play, after the show, the spectators in Homs and Amman and talking together—saying, "Hello! How are you!" "We are with you and …"

It was, it was very emotional.

Very much everyone crying.

And laughing.

For me, I, my time in Zatari, it's about the experience. For me the result—the play, at the end, it's like my ass. I'm sorry. Like my ass, really. I don't care how good the performance. But, the four monthes for rehearsal, this is the treasure. With the kids, this is my target, my purpose. We studying a lot, the kids. All things. Education, theatre, playing, singing, drawing, eating, dancing. All these stuff.

This project, it so far from politic. It's so far from revolution. War, that is a game for adults, this is not our game. We want to play.

It's like sir Lawrence Olivier—what he say, "I'm not acting, I'm playing."

So, we playing. We play. That is all we want to do. Is play.

(The actor playing Nawar strikes the set. He calls everyone else on.

They all sit on the floor and watch the upstage video projection:

One final airport walk. Only this time, the characters dance. They are having fun. They are at play. The actors watch them playing.

Lights fade.)

End of play.

NOTES

[1] Tippett began with a radio program titled *Speaking of Faith in 2001* then changed the name to *On Being* in 2013. At the time of publication, the *On Being with Krista Tippett* podcast is the flagship podcast for the On Being Project.

[2] Civil Conversations Project. "Better Conversations: A Starter Guide." On Being with Krista Tippett. Accessed 20th February 2024. https://onbeing.org/wp-content/uploads/2020/07/8.5x11_BetterConversationsGuide_July2020_FINAL.pdf.

[3] Skipper, Clay. "'Hope Is a Muscle': Why Krista Tippett Wants You to Keep the Faith." *GQ*, July 21, 2022. www.gq.com/story/krista-tippett-on-being-interview.

[4] Grimm, Ernie. "America Broke My Heart, Tijuana Blew My Mind." *San Diego Readers*, June 24, 2004. https://www.sandiegoreader.com/news/2004/jun/24/america-broke-my-heart-tijuana-blew-my-mind/.

[5] Foley, Elise. "18 U.S. Mayors to Obama: We'll Take Even More Refugees." *The Huffington Post*, September 27, 2015. www.huffpost.com/entry/mayors-letter-refugees-obama_n_56044aefe4b08820d91c1b86.

[6] Guo, Jeff. "Analysis: Where Refugees Go in America." *The Washington Post*, November 25, 2021. www.washingtonpost.com/news/wonk/wp/2015/09/11/where-refugees-go-in-america/.

BIBLIOGRAPHY

Béjar Lara, Adolfo. "Narrating Cross-Border Migration, Writing Subjects Without History: On Luis Alberto Urrea's *The Devil's Highway* and Francisco Cantú's *The Line Becomes a River*." *Melus* 47, no. 2 (2022): 170–91.

Civil Conversations Project. "Better Conversations: A Starter Guide." *TALON Teaching and Learning Online Network*. Accessed 20th June 2023. taloncloud.ca/Guide-Better-Conversations.

On Being with Krista Tippett. "About On Being." *American Public Media*. Accessed 20th June 2023. web.archive.org/web/20150222143040/https://onbeing.org/about.

Sanchez, K.J. *You Are Here*, directed by KJ Sanchez. Minneapolis, MN: Guthrie Theatre, April 2018.

Tippet, Krista, and Patrick Bellegarde-Smith. "Speaking of Faith: Living Vodou." *Journal of Haitian Studies* 14, no. 2 (2008): 144–56.

Urrea, Luis Alberto. *Wandering Time: Western Notebooks*. Tucson: University of Arizona Press, 1999.

5

THE ETHICS OF LISTENING

Every journalist, filmmaker, writer, or theatre maker has to develop their own ethical compass. Of course, journalists and news outlets have formal guidelines (to lesser and greater degrees), but nevertheless, we must all make our own rules for what is ethical in our practice. My own ethical compass remains a work in draft. It's constantly changing as I work and learn along the way, as I listen to peers and what they are feeding back from the field. The ethics of our practice are very much on everyone's mind right now, as they should be. What I offer here are a few questions about the ethics of listening that might help readers develop their own guidelines and compass.

HOW TRANSPARENT SHOULD I BE?

There are two kinds of transparency I propose for consideration. First, there is transparency with those we are representing: Are we clear with them about what we are doing and how we plan to represent their lives and experiences? Second, there is transparency with our audience: Are we clear with them about what is and is not fact? In my own practice, as it relates to the people I listen to, I try my best to be up-front about what I am doing and why. I'm not sure there would ever be a situation in which I would record or represent someone without their knowledge or be clandestine in any other way. I've found that almost everyone is willing to talk to me as long as I can earn their trust. Most practitioners—myself included—use release forms, which we ask those we interview to sign. It's a simple letter of agreement that states that the person understands the author is interviewing them for a play and that they give them permission to use their words and likeness. Most often these releases go in only one direction: The interviewee agreeing that they understand they are giving the interviewer permission to use their words and experiences, in whatever current or future mediums available.

I have been wondering if this is enough. Should there be anything in this letter of agreement that asks *us*—those conducting the interview—to offer something to our interviewees? Do we have the right to take someone else's lived experiences and use them any way we like? Do we have the right to edit at will? I've been testing out some answers to these questions, adding to my standard letter of agreement a clause that acknowledges my responsibilities: I will not edit the material in any way that changes the person's intentions, and prior to any public performance, I will either invite the individual to a closed reading of the script or provide them with a draft to read on their own. At this point, the person has the right to withdraw any text that came from transcriptions of their interview. I make it clear that they cannot tell me how to re-write my play, but they do indeed have the right to withdraw any of their own content. I also include a clause that says I will change their name and any identifying traits in order to protect their anonymity, *if* they wish to remain anonymous—some people prefer to be known, depending on the situation and story, so I always give them the choice. To date, after 20 years of work, dozens of plays, and hundreds of interviews, I have never had anyone ask for their material to be removed. There was one instance in which someone questioned whether they should let me keep their words (they were concerned about how their comments would reflect on their community), but after we talked, I did a select revision, including more context and the misgivings expressed by this person. I had the characters talk about their concerns and whether they should trust me or not, and *that* conversation was baked into the dialogue in the play, in tandem with the original interview. This conversation made the play better, so I always lean into concerns rather than trying to avoid or shut them down. People have agreed to let me use their interviews even when they come off as not exactly heroic or virtuous figures. I've shared things that one might assume the person would not want to be made public. I've wondered why people are happy their voice is heard even when they are not painted in the best of lights. Perhaps being seen and heard is what's most important?

My other big question about transparency concerns my relationship with my audience: Am I obligated to make clear to them what is fact and what is fiction?

When I watch a documentary film, by the very nature of the frame, I'm aware of the camera and so am conscious that there is a filmmaker's point of view at play. There's a given transparency right off the bat, but even still, "captured footage" can have the imprimatur of truthfulness but can be quite fictional, as we all know. The footage is easily manipulated—as we've seen with the rise of fake documentaries used to promote extreme political agendas and conspiracy theories. We are a society that was raised on the idea that we can believe our eyes, and this assumption is currently in a state of major revision. For the sake of our examination of ethics, though, I'd like to set aside the world of intentionally manipulated media and speak instead to those who are striving towards truly ethical practices. And in this world, I still think the medium of film or video helps me remember that there is a person making decisions about what I see. Hence, a valuable transparency.

Some filmmakers find creative ways to go even further in reminding us that what we are seeing is curated: Erroll Morris, in his film *Fast Cheap and Out of Control,* combines interviews with four specialists in their field—a topiary gardener, a circus lion trainer, a robotics engineer, and an expert on the naked mole rat—with found footage that he edits to have a dreamlike quality. This combination of dreamy imagery and real people talking directly to the camera reminds us that there is an artist, Morris, who is behind that camera, and is putting things into a specific sequence for effect. Transparency. Another example is Werner Herzog, who narrates some of his films and includes his own musings, questions, and prompts, which are sometimes poetic, sometimes mundane, often with wit and humor. By placing himself in the film, he makes us aware that what we are watching is information processed through the point of view of one particular person. Again, transparency. However, I submit Herzog as an example of transparency with a major caveat: He isn't always transparent. He is known to have put fictional events into some of his documentaries, which he freely admits to and has vociferously defended. Herzog has explained in his "Minnesota Declaration" that he is after an "ecstatic truth." He asks us to think of poetry: When we read a poem, we will recognize deeper truths about human nature. We might feel there is a truth to the poem even if there are no journalistic facts; this, Herzog calls ecstatic truth. This kind of truth, as he sees it, can only be realized with imagination and play. Some find Herzog's approach to truth unethical, while others find inspiration. In his video essay, *The Inner Chronicle of What We Are—Understanding Werner Herzog*, founder of Like Stories of Old, Tom van der Linden suggests that while some documentary filmmakers try to chronicle our reality, Herzog is trying to chronicle our dreams.

I think (I hope) most of us understand that when we are watching a biographical film, AKA a biopic, we are to take the truthfulness of what we see and hear with a healthy dose of skepticism, given that it is a work of dramatization. Nevertheless, it's easy to be so drawn in by the representation that we might fall into the trap of thinking everything we're being shown is true. And these films can have a very real impact on how historical moments or people are remembered. How much of our culture's collective memory of historical events are informed by films like *Schindler's List, Lincoln, Hotel Rwanda, Argo, Zero Dark Thirty, Milk*, and *Oppenheimer*? What is the ethical spectrum for filmmakers between being true to the historical facts and making an engrossing and entertaining film? Can they be the same thing or are they mutually exclusive? And what is the spectrum of consumer savvy that the audience must bring to this equation? Do we assume it's all true because we were emotionally moved, or is it our job to educate ourselves so that we can tell the real from the dramatized?

When it comes to documentary theatre, things get rather tricky, especially when we include verbatim dialogue. When we use real facts and dates and represent real people, it's extremely easy for the audience to assume that everything they see on stage is true and nothing invented. Archived source material or verbatim dialogue creates a sense of historical authority that a play can't really live up to. Theatre scholar Amanda Stuart Fisher, in *Performing the Testimonial; Rethinking Verbatim Dramaturgies,* calls the dramaturgical use of factual source material "truth claims." She suggests that when we see live actors speaking text that we know came from transcriptions of interviews, combined with found footage or samplings of journalistic or historical documents, the audience easily trusts that everything they are seeing must be true. And she has a point. Even when a playwright is trying their level best to represent the truth as they see it, is there really such a thing as objective truth on stage?

What happens when an actor who is playing a real person embellishes different character traits? Is that still true? What happens when the material is edited, like the crafting of a composite character from several people? Is that still true? What happens when we leave traits or facts or timelines out in order to craft a more dramatic impact? Still true?

These questions are important, but—fair warning—they can also paralyze us. We can be so afraid of not being truthful that we either try to "boil the ocean" by including every reference we can or we don't follow our artistic impulses and get stuck in fear and trepidation. What's the solution? More transparency? Perhaps. I think this dilemma provides an opportunity: We can find creative ways to let the audience know what is real and what is not. Cinema Verité, French for "film truth" was a movement in filmmaking pioneered in the early 1960s. Verité filmmakers were committed to both an "authenticity of action" as well as a clear transparency, which highlighted the subjectivity of the filmmaker behind the camera. Verité director Dan Kraus once said "no documentary can ever show you the truth, because there are multiple truths, but Vérité can at least relay the truth as seen by a single observer..."[1]

For theatre makers, what are the ways we can be true to what we hear and see, yet still include poetry and imagination? How can we tell an engrossing story *and* remind the audience that what they are seeing has been processed through an artist's point of view? Here are a few examples for consideration:

When Moises Kaufman, Leigh Fondakowski, Steven Belber, and other members of the Tectonic Theatre Project[2] crafted their play, *The Laramie Project,* about the torture and murder of Matthew Shepard in Laramie, Wyoming, they included not only interviews with citizens of Laramie but also text from their own journals, which married the fact-finding nature of the documentary process with the personal, subjective points of view of the artists involved. This gave the play a more personal touch, and bringing in the artist's point of view allowed for moments of visual poetry, as well as textual prose. Leigh Fondakowski (who I interview in Chapter 8) also writes her own plays exclusive of Tectonic Theatre Project, and she recently offered me an idea that not only leans into transparency with those she is listening to but gives those we listen to the agency in the process; it's simple yet rather revolutionary: Instead of referring to those we listen to as "interviewees" she calls them participants. Of course, they are participants in the writing process—how they tell us their story, what they share when, how they craft it... this is when the writing process starts, with the participant. *They* write the first draft. We are not extracting raw material, and then going off to our little corner to write the story, but rather, the participant and the writer create the work together, in that very first conversation.

The Argentinian playwright Lola Arias goes even further giving participants agency in the playmaking process by devising and developing the work *with* them. Her play *Minefield,* commissioned in 2016 by LIFT (London's International Festival of Theatre), was co-created with three Argentine and three British combat veterans of the Falklands War. These former warfighters—Lou Armour, David Jackson, Ruben Otero, Sukrim Rai, Gabriel Sagastume, and Marcelo Vallejo—play themselves, directly addressing the audience. During the performance, they reference their auditions at the start of the process and share journal entries, and the integrated media design includes projections of personal photos and mementos. There is no doubt that this is a play about war, but it is also a play that makes clear that this is about these six unique individuals' experiences and in no way intends to represent *all* experiences of war. And what I most appreciate about this stunning work is that the men are not only defined by who they were and what they did in the theatre of war. The production also represented their current lives—one was dressed in bike shorts and talked about being an Iron Man while another was a drummer and played during the show. This not only added to the transparency of the process but also gave the audience a sense of a fully defined person, rather than a two-dimensional character confined to only one significantly traumatic experience. In this process toward transparency, by connecting their experiences of the past with who they are in the present, the play and production offered beautiful examples of the enduring resiliency of the human spirit. By inviting men who at one time fought on opposite sides of a war to collaborate together on the making of a work of theatre, *Minefield* also spoke volumes about the healing nature of art without ever having to say it.

Anne Washburn, in her play *The Ladies,* "explores the lives of infamous first ladies Elena Ceaușescu, Imelda Marcos, Eva Perón, and Jiang Qing (AKA Madame Mao)"[3] made transparency the very spine of the play, as Washburn included herself and director Anne Kaufman as characters in the play (played by actors). Washburn and Kaufman met often to discuss these ladies, and the transcriptions from audio recordings of these conversations became a narrative road map through the play.

An artist can even offer transparency in the simplest gestures, such as how they craft the title of the work, or how they list writing credit. For example, the London theatre company Tricycle Theatre, founded in 1972 and known for the creation of Tribunal Plays (plays in which all dialogue comes from extant court transcriptions) commissioned and produced a play called *Half the Picture,* with writing credit listed as: "adapted and redacted by

Richard Norton-Taylor with additional text by John McGrath." That word: "redacted" does so much work here. It offers the audience a clear insight into the playmaking process. The title comes from one of the court transcripts included in the play, in which a witness notes that testimony only offers half the picture of what actually happened; it's such a smart choice because it immediately suggests that we, the audience, will not get everything. Then that brilliant word—redacted—brings home the very nature of using found source material: Inevitably, things will be left out.

Steve Cosson and The Civilians have often found creative ways of letting the audience understand where truth and fiction sit in regard to what they see on stage. In the first ten minutes of their play, *Conard, Conard Goose,* one of the actors addresses the audience and lets them know that "everything is exactly as it occurred, *as we managed to remember it*."[4] What a well-crafted caveat. The scene that follows this statement reveals the cast in a recreation of one of their first company meetings, as they embark on the investigation that eventually becomes the play. The actors flit between discussing the subject which will be investigated and then getting extremely side-tracked by the snacks laid out. It's a funny and charming scene that disarms any assumptions that what we are watching is journalism but rather is a representation of real people—with all their wonderful real quirks—honestly trying to figure something out. One of the many things I have admired about Cosson's work is his ability to resist putting anything remotely sacrosanct on stage.

Another example of a play in which one can assume the creator's desire for transparency informed the artmaking is Lucas Hnath's play *Dana H.*, which received its world premiere at the Kirk Douglas Theatre in Los Angeles in 2019. *Dana H.* is based on interviews with Hnath's mother, Dana Higginbotham, a chaplain, educator, and writer who provides council to people living with the effects of trauma. In 1997 Higginbotham was abducted by a former patient and held captive for five months. As we can all imagine, a son representing his mother's traumatic experience would be an extremely sensitive process. Higginbotham did not interview Dana H. himself, but rather, The Civilians' Steve Cosson conducted the interview. Hnath, working with sound designer Mikhail Fiksel, then edited the audio recordings into his play. The audio recordings make up the entirety of the play's dialogue. Les Waters directed the premiere production, with actor Deirdre O'Connell sitting on stage in a replication of a hotel room, alone for nearly the entirety of the performance. O'Connell wears headphones; the titles above the stage read, "the actress sitting in front of you is going to lip-sync to my mother's voice." And she does. The headphones help O'Connell sync her body to Higginbotham's actual voice. No easy feat, to pull this off. O'Connell worked with a coach to train her body to perfectly lip sync to Higginbotham's voice. This approach made clear that O'Connell is not Higginbotham, but instead *embodying* Higginbotham's voice. It creates a double image where the audience sees both women at once... transparency. Hearing the actual recording undermines any expectation or temptation to represent the story with dramatic action. What I mean by dramatic action is that in lesser hands, the real person might be portrayed in histrionic ways: Animated body gestures, trembling voice, etc. In real life, we often underplay those things that are most terrifying, yet too often we see such experiences represented onstage with heightened emotion. The over-acting becomes a lie. In a February 12, 2020 interview with Laura Collins-Hughes of the *New York Times*, Hnath would not discuss biographical details or the content of the play, but he did discuss why it was important to him that the audience hear his mother's actual voice: "We sort of judge the legitimacy of what people are saying by how they perform it, which I think is extremely dangerous."

It's also dangerous, in my opinion, to let the audience think a story is recounted in perfect narrative structure. When we retrieve memories in the act of telling someone what happened to us—unless we are well-practiced at telling the story—we often talk in circles and syntactic loop-de-loops. If I were being interviewed about something that happened to me years ago, I might start at the end of the memory, then jump to something that happened in the middle, then jump forward to clarify why I brought up x, y, z—my retrieval system would be wobbling from one memory to another; one memory is triggering another, and

I may be jumping all over the place in time. The journalist or author who interviewed me would then edit my interview into a chronological sequence that is easier for the reader/audience to consume. Lucas Hnath and Les Waters' collaboration reached another kind of profound transparency because after the edits were made, which required sound designer Fiksel to move audio samples around for narrative clarification, there appeared a clear tonal difference between one part of the audio recording and another. Instead of doctoring the audio files so that they all sounded the same, the decision was made to add the sound effect of a beep, whenever there is an edit in the original recording. By resisting common devices to dramatize or homogenize, Hnath, Waters, O'Connell, and Fiksel ended up putting onstage the most dramatic and artful thing there is: Reality.

The great Scottish writer/director Bill Bryden's work offered his audience transparency by leaning as far into verisimilitude as he possibly could go. His 1990 play *The Ship,* about the declining shopworkers industry and struggling shipyard communities on the Clyde River in Scotland, actually took place in an old Harland & Wolff engine shed, in a shipyard in Govan. As the performance proceeds, a ship is being assembled, and at the end of the play, the ship is launched into the water. By immersing the audience in the very real objects, space, and context, the performance reveals that the one element that is *not* intrinsic to the surroundings is the audience itself, thereby creating an interesting version of the alienation effect and highlighting the curatorial hand at play in the process.

Another Scottish play worth considering, and a production that I will never forget, is the 2006 National Theatre of Scotland's *Black Watch* by Gregory Burke, directed by John Tiffany with movement direction by Steven Hoggett. *Black Watch* is about the history of the storied Black Watch regiment, its involvement in Iraq, where in 2004 it was ordered into an area later named the "triangle of death," and the political fallout when British military leadership tried to amalgamate the Black Watch into a larger Royal Regiment of Scotland, which would have stripped Black Watch of its historically significant autonomy. Originally staged in an old drill hall in Edinburgh and later built to tour non-traditional theatre spaces like warehouses, an old skating rink, and even an abandoned electric plant, the play starts in a pub. A group of off-duty Black Watch soldiers are talking to a writer who wants to interview them for a play. It feels like a rather naturalistic, traditional documentary structure. It's a nice set-up of theme and leads the audience to assume the rest of the play will follow in this fashion. But that's not what happens. Suddenly the middle of the pool table rips open and soldiers in full battle gear burst forth. The pool table becomes the back of a transport vehicle, and just like that, we are in Iraq. *Black Watch* is as much a dance piece as it is a play: There's a physical review—a kind of ballet—of the history of the regiment, with one soldier marching as he narrates while other soldiers pick him up, flip him over, change his uniform over and over again; there is a dance built off physical gestures around getting mail from loved ones; there's an extremely high-energy sequence of training and marching drills. The dance, along with sampled news excerpts, video, and original and adapted music creates a highly theatrical work that not only communicates the facts but helps the audience *feel* the visceral layers of experience, all the while being quite transparent that this is an artistic interpretation.

The director, producer, and cultural organizer Mark Valdez (an interview with Valdez is included in Chapter 12) who for several years worked with Cornerstone Theater Company and is currently the artistic director of Mixed Blood in Minneapolis,[5] has taken source material collected via story circles and interviews and put them through the filter of a canonical text. For example, he directed Cornerstone founding company member Peter Howard's adaptation of Federico Garcia Lorca's *Blood Wedding*. The basic skeleton of the play was Lorca's narrative structure, but set in rural unincorporated farming towns in Stanislaus County, California. The making, producing, and performing of this piece was for and *with* community members. The combined population of these towns was about 2,000 and 35 of these residents were in the cast and 10 on the crew. Combining the plot of an extant play with very real communities today naturally allowed for transparency, poetry, and the ability to *literally* say, "We see you, we hear you, you matter."

I offer my own learning curve on the road to more transparency: In the first chapter of this book, I wrote about my play, *Highway 47*, which was one of my first forays into documentary playwriting and was about my hometown of Tomé, New Mexico; my family; and the centuries-old land feud that divided both. Years after finishing this play, I kept thinking about the thing that I had not included in that first iteration, which was my own father's involvement in the land feud and my conflicting feelings about whether his participation helped or hurt people. And so, I wrote a second version of the play, in the form of a solo monologue that I would perform. The text included sampled transcriptions of interviews, court documents, state historical records, etc., and was a chronological overview of my father's life and his involvement in the Tomé Land Grant feud. Once it was done, I sent the script to my sister Martha. Martha, being one of the older of the 12 kids (I'm last), was around during the most intense years of the feud, and I wanted her feedback on what was true or not. Weeks went by, and I heard no response from her. I finally got the nerve to call her up and ask for feedback. I said something to the effect of, "I really want to hear what you think because it's important to me that all of this is true." Her response was "True? Oh, I didn't realize that you wanted this to be true." Hardest yet best feedback I have ever received. I realized that what seemed true to me was not her reality *at all*, and the notion that nothing is ever really true but rather subjective to one's point of view hit home, hard. First, I had to take her notes, go back to the research and revise sections for accuracy. Her notes were not the only barometer for the facts, but they led me to where I could find more research to triangulate primary resources. Second, I had to make it crystal clear in the play that this was all from my personal and subjective point of view, and I had to invent some theatrical way of letting the audience know what was what—what was a memory, what was something I heard from someone else in the town, what was a court document, etc. I had to put myself into the storytelling, I had to walk the audience through my point of view, and I had to include more questions than answers. I had to find a way to bring the incompleteness of my research to the stage. Eventually, I created a scene between me and my father, Gillie. I made quite clear to the audience that this scene was entirely fiction, describing how my father was deceased and the research runs out and I was never able to ask him all the things I wanted to ask him so what they are about to see is pure fabrication, made up by a child who needed to find a way to resolve questions with her father. Gillie is a puppet, in the form of a rock from the very land everyone fought over, and this rock-puppet-father-stand-in says to me, the author of the play:

> ... you got this thing with right and wrong so you think you have to love me or hate me. That's why you're telling this story, not for no-se-que promise to Mom. You need to figure out how you feel about me. Because then you'll know how to feel about yourself...
>
> ... You want to write a play that people will buy tickets to. You want to sell this story. And if you make it about me being good or bad you think no one's gonna notice that you're an opportunist, just like me.

Not an easy thing to write, but it felt to me the only way to wrap up a play about a history and a lot of people who were not there to represent themselves... to make it clear that there was one human, with all her human biases and failings and attempts to be accurate and honor what was true to the best of her abilities, a human who will always be working with limited research and a specific point of view.

AM I AN AMPLIFIER OR A TAKER?

When we tell someone else's story, we become curators, whether we realize it or not. And if we are curators, what responsibilities do we owe to those whose lives we are curating?

I think there are two curatorial modes:

1. We are Amplifiers when we amplify an unseen, under-heard, under-represented, misunderstood, or marginalized story or community. Sometimes a known author or established practitioner will have access and resources that can help tell

someone's story, when that someone might not have the access and resources themselves. The author becomes a bridge between a person's experience and others who may not know anything about what this person has gone through. We become Amplifiers if our work can say, "we see you, we hear you, you matter" and then share what we see, hear, and what matters with our audience. We become Amplifiers if our work creates a bridge between people.

2. We are Takers when we take what we see and hear, consume it, process it, craft it into a work that is in our own unique voice or writing style, and the final product benefits the author as much—or perhaps more—than the community it came from. In this scenario, we are Takers. We are Takers when the work directly benefits our own careers more than it directly benefits the community that we took the stories from.

Both Amplifiers and Takers have their place. Neither is necessarily better than the other. They are, to me, just different equations that might change our relationship with the people we are representing and might ask us to reconsider what we owe them.

When Emily Ackerman and I wrote *ReEntry*, I considered that play and process one of amplification. We were interviewing warfighters at the very start of the wars in Iraq and Afghanistan, and at that time the United States had a military that represented less than 2 percent of the general population. We heard from many service members in between combat deployments who said that when they came home they felt civilians had no understanding of what they were dealing with. These wars were not like Vietnam; they were not like the World Wars or the war in Korea. This was a different kind of fighting and different circumstances and very different deployments, and given how few Americans were serving, it was likely that most of our country knew no one doing the fighting. This disconnect was expressed to us in both profound as well as seemingly banal ways. We were sharing Marines' stories with civilians in theatres across the country, we were sharing these stories with medical staff in VA hospitals as sensitivity training, and we were sharing these stories on bases in an effort to let warfighters know they were not alone. We never paid any of the combat veterans we listened to. We felt that we were working under "journalistic-adjacent" principles for this one. And to this day I feel good about that. We were representing the experiences of a few individuals who did not have the platforms that were available to us and we were giving back by amplifying what we saw and heard.

I also found other ways to give back to this community, by serving on the board of a non-profit organization that gave scholarships to Marines, by volunteering to teach free playwriting classes for current and former service members and their families.

On the other hand, there have indeed been times when I have been a Taker: I made two jukebox-documentary musicals about the history of King Records, a record label out of Cincinnati, Ohio. King Records was the first major label to have a Black record executive and a racially integrated staff—from the executive offices to the record pressing plant—notable because this was in the late 1940s and early 1950s.[6] The first of these two musicals, *Cincinnati King,* was based on my interviews with the great drummer Philip Paul, who played on hundreds of King records. Mr. Paul, then in his late 80s, told me stories of playing with all of King's stars; told me about working with the record label's founder and owner, Syd Nathan; and talked about the ups and downs of the record industry. One of the themes of *Cincinnati King* was the question: What were musicians owed for their work? Very often studio musicians were paid for recording sessions but saw no royalties from sales. Given this theme, it felt absolutely unethical for me to just take Mr. Paul's life experiences without giving anything back, so I shared my box office royalties with him. I've never made a lot of money on royalties, but it was important to share what I could with the person whose stories I was taking for my own benefit.

The second, *Need Your Love,* was about the life of the 1950s King recording artist Little Willie John.[7] In his time, Mr. John was a huge star. He was the first to record the tune that Peggy Lee got all the credit for: "Fever." Many people today don't recognize his name because he died in prison at the age of thirty. His is a remarkable story, and I *highly* recommend listening to his records—you can hear so clearly how his brilliance influenced nearly everyone that came after. I interviewed his sister, Mabel John, also an R&B star in her younger years before she left the music business to be a preacher and minister to the poor. This was another instance in which I considered my role as one of Taker, so I offered her payment to be interviewed.

Yes, I could argue that I am amplifying Little Willie John's story and wrongful death, and that was very much my intention, but, as I've said, we all need to design our own moral compass and honor what we feel is right. It's not clear-cut. It's often gray. But the good news is, if we feel we are Takers, we can find so many ways to give back to the people we take from. We can volunteer our services with a non-profit organization or donate money or resources to groups that serve that community; we can put in our programs or websites or lobbies links to places that audiences can go to learn more, donate, or get involved; we can offer community members creative workshops, space, money, and other resources so that they can ultimately tell their *own* stories.

The Writers Guild of America, through the Writers Guild Initiative, offers free and well-supported writing and storytelling workshops. Their mission is to make "the art of storytelling accessible to people of all ethnic, cultural, and economic backgrounds, with special attention to the underserved."[8] Members of the guild—some of the best writers of our time—volunteer as mentors, and the initiative has held workshops for communities such as immigrant youth, Wounded Warriors, spouses and children of veterans, and medical staff working during the height of the COVID-19 pandemic. They have worked with community partners such as The Black List, United We Dream, LGBT Asylum Task Force, and Muslim Writers Collective.

0-Dark-Thirty,[9] founded by Ron Capps, is a literary journal that features service members and veterans writing their own stories. Many of those published in *0-Dark-Thirty* began writing in workshops the journal organized. These workshops are led by professional journalists, authors of fiction and poetry, songwriters, and playwrights, all helping this community find their own style, craft, and voice so that they can represent and amplify themselves.

Whatever you do, whether you amplify or take, it's very hard and possibly unethical, if not inconsiderate, to just walk away from a person or people who have given you such an extraordinary gift: Their lived experiences.

DOES THE MEDIUM MATTER?

As Marshal McLuhan wrote in *Understanding Media: The Extensions of Man*, his 1964 examination of content delivery systems: "The medium is the message." My takeaway from this seminal book (which goes through cycles of celebration and excoriation but is always good food for thought) is that technologies—AKA delivery systems—affect how content is received. If a vending machine delivers our food, the medium—the machine delivering the food—affects our relationship to the food we are consuming. So, how does the medium of presentation affect representation in art?

McLuhan coined the terms hot medium and cool medium. A hot medium would be a medium that holds a great deal of detail and definition, like a movie—we see every detail. For example, a close-up shot: We see every tiny line of the actor's face, all the way down to even the flecks of color in their iris. Or perhaps the movie takes place in a library: The art direction is full of details: Hundreds of books, desks, and light streaming in with such detail we even know what time of day it is, all are in high definition. It's a full and complete picture. McLuhan suggests that a hot medium, like film, which does all the work for us, allows the audience to sit back and be a passive viewer. We don't have to work very hard when watching a movie. However, a medium like animation is a cool medium because the image is just a few simple lines without a great deal of detail, and we, the audience, complete the image with our imagination. I see a circle with two smaller circles on top of it and my brain fills in the details to understand that I am seeing a representation of Disney's Mickey Mouse. A cool medium requires more participation by the viewer.

A film that employed the cool medium of animation is the 2016 documentary film *Tower*, directed and produced by Keith Maitland, about the first mass shooting on a university campus, at the University of Texas in 1966. The film's audio is mostly the real recorded interviews with some of the survivors of that terrible day. However, everything we see—from someone in 2016, sitting in a chair recalling their memories of that day, to a reenactment of the shooting back in 1966—is animated, in an elegantly simple style. The only time the audience is not watching animated representation is at the very end, and that reveal packs quite an emotional punch.

With *Tower* presenting a simplified, low-definition representation—a cool medium—I, the viewer, had to be more involved in filling in the incomplete images. And I think this need to lean in and participate in completing the image asked me to bring my own feelings to what I was seeing. If I see only a few lines sketched on a piece of paper that is meant to represent a person doing a thing, I bring more of my own personal experiences to the image in order to fill in the details. So, when I watched *Tower,* the medium asked me to lean in, to fill in the missing imagistic details, yes, but I also became an active participant in the storytelling. I was not seeing a real face with real tears; I was seeing a simple outline of a face, so *I* was bringing my own emotions to the moment. In the acting profession, we have an old saying: The less the actor feels, the more the audience will. My own acting experience has proven this over and over again—if I am on stage emoting my heart out, the audience lets me do the work and will feel less themselves, but when I hold back my tears, I'll always hear more sniffles and see more tissues in the audience. *Tower* did less work for me, and therefore its cool nature invited me to bring more of myself to what I was watching. So, the viewing experience became much more emotional and personal. The medium can further deepen our connection to the message and increase our empathy with the subject.

There are also times when the medium can have the opposite effect: Its influence can limit the empathy an audience might have for a particular story. In *Performing the Testimonial*, Amanda Stuart Fisher considers the play *Talking to Terrorists* by Robin Soans. This 2005 verbatim play is a collection of interviews with politicians, military officials, former members of known terrorist groups, and victims of terrorist acts. The incidents referenced in the play cover a great deal of time and come from many different parts of the world, and the only thing that connects the characters is that all their stories involve the ramifications of an act of terrorism. Fisher notes the difference in presentation—the medium—between those identified as former terrorists and everyone else represented in the play. For example, Fisher describes a scene with a British former secretary of state: The scene takes place in the secretary of state's home as she is cleaning her house and discussing terrorism. What the audience sees is a familiar setting, very relatable action. However, the characters who had formerly associated with terrorist groups are all represented in abstract settings, almost in a void of context, and only reference their past actions, which they regret; there is no reference to who they are in the present. Fisher suggests that the audience is more likely to see the humanity in the more familiar home setting and therefore have more empathy with the secretary of state rather than those associated with terrorist groups. And I think she's got a point. The semiotics of presentation and representation are powerful stuff. The medium can be extremely influential; artists can control how passive or active our audience will be, and we can influence how our audience feels about the people they are listening to simply by how they are physically manifest on stage... and it's likely that the audience might never even be conscious of the manipulation.

WHAT ARE THE ETHICS OF EDITING?

Another tool of manipulation that the audience might not be conscious of is the editing process. We can never put everything we hear into the work, nor should we. We also need to construct the arc of our story in ways that make for compelling, engaging, and consumable art. This means we will always make decisions about what goes in, what stays out, what goes after what, and what we put next to what.

Plays with extensive source material require rigorous editing. Plays such as Peter Weiss' *The Investigation*, which sampled just a small percentage of hundreds of hours of testimony, or Tricycle Theatre's Tribunal Plays, which took select sections of weeks of court transcripts, required that their playwrights make big choices about what to feature and what to redact. When it comes to editing, in his 2015 interview with Jessica King for Indie Wire, filmmaker Joshua Oppenheimer described some mentorship he'd gotten from Werner Herzog: Herzog showed Oppenheimer his notebook—while Herzog is reviewing footage, he keeps a running list, jotting down one, two, or three exclamation marks depending on how excited he is about each section. Then he only keeps footage that scored three exclamation marks. I think this is brilliant and want to try it in my next process, but I wonder where the traps are. Care would need to be taken so that the audience is not sitting through only a sequence of big events, which can feel repetitive and exhausting when adapted for the stage. Work for the stage tends to want highs and lows, big moments, small moments, and moments of stillness when the audience gets a chance to breathe. With this need for drastic cutting, do we include the sections that will enrage the audience? Or the parts that comfort them? The confusing parts or the crystal-clear sections? Probably a little bit of all these, yes? Do we choose what will defend the character or what will prosecute the character? Say, for example, we are representing someone on stage who has told us about a time when they did something very wrong. At the end of that story, the person tells us they now know how wrong they were and have remorse. If we only tell the story of the wrong committed, are we robbing that character (a person becomes a character once we put them on stage) of redemption? It's a ham-fisted example, but my point is that it's quite easy to manipulate what the audience is taking for granted as fact.

A photographer makes similar decisions about what they put inside the frame and what they leave out; the frame really does control the story. With writing for the stage, we must decide when to start the story and when to end it. When our play is based on real events and real people, clearly, there are never clean beginnings and endings. Real life is a continuum. But we writers must start somewhere and end somewhere else. There's an adage in writing classes that goes, "get in late, leave early." Meaning, don't take too much time setting up a story, and end a story leaving the audience wanting more. But are there ethical ramifications to consider?

Lisa Loomer's 2016 play *Roe*, about the real Jane Roe of the US Supreme Court case *Roe v. Wade*, does not fall into the category of Verbatim or Tribunal Play, as Loomer brought her own quirky (her word, not mine), funny writing style to the dialogue.[10] However, most of the characters in the play are based on the very real people involved in this case. I agree with Loomer when she called it a History Play. It's quite a feat, what she has done with *Roe*. She has taken one of the most serious issues in our lives, honored the gravity but also brought humor to such a sobering subject. The humor and humanity of the play give the audience space to feel whatever they feel, without being pushed into a corner. I recently sat in a full theatre in Austin, Texas to see *Roe*, and everyone around me was quite engrossed. This recent production[11] was part of a series of productions around the United States, for which Loomer made revisions to better connect to the current state of abortion law. The play's two protagonists are Norma McCorvey (the real Jane Roe) and Sarah Weddington, the lawyer who argued Roe's right to an abortion. The play starts with an aged Weddington looking back on the case, then travels back to the very beginning of McCorvey's story. The second act covers the dramatic turn McCorvey's life took after the case was won: McCorvey became an evangelical Christian, then later a Catholic, and the spokesperson for anti-abortion activists. A pretty stunning turn-around—and Loomer shapes this story with skill. What's interesting, however, is where Loomer chose to end the play. In the 2020 documentary *AKA Jane Roe*, by Nick Sweeney and produced by FX, McCorvey flips once again shortly before her death.

She states—on camera—that she was never against abortion but did it for the money. However, two people in her life, both anti-abortion activists, affirm that at the very end of her life she said once again that she was against abortion. Loomer's frame ends before this muddied and complicated final act. Without the third reveal, it's a simpler story. The play ends with two equally opposing views: Weddington's conviction that all women should have a right to an abortion and McCorvey's stance against it. It's a cleaner version of what happened: Balanced scales that seemingly allow the audience to leave with both sides squarely on stage, to decide for themselves. Which is the more dramatic choice? Likely the one Loomer made. Which is the more ethical? Should it matter if the audience leaves without knowing that McCorvey gave a "death bed confession"[12] and recanted her previous recanting? Or is it the audience's job to go home and research that final act?

Sometimes playwrights leave things out deliberately, and sometimes we just make mistakes, which we can hopefully correct before production and publication. For me, when I've been able to have a closed reading of the play in front of the stakeholders—the people represented in the play—it has proven to be very helpful in catching mistakes or places when I'm unknowingly telling only half of the story. In a 2007 conversation with Will Hammond, co-editor of *Verbatim: Contemporary Documentary Theatre*, and Max Stafford-Clark, director and founder of Out of Joint theatre company, the British playwright, screenwriter, essayist, and poet David Hare describes missing something in his play *The Permanent Way*. *The Permanent Way* was about the privatization of the British railway system but is *really* about how people deal with grief and suffering. There was a train crash in Hatfield, Hertfordshire, and in Hare's play, when the executive of the railway company arrived on the scene and was told that the fault was in the track and not the train, he's quoted in the play as saying, "Thank Christ it's not our crash." This was something that this executive had told the actors of the company Out of Joint, and they relayed this interview to Hare, who put it in the play. After the play premiered, the executive called the producers and complained that he was grossly misrepresented. He had also told the interviewers, right after this first statement, that he was very upset about the crash. When Hare heard the complaint, he said, "I agree" and subsequently added a second line for future productions.[13] But this was after the premiere, and who knows how many people in those first audiences walked away with half-informed rage toward this executive? I think Hare is a terrific writer of nonfiction and documentary plays, so in addition to a cautionary tale, I find comfort that someone with such great skill and craft also needs revision. This anecdote is a good reminder of the value of conducting your own interviews. We can't always be at every interview, and having the actors interview the people they would play was an intentional and effective methodology of Out of Joint's, but nevertheless, it can prove useful to hear things for ourselves when we can.

This is obviously impossible when we are constructing a work from a historical event, even if that event took place in the not-too-distant past, such as Heiner Kipphardt's 1964 play *In the Matter of J. Robert Oppenheimer*. Kipphardt distilled 3,000 pages of material from the 1954 US Atomic Energy Commission (AEC) hearing to determine Oppenheimer's government security clearance. (Those who have seen Christopher Nolan's blockbuster film will recognize dialogue.) Obviously, Kipphardt could not put all 3,000 pages into one play, and he writes in his forward to the published script:

> As the author's business is the stage, and not the writing of history, he endeavours to follow Hegel's[14] advice and lay bare "the core and significance" of a historical event by freeing it from the "adventitious contingencies and irrelevant accessories of the event." to "strip away the circumstances and aspects that are of merely secondary importance, and to replace them with such that allow the essence of the matter to appear in all clarity."

Kipphardt forged several individuals into one in order to get at that clarity. I get it and do the same. The other action Kipphardt took, which I have done as well, is that he *added* text that was not in the source material. At the top of the play, the character Oppenheimer walks downstage and addresses the audience, setting up what the audience is about to see. Between scenes, other characters deliver direct-address monologues defending their point of view. At the end, Oppenheimer has a monologue in which he questions whether a scientist should be loyal to governments or not. These monologues are Kipphardt's fiction. He states in the forward that they were informed by what the individuals had said in other media, but nonetheless, they are pockets of fiction in a play that presents as non-fiction, albeit theatricalized non-fiction. Do I think an author should follow rigid rules? Absolutely not. Do I think historical plays should not take a flight of imagination? No. Where would we be without Shakespeare's history plays, or the very recent and wonderful *Oslo* by JT Rogers, which fictionalizes the real and remarkable "back-channel talks" behind the 1993 Oslo Peace Accords? The reason we are drawn to real events is that they are often better than fiction, and frequently authors have to fictionalize in order to adapt the story into the media of presentation. Perhaps I'm curious about Kipphardt's play because I'm curious about my own ethics: When I signal to the audience, "This is real! This person really said this!" and then slide in my own writing, informed be the real person but my own fiction nonetheless… is that ethical?

When the audience believes that what they are hearing is true, it pulls them into the experience, and when they are listening to someone recount the event as a primary witness, it can hook the audience even more, and this can be a seductive fix. It can tempt us to cut corners to get that fix.

WHAT ARE THE ETHICS OF A DELIBERATE SEQUENCE?

In *Understanding Comics,* Scott McCloud defines comics as a sequential art. One image is placed in sequence with another. The same goes for theatre. Because time and space are compressed on stage, we are in fact writing a sequence of moments. And we can put this sequence in any order. I firmly believe that theatre's closest cousin is not TV or film, but comics. Especially because of the "gutter." The gutter, in the parlance of comics, is the space between one image and the next. Usually, there is some sort of jump in time, character, or perspective between one image and the next. For example: Imagine a comic strip in three boxes, with an image in each. In the first box, we see two people facing each other, one red in the face and clenching their fists; in box two, we see an extended arm, an oversized fist, and the word "POW!"; in the third frame, the silhouette of a body on the pavement.

We did not see the fight. We only saw three still images separated by gutters. Our brain jumped those gutters and filled in the details. We *think* we read the whole story, but really, we are just jumping across gutters, filling in missing parts. The sequence of images determines the story we complete. All this holds true for the stage. The audience is watching a sequence of limited images—a couch and coffee table represent a living room, a circle is the moon. Even in examples of American realism or naturalism, and even if the entire play takes place in real-time, I would bet good money that we are still only seeing a limited representation, quite literally in a box.

When we juxtapose these images/moments/text that sit between gutters, that act of jumping the gutter creates meaning and can trigger emotion in the audience. A collaborator of mine, Jenny Mercein,[15] and I made a play for Berkely Rep and Baltimore Center Stage called *X's and O's* which was about American Football. I was a football fan but was turning sour on the sport because of the head injury crisis, and I conceived the play because I needed to figure out how I felt about it and whether I could continue to be a fan. Jenny's father had been a professional football player, and she and I set about interviewing retired players, young athletes with dreams of playing professionally, superfans, coaches, researchers studying Chronic Traumatic Encephalopathy (CTE), and wives of players who took their own life and were diagnosed postmortem with CTE. We juxtaposed the verbatim dialogue of a high school player in the full flush of his athleticism, talking about how strong he's getting and how good his playing is becoming, with a retired football player who still loved the game talking about his over 60 surgeries from injuries. The young player was on one side of the stage, working out and running drills as he spoke, the older on the other, sitting in an armchair. Jenny and I knew that when the audience "jumped the gutter" between these two juxtaposed moments, there would be some emotional resonance. It's manipulative. It's effective. We didn't make up either experience, we were very honest with how we edited our interviews, but we were very deliberate in what we put next to what.

Sequence and juxtaposition are very powerful tools.

CERTAINTY OR AMBIVALENCE: WHICH WAY SHOULD I LEAN?

As I crafted *X's and O's* with collaboration and feedback from Jenny and the director, Tony Taccone,[16] my goal was to lean into my ambivalence. I didn't want this to be what scholar Christine Simonian Bean terms Activist Documentary Theatre.[17] I did not want to write a play that said football is bad, because when you talk to enough of those doing it, they'll give you lots of reasons why they love it. My hope was to simply lay out the math, to follow my own questions about what the sport gives us and what it takes away, and ask the question: "Are we willing to live with that math?" However, in the course of the two years conducting interviews, my own views started to fall pretty hard on one side of that equation. I haven't watched much football since, and I don't doubt that my change of heart seeped into the play, informed my decisions about what I put where and what was in that gutter. I don't doubt that for many in the audience, the play was not as ambivalent as I had planned.

When it comes to political theatre—and I'm using the word political as German theatre director Erwin Piscator used it, as "being of general concern"—I wonder if my responsibility is to take an issue and clarify, simplify, and take an unambiguous stance, or is my job to show complexity, incompleteness, the messiness and muddiness of a political issue?

I can think of no better voice in favor of ambiguity than David Hare. In a 2022 interview with *The Guardian*, Hare argues for complexity. Though he admits to his own guilt in doing the same at times in his own plays, he says, "There is an awful lot of pious theatre at the moment." What he means is that he's seeing lots of plays in which the writer takes a complex subject, simplifies it, and serves it to an audience that is likely already on the political side of the argument. Hare declares that too many playwrights today are writing plays that are preaching to the choir. He warns that audiences are leaving with previously held beliefs simply reinforced and says he thinks the best documentary theatre surprises the audience, rather than confirms what is known. His is a rallying call to leave the audience confused and conflicted and describes his own job as "to examine the ills of the world and leave people with very ambiguous feelings about what can be done about them and their own involvement."

Whichever side a writer lands on, I have no ambivalence when it comes to my opinion of the value of ambivalence in the research and development process: It's really, really helpful. If we begin with what the Australian playwright Alana Valentine, calls an "unanswerable question," then there is no telling what trove of great source material will come our way. If we are insatiably curious, confused, and uncertain, then we look in all directions for answers.

WHOSE STORIES DO I HAVE A RIGHT TO TELL?

This might be the hardest question to answer, and my own offerings remain very much in draft. I am an interloper when I represent a community that is not my own. I felt like less of an interloper when Emily and I built *ReEntry* because I had five brothers who served in the military during the Vietnam War, and even though I was interviewing combat veterans from very different wars, I felt enough of a kinship with these veterans' families that I was confident in our representations. I do, however, wonder about telling the stories of Philip Paul and Little Willie John. Both Paul and John are Black, both musicians; I am neither. Do I have the right to tell their stories? Mr. Paul watched rehearsals and performances and expressed his support for my representation. But Mr. John never got a chance to give me his permission. I eventually received support from his sister, Mabel, after she read the rehearsal draft, but when I first called her, she let me know in no uncertain terms that I was an interloper, and I was extremely grateful to her for doing so. She pointed out that no matter how extensive my research, I was painting a picture of a man based on a limited glance: Limited newspaper articles, a few boxes of artifacts, interviews with *some* of those that knew him… she let me know that this was an incomplete view. Mine was a character, hers was a brother. So, I put this sentiment in the play. The actor who plays Little Willie John, when thumbing

THE ETHICS OF LISTENING 119

through a box full of King albums, pulls out one of James Brown's records and says to the audience:

Look, I knew Brown as an artist, I knew him as a person, but even I, who knew him fairly well, I only knew a small piece of his life.
What do you know of James Brown?
His records, his music, of course.
And then...
What you read about him or heard on the news?
The drug problems?
The arrests?
The down-and-out times?
His death?
We sketch together a man from a cultivated performance and reportage from a lot of people who had something to gain from what and how they told you his story.

Later, when talking about his own life, the character Little Willie John walks over to a box of (real) newspaper clippings about him and mementos of his career and says:

Maybe there's something in one of these boxes that'll explain how it all went south.
Is there a cardboard box somewhere of things about you?
If this is how you'd be remembered, what would be in your box?
What would you want in there?
And what would be in there regardless of what you want, what you need?

My intention was to be as transparent as possible, but nevertheless, I can't help but wonder if I'm the person who *should* be telling these stories.

On the other hand, I think of Studs Terkel. I think about all the lives, all the stories, that would have gone unchronicled if he had limited his listening to only people in his own communities. Appropriation is real and does real damage, but on the other hand, locking ourselves into silos of experiences creates its own problems. This essential question about who has the right to tell what story is further discussed in Chapter 14 in my interview with playwright and artistic leader Idris Goodwin.

I also think that there are certain times and certain stories that are well served when the writer has distance from the experience. Sometimes people would rather talk with someone who is not a stakeholder. Sometimes people feel more comfortable sharing things with someone outside their circle.

Perhaps this need not be such a binary. There's a whole lot of room in the middle and a lot of ways we can tell a story from the inside *and* the out. The work of Cornerstone Theater Company, as I've discussed, is a great example. So too the work of Ping Chong and Company and The Telling Project. These companies not only offer community participants skills and resources to tell their own stories but also invite them into the making of the company's work, to tell their stories *together*—by, with, and for. Ping Chong, a National Medal of Arts recipient, has made an extraordinary contribution to theatre over his career. And the company he founded, Ping Chong and Company, has many branches and programs: They have created and produced over a hundred new works that "dismantled history, chronology, geography, race, and culture"[18] including a series of plays in their "East West Series" which included:

- *Deshima* (1990) tracing East-West interactions in Japan from the Sixteenth Century Dutch traders to the economic bubble of the 1980s.
- *Chinoiserie* (1994) an opera sprawling Chinese history from Chinese-English trade in 1793 to Chinese settlers in the US to the killing of a Chinese American in Detroit in 1982.
- *After Sorrow* (1997) a dance piece about the legacy of war in Vietnam.
- *Pojagi* (1999) an expressionistic meditation on Korean-European history spanning four decades.

In addition to a substantial body of theatrical reflections and reclamations of history, Ping Chong also founded the Undesirable Elements (UE) project, which has produced hundreds of performances for over two decades. Participants in a UE project are interviewed, and that material gets edited and crafted into a script that is then performed by those same individuals; it's people telling their own stories on stage. An interview with Sara Zatz, who serves on the current artistic leadership team of Ping Chong and Company and has been working with UE for 20 years can be found in Chapter 11.

The Telling Project, founded in 2008, works in a similar fashion in that the company of artists work with participants to help them tell their own stories on stage. Founded by Jonathan Wei in 2007, The Telling Project began with the focus of US military veterans sharing their own stories and has since expanded to telling stories of immigration, migration, and seeking refuge. All stories are performed by the people who lived the experience. The staging, like Ping Chong and Company's EU, is simple: Only chairs and music stands so that the focus is on the story, with nothing else to get in the way or create any illusions. The company's mission is "It's time to speak. It's time to listen."[19]

WHAT IS "FAIR"? WHAT DOES "HEARING ALL SIDES" MEAN?

I started this book by writing that I used to believe that I had to hear all sides of every story. Then, when I was no longer capable of listening to some voices, everything I thought I knew about my work fell apart. But now, I think I'm moving toward a new understanding of "all sides of a story." First, what does that even mean? Equal balance in any given situation only exists if all arguments hold equal weight. And equal weight does not mean that all sides get equal airtime, but that all sides are *weighted* relative to the context and assessment. If they are not, then it's a false equivalency.

Here's an example of false equivalency: Ninety-nine percent of climate scientists say that climate change, caused by the actions of humans, exists. One percent of climate scientists deny human-caused climate change. So, if I'm reporting on climate change, it's a false equivalency to think that what is fair is to have a climate denier speak every time I hear from a scientist who says climate change is real. In fact, the *truly* fair and balanced thing to do is give the climate denier voice only once to every 99 times we hear from a scientist who confirms climate change.

Another way to think about false equivalency is to imagine any object's center of gravity. The center of gravity is the location in any given object where the entire weight of the body is centered. Think of a see-saw: A long piece of wood balancing on a crossbar. If the wood has equal weight on both sides, then perfect balance exists when its resting place on the crossbar is at the very center of the board. That's the center of gravity for the wood. However, if one end of the wood is heavier than the other, then the center of gravity must be moved closer to the heavier side in order to find balance.

I feel like Nero at the end of the first Matrix movie! Now that I understand false equivalency, I can see it all around me. And I feel so much freer to lean further toward one side. I'm going to lean toward what has weight. I'm no longer going to confuse fairness and balance with false equivalency. And I know that in order to be truly balanced, sometimes I will need to move in one direction or the other.

I'll end this chapter with a discussion of the Australian playwright and director Alana Valentine. Valentine's work, which is often in the verbatim or non-fiction milieu, connects with many of the questions surveyed here. Her play *Parramatta Girls* got me thinking about the relationship between the author and those she listens to. *Parramatta Girls* is based on the experiences and lives of a group of women who, as children, were incarcerated at the Girls Training School at Parramatta. Despite the bucolic-sounding title, this was a brutal place where young girls ages 13–18 were incarcerated. In Australia's not-to-distant past, there were hundreds of thousands of women over the course of nearly a century who were incarcerated—some sent for truancy, some committed after parents abandoned or abused them and the girls were charged with "neglect." There was much abuse and cruelty suffered at Parramatta, and the majority of Australians had no idea. Valentine interviewed a group of these women who had been incarcerated as children, and her play was part of the building of a bridge between these experiences and the general public who had not heard of Parramatta or what went on there.

Valentine starts the play with the characters, based on the real women she interviewed, returning the Parramatta for a reunion. In a 2018 interview with Martin Portus for a State Library of New South Whales Oral History Project, Valentine states that she will often conduct interviews in groups, particularly during reunions, because these are moments when people are often in a state of great change: They are in a moment that is both in the past and present. They're revisiting their past, wrestling with who they were and what they felt, while reflecting on who they are now.

In that same interview, Valentine noted that she only interviewed women who had a strong support network in their lives, which is a helpful model for ethical practice. Retelling a traumatic event can be triggering for some, and though we are not trained medical practitioners or social workers—nor should we act as such—we can take time to check in to see if those we listen to (based on the content of the story) might have family, friends, health providers or others in their circle who can be there to help them if the process of remembering becomes triggering or in any other way disruptive. The National Institute of Health (NIH) Library of Medicine has many references for understanding the impact of trauma. But I reiterate: We are not mental health practitioners. We are not there to *treat* the person; we are there to listen. And if the individual might be harmed by the interview process, then it's not the right time to listen. Valentine is honoring transparency with those she is listening to. She in no way pretends that the act of listening has no ramifications.

The structure of Valentine's play also has transparency, in that it is clearly *her* play. The dramaturgy makes it clear that there is an author's hand shaping the delivery of the story. The events are authentic, but Valentine puts them into a crafted structure: It begins with a reunion at the gates of Parramatta and then the plays sweeps back and forth between moments from the past, present, and timeless dream-like sequences that bring to the stage shards and glimpses into emotional spaces. Valentine combined interviews with 35 women into eight characters. When she takes material from several lives and crafts them into one, she always asks the participants' permission to do so.

In my opinion, Valentine resists the trap of torture porn by showing well-rounded humans on stage, not two-dimensional victims. The term torture porn is commonly used when referring to horror films that spend an inexorable amount of film time on violent scenes, showing gore and suffering in great detail. I've stolen this term and use it in my own line of work when I suspect that I am giving too much focus to descriptions of human suffering, as I fear I am getting some sort of subconscious, emotional "fix" from hearing the gory details of someone's trauma. In *Parramatta Girls* we see moments of resiliency, humor, and fancy, and we see them at times behaving badly toward each other— we see children being *real* children. The characters are not only angelic victims, but they are very real humans with real human failings. The play is as much about the women coming to terms with how they treated each other as it is about how Parramatta treated them. Valentine's work strives to break through the mythology of a monolithic community by showing how all communities have internal conflicts and that people of one community never think, feel, or act in monolithic ways.

Valentine has said in several interviews that now, even after the play has been produced and published, that she gets calls from other women who had been incarcerated at Parramatta, wanting to tell her their story. She stays on the line and listens. Even though the play is finished, she listens because she understands that sometimes people just need someone to listen to them. And I think she offers another example of a way of giving back. When we amplify, when we take, we can't just turn the recorder off and walk away. A simple way to give back is to just keep on listening.

NOTES

[1] New York Film Academy. Cinéma Vérité vs. Direct Cinema: An Introduction. NYFA, November 16, 2022, www.nyfa.edu/student-resources/cinema-verite-vs-direct-cinema-an-introduction/.

[2] Greg Pierotti, Barbara Pitts, Stephen Wangh, Amanda Gronich, Sara Lambert, John McAdams, Maude Mitchell, Andy Paris, and Kelli Simpkins.

[3] From the description of *The* Ladies released by the publisher, Playscripts, Inc. Accessed February 26, 2024, https://www.playscripts.com/play/1668.

4 Spoken by the character (and actor) Colleen Worthman.
5 Mixed Blood Theatre Company was founded in 1976 by Jack Reuler, and the company describes "Radical Hospitality" as "core to all Mixed Blood does." Mixed Blood Theatre Company, "About." Accessed February 26, 2024, https://mixedblood.com/about/.
6 Henry Glover (1921–1991).
7 Both *Cincinnati King* (2018) and *Need Your Love* (2021) were commissioned by and received their world premieres at Cincinnati Playhouse in the Park, Blake Robison Artistic Director.
8 Writers Guild Initiative. "About the Initiative." Accessed February 26, 2024, https://writersguildinitiative.com/about/.
9 O-Dark-Thirty. "Home." Accessed February 26, 2024, https://o-dark-thirty.org/.
10 Lisa Loomer. "Interview with Lisa Loomer," filmed August 13, 2015 with the Association for Theatre in Higher Education, video, https://www.youtube.com/watch?v=oZYvGQCYpZU&ab_channel=AssociationforTheatreinHigherEducation.
11 *Roe* by Lisa Loomer, directed by Jenny Lavery, ZACH Theatre, Austin, Texas, April 5–30, 2023.
12 Which is what McCorvey calls it in Sweeney's documentary film.
13 Hammond, *Verbatim*, 61.
14 Hegel. *Äesthetik*, 897. Berlin: Aufbau-Verlag, 1955.
15 Associate Professor, Tulane University.
16 Taccone has had a significant impact on the American theatre. He is the former artistic director of Berkeley Repertory Theatre in Berkeley, California, and has collaborated with artists such as Tony Kushner, Sarah Jones, John Leguizamo, and Carrie Fisher.
17 Bean wrote a fascinating case study of the ethical complexities involved in producing Blank and Jessen's *The Exonerated* in 2014: "Dramaturging the "Truth" in The Exonerated: Ethics, Counter-Text, and Activism in Documentary Theatre." *Theatre Topics* 24, no. 3 (September 2014): 187–97.
18 Ping Chong and Company. "Company." Accessed February 26, 2024, https://www.pingchong.org/about/company.
19 The Telling Project. "Home." Accessed February 26, 2024, https://thetellingproject.org.

BIBLIOGRAPHY

Arias, Lola, and Daniel Tunnard. *Minefield*. London: Oberon Books, 2017.

Bean, Christine. "Dramaturging the 'Truth' in *The Exonerated*: Ethics, Counter-Text, and Activism in Documentary Theatre." *Theatre Topics* 24, no. 3 (2014): 187–97.

Cosson, Steven, ed. *The Civilians: An Anthology of Six Plays*. New York: Playscripts, 2009.

Ebert, Roger. "Herzog's Minnesota Declaration: Defining 'Ecstatic Truth.'" Ebert Digital LLC, April 30, 1999. https://www.rogerebert.com/roger-ebert/herzogs-minnesota-declaration-defining-ecstatic-truth.

Fisher, Amanda Stuart. *Performing the Testimonial: Rethinking Verbatim Dramaturgies.* Manchester: Manchester University Press, 2020.

Franklin, Corrinne. "Belonging to Bad: Ambiguity, Parramatta Girls and the Parramatta Girls Home." *Geographical Research* 52, no. 2 (2014): 157–67.

Hammond, William, and Dan Steward, eds. *Verbatim, Verbatim: Contemporary Documentary Theatre.* London: Oberon, 2008.

The Herald. "Raising the Curtain on 1990 Events." February 2, 1989. https://www.heraldscotland.com/news/11993510.raising-the-curtain-on-1990-events/.

Kipphardt, Heinar. *In the Matter of J. Robert Oppenheimer: a Play Freely Adapted, on the Basis of the Documents.* Translated by Ruth Speirs. North Yorkshire, England: Methuen Publishing, 1967.

Like Stories of Old. "The Inner Chronicle of What We Are – Understanding Werner Herzog." Mubi, YouTube, February 28, 2019. www.youtube.com/watch?v=k1W5wAGzCpU.

McCloud, Scott. *Understanding Comics: The Invisible Art.* New York: Harper Perennial, 1994.

McLuhan, Marshall. *Understanding Media: The Extensions of Man.* Cambridge: MIT Press, 1994.

Reisz, Matthew. "David Hare: 'There Is an Awful Lot of Pious Theatre at the Moment.'" *The Guardian*, August 6, 2022. https://www.theguardian.com/books/2022/aug/06/david-hare-there-is-an-awful-lot-of-pious-theatre-at-the-moment.

Rogers, J. T. *Oslo.* New York: Theatre Communications Group, 2017.

Sanchez, K. J. *Cincinnati King.* Directed by K. J. Sanchez. Cincinnati, Ohio: Cincinnati Playhouse in the Park, November 2018.

Sanchez, K. J. *Need Your Love.* Directed by K. J. Sanchez. Cincinnati, Ohio: Cincinnati Playhouse in the Park, November 2021.

Sanchez, KJ, and Jenny Mercein. *X's and O's.* Directed by Tony Taccone. Baltimore, MD: CenterStage, November 2015, and Berkeley Repertory Theatre, Berkeley, CA, March 2015.

Sullivan, Corrinne. "Aboriginal Inmate Experiences of Parramatta Girls Home." *Australian Aboriginal Studies Journal* 2 (2017): 84–98.

Valentine, Alana. *Parramatta Girls.* Strawberry Hills, NSW: Currency Press, 2007.

Valentine, Alana. "Item 1: Alana Valentine Interviews by Martin Portus, 16–17 April 2018." Interview by Martin Portus, Mitchell Library, State Library of New South Wales, April 16–17, 2018. Audio, 02:15:41. https://collection.sl.nsw.gov.au/record/YzOmVbO9.

6

STUDS

When I'm feeling cynical, I think of Gore Vidal's conviction that "We are the United States of Amnesia, we learn nothing because we remember nothing." And when I fear that this amnesia will be our demise, I try my level best to focus on people who are helping us remember. I think of writers like:

Zora Neale Hurston, who in 1927 in Plateau, Alabama interviewed Oluale Kossola, also known as Cudjoe Lewis, an 86-year-old formerly enslaved person who at the time was the only known living survivor of the Middle Passage, on the human cargo ship *Clotilda*, which was operating illegally 52 years after Congress passed the Act Prohibiting Importation of Slaves. Hurston and Kossola spent weeks together, eating together, cleaning the local church together, and getting to know one another. She included these conversations, along with her own memories and reflections of her time, in *Barracoon: The Story of the Last Black Cargo*. One of the many things that makes Hurston's book special, for me, is that she preserved

Oluale Kossola's vernacular. Believe it or not, this book was not published until 2018, *91 years* after Huston interviewed Kossola. It sat on a shelf at Howard University all those years because publishers did not have faith readers would follow Kossola's vernacular, there were tensions between Hurston and her patron, and there were some questions about an article the young Hurston had written when she was just starting out that lacked proper citation.

Joan Didion, was one of the pioneers of New Journalism, a style that writers like Didion, Tom Wolfe, and Hunter S. Thompson developed in the 1960s. Whereas traditional journalism strives to be objective, with journalists attempting to remove themselves from the reportage as much as possible, New Journalism is a form wherein the writer puts themselves into the narrative and blends objective facts with subjective points of view. This allows the writer to not only chronicle the hard facts but also chronicle the mood and spirit of the time. By including their own subjective responses to the factual events, they are able to chronicle how they are experiencing the events, which I think is a great way to capture the vibe of a time. Didion's *The White Album* is a searing collection of previously published articles that chronicles some of the cultural and civic structures of Southern California of the late sixties. *The White Album* covers a wide array of subjects: From the women's movement to city planning (and her obsession with how malls are built) to her own strange connections to the Manson murders. If we are to remember the past, I think it's helpful to balance traditional journalistic reportage with first-person sources alongside subjective reportage that not only tells us what people were doing, but how people *felt* about what they were doing. Didion's very first line in *The White Album* is what I consider one of the most perfect sentences in literature:

> We tell ourselves stories in order to live.

Lt. Gen. Harold G. Moore and Joseph L. Galloway, a commanding officer and journalist, respectively, who fought in and reported from the Battle of Ia Drang, one of the first and bloodiest battles in the US war in Vietnam. In the early 1980s, Moore and Galloway collected statements from warfighters who survived Ia Drang. They also returned to Vietnam to revisit the battlefield and interview North Vietnamese commanders—the very leaders Moore battled just a few years earlier. These interviews and personal experiences make up their seminal *We were Soldiers Once ... and Young; Ia Drang—The Battle That Changed the War in Vietnam.*

Arthur Taylor, whose 1977 book *Notes and Tones* holds some of the finest interviews with some of the greatest musicians of all time such as Philly Joe Jones, Max Roach, Dizzy Gillespie, and Nina Simone. In this collection of conversations, Freddie Hubbard talks about his connection to his audience:

> The older I get, the more I'm trying to get involved with other people's feelings listening to me, whereas before I used to play whatever I felt I ought to play. But now the whole thing works off vibrations. If I feel the people are cold, I think maybe if I do this, it will warm them up. That's what music is about. You try to connect emotions no matter what you play. Even if there are only one or two people, you want to be able to get to them; otherwise, you're just playing for yourself.

I think of documentary filmmakers like:

Joshua Oppenheimer, whose shattering film *An Act of Killing,* co-directed by Christine Cynn and an anonymous Indonesian director (who has to remain anonymous because exposure remains unsafe), is about the 1965–1966 genocides in Indonesia. This film completely redefined what a documentary film could do. The production team established relationships with two executioners known for killing hundreds of innocent people. These executioners were celebrated as national heroes in Indonesia because, as one executioner says in the film, "War crimes are defined by the winners." The second thing that makes this film so unique is that instead of just interviewing these killers, the directors gave them cameras, crew, and actors, inviting them to make their *own movie* about what they did, in the genre of the old 1940s Chicago gangster films that these executioners loved so dearly. Oppenheimer and his team then filmed these executioners as they made their own movie, and though the killers' goal was to make a film that glorified their crimes, the process takes them places entirely unexpected; what is revealed about their sense of responsibility and guilt is truly revelatory.

An Act of Killing was not made overnight. It took nearly a decade to make. Oppenheimer and Cynn originally traveled to Indonesia to help make a film about plantation workers trying to unionize. Through that first project, Oppenheimer got to know non-governmental organization workers, scholars, and activists who were risking their lives documenting the Indonesian government's brutal oppression of its people. Oppenheimer realized that he, as a non-Indonesian, could take risks that Indonesians could not. As he describes in a 2015 *IndieWire* interview with Jessica Kiang:

> I think gradually I felt charged with work that they couldn't do. I never felt like the American filmmaker coming in to expose barbarism in this far-off country, to "save Indonesia." On the contrary, I felt like an agent of people with whom I was living, and deeply close, who asked me to do something that was not possible for them.

Ari Folman, who wrote, directed and produced the 2008 award-winning *Waltz with Bashir*. I cannot recommend this film more enthusiastically but to say: Any and all documentary theatre, film, radio, or podcast makers really must see this film. It's about the 1982 Israeli invasion of Lebanon and the siege of Beirut. During the invasion, Israel's allies, the Lebanese Christians, killed scores of Palestinians in refugee camps, and it was Israeli leaders and their soldiers that gave them assistance. Folman served as an Israeli soldier in this war and was experiencing nightmares and memory loss about where he was and what he did during the massacre. He began talking with his friends, fellow combat veterans. The dialogue in Folman's film was taken directly from these recorded conversations, and most of the voices heard in the film are the actual voices of the real people involved—a few asked that actors portray them, to protect their emotional and physical safety, but the actors read the transcriptions word for word. We *hear* these real people dealing with the very real aftermath of war, but what we are seeing is an *animated film,* accompanied by an outstanding and emotionally full musical score designed by Max Richter. This film is so special that it invented its own genre: "adult animated war documentary drama film." The dialogue keeps the film rooted in the real, and the animation allows for metaphor, dream, and imagination, which invites the audience to tap into a different set of truths: Emotional truths and visceral realities that we might not have words for, and the broken, shattered, incomplete truths of the psyche. In a 2008 interview on *National Public Radio's All Things Considered* Folman discussed why he felt urged to produce this film:

> For me, it was very essential to bring young audiences to the theaters to watch the film because I thought that if this film could influence even one teenager making the decision not to go the war, it doesn't matter where I did my job, I earned it ... All wars are useless ... and sometimes in films we tend to glorify them by making all of those great characters and they show you it's all about bravery and brotherhood of man. And I don't believe in that.

When I fear that we, as a society, are sliding into Gore Vidal's United States of Amnesia, I remember these writers and filmmakers, who are just a few of the many good people exposing necessary truths and chronicling the darker and more pivotal times of human experience so that we don't forget who we are, what we did, and how we *felt* about what we did.

"What people do and how they feel about what they do" is a phrase I often rely on when I talk about Documentary Theatre. I aspire to capture not only what they did but how they felt/feel about it. And I stole this phrase and approach from an incredibly prolific oral historian, **Studs Terkel.** The title of one of Studs's books is *Working: People Talk About What They Do All Day and How They Feel About What They Do.*

When it comes to the radical act of listening, Studs Terkel is the real deal, and if you don't know him, run to your library and dive into any number of his books, such as *Division Street: America* (1967)—a study of the city of Chicago through interviews with residents of all walks of life, or *Hard Times: An Oral History of the Great Depression* (1970) which, as the title describes, remembers what it took and how it felt to survive the Great Depression.

One of my favorite books by Studs (I realize that I usually use last names when referencing people in this book, but I am choosing to always use 'Studs' instead of "Terkel' because Studs is a great name and everyone knew him as Studs) is *"The Good War": An Oral History of World War II* (1984). This Pulitzer Prize-winning book holds countless and surprising portraits of people living, working, entertaining, loving, protesting, fighting, and dying in the Second World War. Studs intentionally places the title within quotation marks and uses the phrase "good war" ironically because he believed there was no such thing as a good war. This collection was published less than a decade after the US war in Vietnam, and I suspect that the Vietnam War (the war no one felt good about) was very much on his mind when reflecting on World War II. In interviews promoting the book, Studs discussed his intention to strip away the romantic mythology of WWII, and that he wrote this book for the Baby Boomers, for the children of silent fathers and uncles who never talked about the war with their children. These silent veterans did, however, talk to Studs. They shared aspects of the war not commonly discussed at the time, such as the internment of Japanese Americans, our segregated military, and the struggles women faced after the war when they had to give up their newfound jobs and freedoms (from Rosie the Riveter to Betty Crocker in a hot minute). This is a book you can leave on a coffee table and open every now and again—just open to a random page and you'll find an interview that will be sure to offer new understanding and insight.

Studs was not always an oral historian. In fact, he came to this vocation later in his life: Born Louis Terkel in 1912, he first studied law, though he had no interest in practicing it. Studs then became a radio soap opera actor, playing gangsters—and sometimes running with real gangsters when they recognized him and mistook him for one of their own. Studs was deeply invested in politics and had a profound commitment to Franklin D. Roosevelt's New Deal, and in the early 1930s, he performed radio plays for the Works Progress Administration (WPA). He married his dedication to politics with his acting career, performing on stage with the Chicago Repertory Group. In his 2007 memoir *Touch and Go,* Studs described this theatre company:

> Its audience was made up of teachers and social workers and cab drivers. It was the Great Depression and this was the theater of then: *Waiting for Lefty*,[1] *Cradle Will Rock*.[2] We performed Street Theater at picket lines and soup kitchens; We regularly appeared before unions, performing *Waiting for Lefty* as various strikes were being organized – performing in Union Halls, Finnish halls, Polish halls, Czech halls. Chicago was full of vitality. High, low ... roller coaster. This was the world I was engaged with and it was exciting.

During World War II Studs served as a clerk in the US Army—he could not fight at the front lines because he had a perforated eardrum. He had a robust sense of humor about nearly everything, and in a 2003 question and answer session with University of California students, Studs joked about his hearing impairment and how it made him a better listener, "It gets you closer to the truth."[3] He described how during Operation Iraqi Freedom—the US government's official name for the 2003 invasion of Iraq—President George W. Bush kept using the term "embedded journalists," but Studs tells the audience that what he heard was "in bed with journalists." The audience laughs and Studs continues, "And so, you see, hearing impairment does away with euphemism."

Studs's humor and showmanship was always a part of who he was; he was a natural entertainer. After the war, he became a disk jockey for a program called *Wax Museum.* Studs would bring recording artists onto his show, and because he was voraciously curious, the conversations would flow from music, to philosophy, to life. He was interviewing artists like Billie Holiday even before he knew he was becoming one of our country's most prolific interviewers. He also had his own TV show, *Studs Place,* about the everyman, the everyday lives of very everyday working people, which he also considered in *Touch and Go*:

> Studs Place was a revolutionary program; we were pioneers. Remember, this was 1949, and TV was a brand-new medium. The radio had brought hearing a voice into your home, but seeing someone, the visual aspect, this was brand new. Aida and I didn't have a TV set when *Studs Place* was on—we used to go over the Win's house to watch. Working on TV at that time it was frontier country, you could do anything—your own impulses could be expressed and nobody was there to stop it.

The *Wax Museum* eventually evolved into a documentary radio program on WFMT where Studs was on air for 45 years.

Finally, a publisher, connected by an actor working with The Second City—a Chicago staple founded in 1959—asked him to write a book, a collection of oral histories that became *Division Street*. And once *Division Street* hit the world, Studs spent the second half of his life chronicling the lives that had gone unchronicled and listening to people who never expected to be listened to:

> I have, after a fashion, been celebrated for having celebrated the lives of the uncelebrated among us; for lending voice to the face in the crowd.

But Studs never took credit for inventing anything new:

> It was Henry Mayhew, a contemporary of Dickens, who sought out the needle workers, the shoemakers, the street criers, the chimney sweeps; all those etceteras; and then one year, 1850, poured forth a million words, their words, in the *Morning Chronicle*.

Studs died in 2008 at the age of 96, and he worked to his very last day. He didn't start writing his first book until he was 55 years old, yet managed to publish *eighteen* books. His secret for such a long and productive life? He said it himself:

> Curiosity did not kill this cat.

When I read Stud's books and listen to archives of his radio program, I find lessons on radical listening:

- He made people feel needed. He needed to hear from them, he needed to understand how they felt, and he needed their help in understanding how things worked.
- He knew the importance of who to listen to. Choosing, as Mayhew did, the needle workers or the shoemakers is not a gesture that comes from any obligation to charity. It's simply a smart way to chronicle history. If we want to understand how things work, then we need to listen to the people actually doing the work.
- By choosing to listen to those doing the work, rather than business leaders, politicians, celebrities, etc., we also gain insights into human nature: What does 'one of the many' think and feel about what they do and how they live their lives? In Touch and Go[4] Studs uses Bertolt Brecht's words to make his case for this approach:

> Berthold Brecht, in a series of questions, put it this way:
>
> Who built the seven gates of Thebes ...?
>
> When the Chinese Wall was built, where did the masons go for lunch?
>
> When Cesar conquered Gaul, was there not even a cook in the army?
>
> When the Armada sank, we read that King Philip wept. Were there no other tears?
>
> That's what I believe oral history is about. It's about those who shed these other tears. Or who laughed that other laugh, during those rare moments of rebellious triumph. Consider some of these heroes of our day, whom I've had a good fortune to encounter. They are an arbitrary few I've chosen out of a multitude of such heroes.

Studs teaches me *how* to listen. He never led with credentials or bonafides, he never tried to be the expert, but just the opposite: His bumbling exemplifies the value of allowing vulnerability, frailty, and inadequacies to be seen. When he fumbled with the mechanics of turning on his recording device, he was never embarrassed, but rather, embraced it as a chance to undermine the notion of the interviewer as expert:

> How do I get people to say things they keep from others and even from themselves?
>
> Simple. It is my ineptitude, my slovenliness. The other, the ordinary person feels not only as good a being as I am; rather he feels somewhat superior ... I make it clear to the person that now and then I screw things up. I say I can't drive a car. I punched the wrong button. A goof up. The other points out to me: look the reel isn't moving, or the cassette seems to be stuck. Of Course, at that moment, the other feels needed, by me.
>
> The feeling of being needed may be the most important to any human, and especially to one who is regarded as no more than ordinary. In that way, there is empathy.

Studs teaches me how to ask questions, but more importantly, he gives me the confidence to trust that I can participate in the conversation and still avoid leading the person I'm listening to toward a pre-determined agenda (in other words, I can talk and still avoid going fishing). I used to think that my job as an interviewer was to simply be a blank canvas—to sit quietly and passively and let the person I'm listening to leave their imprimatur on me. I thought it was a passive job. Studs teaches me that listening is radically active. Because, like Krista Tippett, he teaches me that listening can be a conversation:

> We think of historians and scholars who research in great scope and detail. What I do in great scope and detail is converse; the phrase oral historian, when it refers to me, carries a somewhat whimsical connotation. People say, oh he's so friendly he makes conversation with anyone. He gets people to talk, he gets things out of people others miss. They attribute that to my generosity of spirit and my open mindedness when the truth is very simple: I like to have conversations, which gives me an excuse to talk as well.

Studs also reminds me to avoid seeking out people who are certain about their beliefs; after all, is there anything less interesting than firmly concretized dogma? Deeper comprehension often comes from people in the middle of change, or have had a big shift in their opinions:

> When I look for people, I'm not looking only for those who share my views, I'm looking for those who have grown to think a certain way, who have changed their views. A number of conservative people are in my books; not as many as more progressive thinkers, but that's not the point of my books at all. I'm looking for those who can talk about how they see their lives and the world around them. Who can explain how and why they became one way or another.

There are thousands of Studs' WFMT interviews archived online at studsterkel.wfmt.com. There, you can listen to Studs interview James Baldwin, which was broadcast by WFMT on July 15, 1961. There are some techniques from this particular interview that I'd like to note:

- Studs starts the program by playing a Bessie Smith record, which the two of them listen to live. This begins the conversation—talking about this Bessie Smith song. Immediately, this relieves pressure; It gives them both space to talk about a third party, to reflect on someone else's work, smartly taking the spotlight off the self.
- Studs then brings in Baldwin's own words, inviting the Baldwin that sits before him to respond to the Baldwin of the past, the Baldwin who wrote those words. It's done in such an effortless and pressure-free way that Baldwin seems immediately comfortable to reflect on parts of his work and persona that have changed, and those that still ring true. Baldwin is not pressured to defend his life or writing, but instead invited to reflect on it, almost as though it belonged to someone else, just as they talked about Bessie Smith's song.
- Studs listens so keenly that he can pluck out a single sentiment: Baldwin, in the first five minutes of the conversation, mentions—almost as if in passing—a sense of shame that his

young self carried, when it came to Bessie Smith, jazz, or such stereotypes as eating watermelon. Studs teases out this one word, "shame," and hands it back to Baldwin as a prompt, or perhaps even a catalyst. Studs isn't trying to make a particular point, nor is he playing any sort of "gotcha journalism" game. No, he simply keys into a term that naturally contains a well of feelings and context and passes it back to Baldwin to go where he will with it. Masterful. It seems so simple, but it takes so much practice and focus and energy to listen with nothing but unsatiable curiosity and unending empathy ... and to do so with ease, never forcing an answer. It takes guts and a lot of faith. And a lot of practice. Being a good listener is a muscle like any other muscle, and it gets stronger with repetition.

- Studs is an unassuming listener, making no assumptions about what Baldwin thinks or feels and no assumptions about where the conversation will go.
- Interviewing in the mode of conversation can feel, in a helpful way, like excavation. Together we are digging, and if we clear away enough debris/dirt/you-choose-your-metaphor, we will, *together,* uncover something special. To do so, we have to work together.

James Baldwin is such a brilliant thinker that just about anyone could have turned a recorder on and let James Baldwin talk, and odds are it would have been interesting. This interview with Studs, though, is outstanding because Studs invited Baldwin into a space where Baldwin could talk about the ways he is changing, rather than asking him to share a declarative, concretized opinion. Studs was most interested in listening to people who were in the midst of change, and that makes for much more interesting content. For example, in *"The Good War"* Studs interviewed a priest who blessed the planes that dropped the atomic bomb on Hiroshima. In the 1980s, when Studs interviewed him, he had become an ardent peace activist, and he tracks through this significant change with Studs.

I began this book because I needed to find my way back to being able to listen to others. It wasn't until I went back and spent some quality time with Studs that I realized why I had lost hope in my art: Because I lost hope in people being able to change their minds. Is it true that people are no longer willing to change? Or is this a mythology, a giant brick wall we have built for ourselves that is a flat-out lie? Was Studs able to find people in the midst of change because he lived in a time when people were willing to change? Or did he find people in the midst of change because he had *hope* that people could change, he had faith that people do indeed change and so he sought them out? Am I not seeing them, or am I asking the wrong questions?

Studs taught me that in order to hear, I must have faith. Not faith in a higher power (Studs was agnostic, which he called a "lazy atheist"). I'm not talking about faith in a higher power, but rather faith in my fellow human. I'm talking about my faith that people can and are constantly changing so that I can and should create a comfortable space and a non-judgmental and ever-curious ear ... so that I can listen once again.

Studs and his thousands of interviews are a remedy against amnesia. I invite you to visit his online digital WFMT archive. Spend an afternoon listening to Studs listen to others. He helps us remember yesterday so that we can know ourselves today. As he tells us:

> When there's no yesterday, a national memory becomes more and more removed from what it once was, and forgets what it once wanted to be.[5]

NOTES

[1] By Clifford Odets, first produced by the Civic Repertory Theatre on January 6, 1935.
[2] By Marc Blitzstein, first produced by the Federal Theatre Project, directed by Orson Wells.
[3] Terkel, Studs. "Conversations with History: Studs Turkel," interview by Harry Kreisler, *Conversations with History*, University of California Television, October 29, 2003. https://www.youtube.com/watch?v=QmDUwlseN4M.
[4] Terkel, Studs, and Lewis with Sydney. *Touch and Go: A Memoir*. New York: New Press, 2007.
[5] Terkel, *Touch and Go*, 236.

BIBLIOGRAPHY

Diamond, Anna. "Zora Neale Hurston's 'Barracoon' Tells the Story of the Slave Trade's Last Survivor." *Smithsonian Magazine*, May 2, 2018, https://www.smithsonianmag.com/arts-culture/zora-neale-hurston-barracoon-last-survivor-slave-trade-180968944/#:~:text=ARTS%20%26%20CULTURE-,Zora%20Neale%20Hurston's%20'Barracoon'%20Tells%20the%20Story%20of,the%20Slave%20Trade's%20Last%20Survivor.

Didion, Joan. *The White Album*. New York: Simon and Schuster, 1979.

Folman, Ari. "Filmmaker Reflects on 'Waltz with Bashir' Reception." Interview by Robert Siegel. *All Things Considered*. NPR, December 26, 2008. https://www.npr.org/2008/12/26/98723606/filmmaker-reflects-on-waltz-with-bashir-reception#:~:text=Filmmaker%20Reflects%20On%20'Waltz%20With%20Bashir'%20Reception%20Although%20Ari%20Folman's,teenagers%20from%20going%20to%20war.

Hurston, Zora Neale, et al. *Barracoon: the Story of the Last "Black Cargo"*, edited by Deborah G. Plant, Foreword by Alice Walker. New York: Amistad Press, 2018.

Kiang, Jessica. "Interview: Joshua Oppenheimer Talks 'the Act of Killing,' How Werner Herzog Works & the Scene That Gave Him Nightmares." *IndieWire*, February 26, 2015. https://www.indiewire.com/features/general/interview-joshua-oppenheimer-talks-the-act-of-killing-how-werner-herzog-works-the-scene-that-gave-him-nightmares-266758/.

Moore, Harold G., and Joseph L. Galloway. *We Were Soldiers Once ... and Young: Ia Drang—the Battle That Changed the War in Vietnam*. New York: Random House, 1992.

Taylor, Art. *Notes and Tones: Musician-to-Musician Interviews*. Expanded ed. Boston, MA: Da Capo Press, 1993.

Terkel, Studs. *Division Street: America*. New York: Pantheon Books, 1967.

Terkel, Studs. *Hard Times: An Oral History of the Great Depression*. New York: Pocket Books, 1978.

Terkel, Studs. *The Good War: An Oral History of World War Two*. New York: Ballantine, 1985.

Terkel, Studs. "The Craft of the Journalistic Interview." Conversation with Mike Wallace, *American Perspectives*, C-SPAN, April 17, 2000. www.c-span.org/video/?156604-1%2Fcraft-journalistic-interview.

Vidal, Gore. *Imperial America: Reflections on the United States of Amnesia*, 7. Nation Books, 2005.

7
LISTENING AS CIVIC ENGAGEMENT

As I was preparing to write this book, a friend suggested that I include an overview of the genres of documentary and investigative theatre. An overview of "the" genres became impossible for me because there really is no clear genealogy of a singular form. There are clusters of work that end up falling under different names, such as Living Newspaper, Verbatim Theatre, Documentary Theatre, Tribunal Plays, Theatre of the Real, Testimonial Theatre, Oral History, Factual Theatre, Theatre of Fact, Non-Fiction Plays, Memoir Plays, Theatre of Found Text, Archival-based Plays, Investigative Theatre, Biodrama … to name just a few. However, I found no one perfect chronological order or one umbrella form. Instead, I found many examples of works with common traits, but one play or artist did not necessarily inform the other. In the study of evolutionary biology, when scientists find common traits in different animal species, but there is no shared DNA, it is called convergent evolution. Convergent evolution is when different species have similar traits yet these traits did not evolve from one common ancestor. Bats, dragon flies, wasps, and blue jays all fly but do not share any ancestral traits of flight. They evolved the ability to fly independently.

An analog that I see in the landscapes of theatre based on listening is the impulse and process of chronicling a time. Even when plays are about events of the past, there is still an immediacy of the moment, there is a reason *why* a group of theatre makers needed to make a play about something that happened in the past, as a way of understanding the present or possibly affecting the future.

The instinct to chronicle can come from different places: A need for closure and healing, a need to bear witness, to prosecute, to vindicate, to amend history, to create history, or perhaps to simply figure out just what happened. The British theatre critic Michael Billington suggested that artists turn to verbatim theatre when they become disillusioned and lose trust in their media and politicians. Playwright David Hare tells Will Hammond and Dan Steard in *Verbatim, Verbatim* that verbatim theatre "does what journalism fails to do."[1] Jerzy Koenig, a Polish theatre critic writing in the 1960s about trends of documentary playmaking in Poland, which he called Theatre of Fact, states that these forms did not come from any commitment or fascination with genre, but rather because the events of the recent past were so significant and overwhelming that the playwright was helpless "in the face of a given problem. How can one write about dropping a bomb on Hiroshima? ... About the Pope's conduct during the Second World War? About the crimes of Eichmann? Auschwitz? Majdanek?"[2] and therefore simply presenting the facts on stage became the only way to tackle such staggering and formidable events.

Whether the impulse to chronicle reality came from a need for healing or prosecution, there are many examples wherein the performance that ensued became a catalyst for—at the very least—conversation, and—at the very most—societal change. I offer a handful of examples of works and artists that chronicled a moment/time/event and in doing so, became catalysts for civic engagement. These works do not fit into a conventional evolution of genre but, rather, their common traits are examples of the convergent evolution of theatre as civic engagement.

THEATRE AS POLITICAL ACTIVISM: ERWIN PISCATOR

> The people who filled the house had for the most part been actively involved in the period, and what we were showing them was in a true sense their own fate, their own tragedy being acted out before their eyes.

This quote comes from the 1978 memoir of German playwright and director Erwin Piscator, who began creating documentary political theatre after World War I and continued to make such work up until his death in 1966. Piscator used the term political "in the original sense: 'being of general concern'" when reflecting on his 1925 play, co-credited with Felix Gasbarra, *In Spite of Everything!* Piscator was a war veteran, a German infantryman who fought on the Western Front in World War I. After the war, outspoken against militarism, Piscator was commissioned by the newly formed Communist Party of Germany (KPD) to create a historical review of events before, during, and after the war. Here are some highlights of Piscator's production:

- It was a huge spectacle; there were over 200 performers on stage.
- He sampled newspaper reports and used them as dialogue.
- He used interactive media, combining live action with filmed and very real war footage.
- The piece flowed seamlessly from one moment in time to another using spectacle, physical transition, and gesture to jump time and place.

The script itself no longer exists, but details of the production have been pieced together from Piscator's memoir, an outline created for the program, and police reports from those in attendance. When I consider *In Spite of Everything!* I can see that, obviously, there was an agenda at play—given that the work was commissioned by the KPD and that Piscator was clearly against warfare. However, I think Piscator saw his job as something similar to that of a scientist laying out the empirical evidence—the instigation of violence, the warfighting, and then the aftermath of the moment.

Piscator believed that by combining grand spectacle with fact-based content (like including actual film footage of war) the audience would undoubtedly be persuaded and moved to action. Piscator writes:

> After all what do I consider the essential point of my whole work? Not the propagation of a view of life through formal cliches and billboard slogans but the presentation of solid proof that our philosophy and all that can be deduced from it, is the one and only valid approach for our time. You can make all sorts of assertions, but repeating assertions does not make them more true or effective. Conclusive proof can be based only on scientific analysis of the material. This I can only do in the language of the stage, if I can get beyond scene from life, beyond the purely individual aspect of the characters and the fortuitous nature of their fates. And the way to do this is to show the link between events on the stage and the great forces active in history.[3]

In 1931, Piscator went to the Soviet Union to direct a film, *Revolt of the Fisherman*, meant to be a warning of the dangers of fascism. There were delays in production, and Piscator was not able to finish until 1934. By that time, his artistic collaborators and friends in Russia were being targeted by Joseph Stalin's purge, and he had to flee. He could no longer go home to Germany, as Hitler was rising to power. In exile, Piscator first lived in Paris and then immigrated to the United States, living on the Upper West Side of Manhattan. The founder of New York's The New School hired Piscator to run a theatre workshop where he taught young artists like Marlon Brando, Eli Wallach, Elaine Stritch, Judith Molina, and Tennessee Williams. After World War II Piscator had to leave the United States due to Senator Joseph P. McCarthy and the House Un-American Activities Committee's persecution of communists. Piscator returned to Germany and eventually ran the Freie Volksbühne theatre of West Berlin where in 1965 he directed Peter Weiss' *The Investigation* based on the 1963–1965 Frankfurt Auschwitz trials which tried 22 Nazi S.S. officers, guards, and doctors for their crimes in the Auschwitz-Birkenau death camps.

THEATRE AS PUBLIC TRIAL: PETER WEISS

In October of 1965, Piscator's production of *The Investigation* was one of 14 simultaneous productions—13 of these productions were seen across both East and West Germany, and one production was in London at the Royal Shakespeare Theatre. Weiss, who was born in Germany and had Czech and Swedish dual citizenship, is probably best known for his play *Marat/Sade* and the historical novel *The Aesthetics of Resistance.* Weiss sat in on much of the Frankfurt Auschwitz trials and read testimonies of over 300 Holocaust survivors. He condensed these testimonies into *The Investigation.* Through the years critics have either praised or excoriated the play—it's the kind of work that is impossible not to have a strong response to, one way or the other. I've not seen a production, but when I picked it up to read, I could not put it down until finished, even though there were times when the naked and unrelenting testimony of atrocities felt too difficult to continue. To be clear, there is no violence physically represented on stage. It is all dialogue, all actual court testimony—essentially, it is a condensed hyperdrive collection of transcriptions from the survivors/witnesses and defendants. We don't see anyone doing anything to anyone else, unlike films like *Sophie's Choice* or *Schindler's List* in which we see reenactments. It is all testimony.

Here are a few elements of Weiss' playwriting that made the play so compelling to so many directors, including Erwin Piscator, and, a year later, Ingmar Bergman:

- He took over 300 testimonies and sampled them into 9 witnesses and 18 accused.
- The form is an "Oratorio in 11 Cantos." An oratorio is "a large-scale musical work for orchestra and voices, typically a narrative on a religious theme performed without the use of costumes, scenery, or action."[4] There is no singing, no music in *the Investigation,* but the structured lines clearly have an exact rhythm and pace.
- The accused are named, but the witness' names are not included. In a 1966 interview with the New York Times, Weiss explained why he chose to include the real names of

the accused: "I used their names not to keep on trying them, but as symbols for the average, ordinary Germans who helped the machinery run."[5]

- There is no punctuation and very few stage directions. The structure of the text on the page is organized in a rhythmic pattern, similar to lyrics. On the page, the dialogue looks like a waterfall. This lack of punctuation and waterfall effect keeps the language tumbling forward; there's an inherent urgency and quick pace, no time or room for pauses or moments of "acting." This is as text-forward as a play can possibly get.
- The text's structure requires the staging to be incredibly simple. It would work with actors standing in one place, with all the lights in the auditorium on. It would work with no lighting cues, no mise-en-scéne, and none of the usual "bells and whistles" of dramatic staging. Piscator put the witnesses in the audience and only the accused on stage, to further break any illusion of a comfortable fourth wall or dramatic presentation. The witnesses' memories and the justifications of the accused are dramatic enough without any help from a theatrical device.
- The play never uses the words German, Jew, or Auschwitz, which resists representing the Holocaust as a singularly German phenomenon and allows the circumstances to be a grave warning for all of mankind, rather than a capsule of just one psychotic event. It allows for the investigation of human nature, not the investigation of the Nazis. This stripping of identity without stripping of any details is likely why theatre companies across the world, in various decades since, have reproduced *The Investigation*. In 1994, Urwintore, a theatre company in the Democratic Republic of Congo founded by survivors of the Rwandan genocide, performed the play across Africa.
- Weiss doesn't follow the chronology of the trials but rather organizes the testimonies in sequence from a prisoner's point of view: From the train arriving at selection processing, to forced labor and experiments, to punishment, starvation, and torture, to the gas chambers and the crematorium. It's unflinching in detailed description. Only at the very end does the lens suddenly expand to connect these 18 defendants with the millions of average citizens who were equally complicit.

A shockingly small percentage of those who participated in the Holocaust were convicted of crimes. Indicting those who ran concentration camps was extremely problematic because judicial precedent established that in a totalitarian government, only individuals at the very top, only those making executive decisions could be tried for murder. All other members of the S.S., even camp commanders, could only be tried as accomplices to murder due to the notion that they were "just following orders." In order to convict someone for murder, the prosecution had to prove that they were "acting on their own initiative." The officer overseeing the gas chambers could not be found guilty of murder because he was ordered to do so. However, if he beat a prisoner to death of his own volition, he could. The Frankfurt trial was focused on defendants who had committed heinous crimes that the prosecution could prove were made on their own initiative. The media covering the trial represented the accused as a handful of deranged monsters. The judge in the case, Fritz Bauer, later said he considered the trials a failure because this representation of the accused as a handful of "bad apples" (as we say today) allowed the average German citizen to distance themselves from these abhorrent events. Weiss's edited text cuts right through this distortion. In the penultimate moment of the play, a witness says:

> Each one of the 6000 camp staff personnel
>
> knew what was taking place
>
> and each at his post did
>
> what was required
>
> for the functioning of the whole
>
> Furthermore every locomotive engineer
>
> every switchman
>
> every railroad employee
>
> who had anything to do
>
> with the transportation of the people
>
> knew what went on in the camp

> Every telegraph clerk and typist
> who passed on the Deportation Orders
> knew
> Every single one
> of the hundreds and
> thousands of office workers
> connected with the widespread operation
> knew
> what it was all about[6]

I invite you to read this passage out loud and note the rhythm Weiss has given us. This play reaches its audience intellectually, emotionally, *and* viscerally.

PUBLIC ART AS A THEATRE OF MEMORIAL: MAYA YANG LIN

Memorializing what we call the unimaginable to remind us that these terrible things are, in fact, *imaginable*, is a core tenet to listening to our time. When I visit Washington, DC, I like to walk the historical sites and I always find a place to sit near the Vietnam Veterans Memorial, designed by Maya Yang Lin. I realize that this is a public work of art and not what some might see as conventional theatre, but—for me—public works of art, especially memorials, *are* theatre. The artist is chronicling a person, people, place, or time; they are channeling this information through their unique point of view and we—the public—have a shared, collective experience. Lin's Vietnam Veterans Memorial, like *The Investigation*, is a visceral experience—you can see it on people's bodies as they walk down and into the work. The overwhelming enormity of seeing 58,320 names etched into that night-black granite, every name of every recorded US service member who is officially listed killed or Missing in Action while seeing your own reflection in the high polish of those beautiful panels ... this experience helps us *physically* understand the magnitude of the event. And I think that when a concept that can easily become abstract in our imaginations is made more real by the physical impact of art, this aesthetic and visceral effect can serve as a political tool to remind us, teach us, and every so often help us be better at being human.

THEATRE AS ECONOMIC AND POLITICAL ENGINE: THE FEDERAL THEATRE PROJECT

There were four years in American history when the US government funded a jaw-droppingly expansive theatre project designed to not only use art to teach but to actually put food on people's tables and roofs over people's heads.

After the Great Depression, between 1933 and 1939, US President Franklin D. Roosevelt enacted the New Deal, a collection of programs and financial regulations designed to right the economy. One particular program of the New Deal was the Works Progress Administration (WPA), which intended to generate jobs across all sectors. Within the WPA was the Federal Project Number One, which created projects for musicians, writers, historians, visual artists, and theatre makers. A subset was the Federal Theatre Project (FTP), formed in 1935. Harry Hopkins, the head of the WPA, tapped Hallie Flanagan, a playwright, director, producer, and professor at Vassar College to create and run the FTP. In her memoir *Arena; The History of the Federal Theatre,* Flanagan describes Hopkins saying to her, "I don't know why I still hang on to the idea that unemployed actors get just as hungry as anybody else."

Flanagan was instructed in no uncertain terms that this funding was limited to *only* paying salaries. The federal government (Fed) would not cover production costs such as lighting, scenery, and costumes, nor would it pay for renting theatres. There was another limitation to this funding: Performances had to be free. The Fed mandated that all productions should be accessible to every citizen, rich and poor alike. Flanagan and her team took on the herculean task of negotiating free space, donations of goods, loans of lights and costume, and props from closed theatres across the country. Eventually, she got Hopkins to agree to allow a price for admission on rare occasions in order to cover production costs, but those prices had to be kept within 10–50 cents, never allowed to exceed one dollar.

In its short lifetime of four years, the FTP produced over 27,000 live productions across the United States, premiering 77 new plays and 3,000 radio dramas per year. In 1936 alone the FTP had troupes performing in 31 states in front of approximately 500,000 people per week.[7] At the end of her memoir Flanagan includes WPA financial statements and notes that "an average of 10,000 people supported an average of four dependents for four years." The gross amount the Fed spent on the FTP was $46,207,779, which Flanagan notes as being the same amount of money spent on "one complete battleship."

In addition to supporting emerging artists like Arthur Miller, Orson Welles, and Elia Kazan, the FTP also produced the Living Newspapers. This subset of the FTP was comprised of journalists and theatre makers taking real events and dramatizing them onstage. It's likely that Flanagan's concept for Living Newspapers came from two trips to the Soviet Union to see the Blue Blouse theater, AKA the "Blue Blouses," performing *Zhivaia Gazeta* (Living Newspaper). The Blue Blouses would travel the Soviet Union performing excerpts of the news for illiterate workers. They used puppetry, dancing, music, circus, sketches, you name it. The structure of the performance was similar to the effect of reading a newspaper in that it jumped from one topic to another without any single organizing thread, other than they were all related to daily news. In terms of content, the material was much more in line with an op-ed section of a newspaper, rather than non-biased reportage. This was Agitprop Theatre with didactic messaging and calls to action. The Blue Blouses had no interest in simply recreating the news. Director Vsevolod Meyerhold, leading an artistic revolt against the realism of Konstantin Stanislavski, wrote:

> Blue Blouse categorically rejects any decorative and realistic set designs. There will be no birch trees or little brooks ... [Blue Blouse] is not a photograph, but rather a construction site.

FTP's Living Newspapers were similar to their Soviet counterparts in name and basic concept only. They differed in many ways: They used scenery and stagecraft and each performance had one organizing theme—they were playing more than cabarets. The name—Living Newspaper—is a bit misleading. The events recreated were not quite as immediate as taking the day's headlines and quickly throwing them onstage; the plays were more slowly cooked, covering events that spanned decades and even centuries. Actually, the form is similar to some documentary theatre practices today, which combine information from reportage with fictional scenes. They were also rather inventive in form, offering audiences a kind of mash-up of Brechtian technique and American realism. In one single play, the audience would be served a grand and impressive stage design, intimate scenes depicting the daily lives of the working poor, moments when characters break the fourth wall and address the audience while referencing the play they are in, allegorical vignettes, *and* sampled text from newspapers, political speeches, and congressional records. In these plays, I see seeds of styles later developed by writers like Clifford Odets (*Waiting for Lefty*) and Thornton Wilder (particularly *The Skin of Our Teeth*).

One-Third of a Nation (1938) by Arthur Arent was an examination of the squalid living conditions of the poor in America. The title comes from FDR's second inaugural address: "I see one-third of a nation ill-housed, ill-clad, ill-nourished." It begins with a recreation of a 1924 tenement fire that killed 13 people. The set, designed by Howard Bay, is impressive: A cross-section of a four-story tenement building in lower Manhattan. The curtain rises on smoke billowing out of the building, people running onto broken fire escapes, and desperately trying to flee. We see a father trying to push his way back into the building to save his family, but he cannot. What follows is an investigation by a city commissioner. Though the event was real, the characters are fictional, and the scene becomes an examination of the economic context of owning property in New York, suggesting that slumlords did not maintain their buildings because the only value of any tenement building was the property it sat on. The next scene goes back hundreds of years to the founding of the city and the genesis of the system of paying rent when one cannot afford to buy. Moving from there and forward to the present and the creation of the US Housing Authority, each scene depicts various struggles for tenement renters and is a lesson in economics and social science through fictional depictions and imaginative theatricality. *One-Third of a Nation* ran for ten months at the Adelphi Theatre in New York and was produced in other cities including Seattle, Washington, where it is given credit for impacting local officials' focus on housing. The University of Washington's Civil Rights and Labor History Consortium's Great Depression in Washington State Project notes that the Seattle Housing Authority became one of the most active organizations against slums and for tenants' rights.[8]

TRIBUNAL PLAYS AND TRICYCLE THEATRE

The term Tribunal Play came out of the work of London's Tricycle Theatre and was a condensed staged recreation of a trial or investigation based on current political events with dialogue taken directly from official testimony. Nicolas Kent, Tricycle's artistic director from 1984 to 2012 was the driving force behind the abundance of Tribunal Plays generated over two decades (1994–2012) working with journalist-turned-playwright Richard Norton-Taylor and novelist-turned-playwright Gillian Slovo.

Richard Norton-Taylor described his work with Tricycle as Verbatim Theatre, which for him was an "extension of journalism."[9] Norton-Taylor was reporting for *The Guardian* covering issues of defense and national security from 1975 to 2016. He was also *The Guardian*'s security editor and now serves on the board of the investigative media organization *Declassified UK*. His path toward becoming a playwright started on a tennis court: In 1994 Norton-Taylor was covering the Scott Inquiry, an investigation into the British government's sanctioning—and then lying to itself about this sanctioning—of British companies selling military equipment and arms-related goods to Iraq during the Iraq-Iran war and Saddam Hussein's invasion of Kuwait. British Parliament had created guidelines prohibiting the sales of arms to either Iraq or Iran, but government officials intervened and loosened these guidelines. Sales were made and neither Parliament nor the public were notified. During the Scott Inquiry, officials were testifying with maddening statements suggesting that because the public did not know, nothing really happened. Every Sunday Norton-Taylor played tennis with Nicolas Kent and would give Kent blow-by-blow details of the inquiry. Kent convinced Norton-Taylor to compile his reportage into a play (Norton-Taylor had never written a play before) and this out-of-the-box partnership lead to seven Tricycle Tribunal Plays by Norton-Taylor: *Half the Picture*, about the Scott inquiry; *Nuremberg*, sampled from testimonies at the Nuremberg Trials (1997); *The Color of Justice* about the racially-motivated murder of Stephen Lawrence and the systemic racism of the London police department (1999); *Justifying War* about the Ministry of Defense's dossier on Iraq's "weapons of mass destruction" (2003); *Bloody Sunday*, based on the 1972 inquiry into the events of Sunday, January 30th when British soldiers shot 26 civilians during a protest in Northern Ireland (2005) *Called to Account* (co-written with Nikolas Kent) based on the inquiry into indictment of Prime Minister Tony Blair for "the crime of aggression against Iraq" (2007); and *Tactical Questioning*, a recreation of the investigation into the death of Baha Mousa, a detainee killed while in the custody of British soldiers in Iraq (2011).

Kent's staging of all of these plays had a unique and rigorous style with verisimilitude being an essential element. The plays were staged as exact replicas of the courtroom: The drab furniture, florescent lighting, and every object to be found in this banal and sterile place. The cast studied the real people they would play to the smallest detail, listening to recordings and watching videos over and over again. When they could, they met with their "characters" to help them better understand intentions. So, if this was a strict recreation of a courtroom, what made the work so vitally theatrical? First, the verisimilitude was its own form of spectacle. The designs were one-to-one life-size replicas, which in and of itself became a sort of virtuosity of the commonplace. In *Half the Picture*, an actor played Margaret Thatcher—resisting caricature, commentary, or sending her up, but rather, playing her as the fully fleshed-out person—and when the lead investigator says to her:

> I am very grateful for you coming. There will be a transcript prepared of everything that has been said on the course of today, which we will supply to you as soon as we can, and, if you have time to read it, and if it occurs to you that there is anything that you wish you could add or that you wish to correct, then we would be very grateful if you would do that.

The character Margaret Thatcher replies:

> I fear there will be much grammar to be corrected.

This line packs such a punch because the audience knows that this is verbatim—it's *exactly* what Thatcher actually said in court. Scott's response is the last line of the first act:

> "Never mind grammar, that is the least of the problems."

Which gets me to the second element that made this work so theatrical: Norton-Taylor's editing. He took over 400 hours of testimony and redacted it—his word[10]—into a two-act play. He had to do so quickly, as it was important to get this play to the audience while the inquiry was still on everyone's mind. I have a personal appreciation for the exquisite pressure of time[11] when we writers have to meet a short deadline. When we have to produce quickly, it can do wonderful things for the process. You have no time to overthink or doubt. You must quiet the noise and work on instinct.

There is only one thing about *Half the Picture* that feels to me at odds with this fiercely inventive form, and it's the inclusion of a handful of fictional monologues written by the political activist playwright John McGrath. These brief moments of direct address come between dense courtroom scenes, they break up the rhythm and work as a sort of palate cleanser, but I'm not convinced the play needed them and can't help but wonder if Kent and Norton-Taylor didn't quite trust the verbatim material yet in this, their first foray.

For me, Tribunal Plays hold a unique space between fiction and journalism. Truth can be so much more complicated than fiction, and when a political issue is examined on the stage, the creative team can get unparalleled access to information because most anyone in charge of protecting "state secrets" is quite afraid of being accused of a cover-up, so they will give a playwright remarkable access. This I know from first-hand experience. If you ever want to get past gates and into official rooms and documents, just make a play. You'll be amazed at where you can go and what you can get. This kind of playwriting can also include moments that often get passed over in traditional reportage. Something that a journalist will ignore can be brought to life on stage. When remembering the making of *The Color of Justice,* Norton-Taylor writes:

> Nick taught me, not only about the power of the theatre in exposing facts to a wider public, but also how apparently inconsequential incidents or anecdotes which a journalist or news desk might ignore, could be very telling. For example, Doreen Lawrence, Stephen's mother, described how when she handed a senior police officer a note containing a list of suspects, he simply "rolled the piece of paper up in a ball in his hand." She added: "I was shocked by what I saw."[12]

This is just the kind of detail that plays well on stage. In addition, because a play can highlight and foreground certain information, it can preserve testimony that, over time, can become an important historical document. For example, in *Half the Picture* Foreign Officer Mark Higson testifies:

> The Iraqi market, after the end of the Iran-Iraq war, was summed up as being "the big prize." However distasteful we found the Iraqi regime, we could not afford to be left behind in developing trade links, and we were in a prime position, to use a motor racing phrase.

Looking at the state of Iraq now, the way *Half the Picture* features this moment—that there was a rush to claim the economic "big prize" of Iraq—adds an important marker for mapping the history of Iraq and the US and European allies' role in its trajectory.

Kent and Norton-Taylor are still making Tribunal Plays today. Their most recent, *Value Engineering: Scenes from the Grenfell Inquiry,* debuted in 2021. It is a verbatim play about the Grenfell Tower, a housing block in the Royal Borough of Chelsea and Kensington in West London. In 2017 a fire rapidly spread through the tower, killing 72 residents, the most lives lost in a building fire in London since World War II. Though this is one of London's richest boroughs, the Grenfell Tower's residents were mostly working-class people of color. Those killed in the fire represented 19 different nationalities, and the four-year investigation exposed gross negligence and malpractice of contractors, building inspectors, and city officials and it was evident that racism played a role in this tragedy; yet no one—at the time of the play's making—had been held accountable.

There are many ways that verbatim playwriting practices, theatre production models, and expectations from audiences have changed since Kent and Norton-Taylor started collaborating. We, as audiences, are much more attuned to the complexities of representation, and we are holding a keen eye on who is an Amplifier and who is a Taker. Of course, an obvious difference between then and now is that there was no social media when Kent and Norton-Taylor first collaborated. When they announced in late 2020 that they were making this play and shared the cast list, it set off a maelstrom of negative feedback on Twitter. In his 2023 article "Scenes from the Inquiry: Tribunal Theatre and the Act of Listening,"[13] Tom Cantrell examines this blow-back, and he notes two kinds of listening that Kent and Norton-Taylor employed when meeting this scrutiny: "macro listening" and "micro listening."[14] The micro listening took place in rehearsals, where Kent and the acting company listened to recordings over and over again, listening carefully to every intonation, every change in pitch and tone, sifting through vocal gestures to uncover motive and intention. The macro listening came into play when Kent and Norton-Taylor heard and responded to the negative reactions on social media. The criticism was in response to the fact that all but one actor in the cast were white. Critics were furious at what they saw as a narrative that centered on whiteness when most of the people impacted were not.

Kent, Norton-Taylor, and all involved in the production created a series of conversations and programming around this critique, opening dialogue around why this casting decision was made. In a 2021 interview with the *Evening Standard*, Kent said, "All the company people—the baddies, villains, the people who lied—are all white, and mainly, but not all, men." This is why the characters in the play were mostly White—because Kent and Norton-Taylor were focusing on the perpetrators, not the victims. Kent also holds nothing back when discussing his mission and motive: "I want people brought to court and charged with corporate manslaughter."

THEATRE AS REBELLION: TEATR ÓSMEGO DNIA

One of Poland's most famous theatre companies, *Teatr Ósmego Dnia* (Theatre of the Eighth Day) has been utilizing theatrical practices as civic engagement—and even outright rebellion—for decades. Known for great spectacle and a playful, punk-rock style, "The Eights" were inspired by the work of Jerzy Grotowski. Founded in the 1960s by students rooted in counterculture and rebellion against the communist regime, The Eights approached their artistic work and their political activism as one and the same. In 1976 they signed an open letter against changes to the constitution and in support of the opposition group for oppressed workers. In response, the communist regime arrested company members, took away passports, cut all funding, took away their performance spaces, and even made it illegal for the press to write anything positive about The Eights. By the early 1980s, many were forced to emigrate to Italy where they kept working. They returned in 1989, with the end of communism, and have been making and performing their work in Poland and touring it around the world ever since. In 2007 they premiered *The Files*. For decades the communist secret police kept extensive and details files on all members of The Eights. These files covered their personal lives and actions but were also exhaustive reports of the theatre The Eights produced. Officers of the secret police attended Theatre of the Eighth Day performances and then drafted detailed reviews of the work. So, in 2007, when it was safe to do so, they were able to obtain their police files and turn them into performance art: Actors stood at podiums, spoke into microphones, and read excerpts from their own files. These excerpts are chilling but also funny and at times profound, as police officers became theatre critics. Because they were documenting the metaphors and meanings in the work they were there to spy on, the officers inadvertently became social critics as well.

THEATRE AS SOCIAL MEDIA: TINA SATTER

A play can tap into the zeitgeist so rapidly that it can go viral, becoming its own form of social media. Recently, a play made its way from Off-Off Broadway in 2019 (The Kitchen), to Off-Broadway (the Vineyard Theatre) to opening on Broadway in 2021. *Is This a Room* was conceived and directed by Tina Satter, founder and artistic director of the New York company Half Straddle, and all the dialogue is verbatim transcription—with every um, uh, and half-sentence—of the 2017 FBI interrogation of Reality Winner. Reality Winner is a US Air Force Veteran who was working as an interpreter for a Department of Defense contractor. Though her job was specifically focused on intelligence related to Iran (Winner is fluent in Farsi), her security clearance allowed her to search for intelligence related to Russian interference in the 2016 US presidential election. Winner told CBS's *Sixty Minutes* that she leaked the intelligence because she believed citizens were misled about Russia's role in US elections. After a plea agreement, she was sentenced to five years in prison, the longest sentence ever imposed for leaking classified government documents. What a testament to the adage "reality is stranger than fiction" (no pun intended), when something as seemingly untheatrical as staging transcripts can become a work of art that the *New York Times* theatre critic Jesse Green called, "one of the thrillingest thrillers ever to hit Broadway." After opening on Broadway, the play was then adapted into a film for HBO. The process of transposing a transcript that moved quickly from the page to stage to film has created a series of time capsules of a moment, and captured a rapidly shifting political climate in the United States.

THEATRE AS A CIVIC MIRROR: ANNA DEVEARE SMITH

Living, breathing time capsules are no easy feat. Anna Deavere Smith makes it look easy. Deavere Smith began her career as an actor and has, for over three decades, written one-person plays based on interviews she has conducted, which she performs. In a conversation with David M. Rubenstein for the American Academy of Arts and Sciences, she said she started writing documentary plays because "I wanted to learn as much about America as I could." Two of what I would consider her seminal works are *Fires in the Mirror*, which premiered in 1992, about the 1991 Crown Heights riots, and *Twilight: Los Angeles, 1992*, about the uprisings in Los Angeles in response to the acquittal of all Los Angeles Police Department Officers involved in the arrest and beating of Rodney King. *Twilight: Los Angeles, 1992* premiered at the Mark Taper Forum in Los Angeles. Deavere Smith interviewed hundreds of people, from city officials to everyday citizens, from diverse backgrounds, ages, races, and lived experiences. She then selected a handful of those interviews and edited them into monologues, listening to her audio recordings over and over again, striving to as accurately as possible replicate each person's syntax, intonation, speech, vocal patterns, tone, dialect, etc. She resists categorizing this process as doing an impression but instead calls these monologues portraits. She strives to capture another person's way of speaking because she believes that a person's identity is embedded in how they communicate.

I remember, quite vividly, driving up from San Diego to Los Angeles in 1993 to see her perform *Twilight: Los Angeles, 1992*. I was a kid just graduating an MFA acting program, and this performance left two lasting impressions on me: First, I was thrilled at how short the bridge could be between real-life events and the stage. These events had *just* happened, and there I was, sitting in a theatre, listening to first-person accounts. (There's that exquisite pressure of time again.) The other takeaway for me was the fact that Deavere Smith was performing all of these portraits herself. As she strived to capture every gesture, every vocal intonation I was as aware of her, the person asking questions, as I was the person she was performing. It reminded me of one of those human anatomy books so popular in the eighties and nineties, with transparent pages, each with a different layer of the human body. If you flipped through the book from back to front, you could see how the body's systems layered on top of one another. Seeing Deavere Smith perform, I could see two people at once—one layer the artist, the other the person she was listening to.

Convergent evolution is a big part of why we have so much theatre based on the real in the world today, but there are other times when *divergent* evolution—when there is a clear lineage—is at play, and this is one of those examples. Anna Deavere Smith has had a significant impact on several generations of theatre makers and the DNA of her process and approach is as prolific as she.

THEATRE AS POETIC TESTIMONIAL: YAEL FABER

Much of the work covered in this chapter, in one way or another, is connected to the act of bearing witness. When I think about the future of these forms, I wonder: Can we tell stories without re-traumatizing our audience or the artists making the work? How do we bring a holistic approach to bringing personal lived experiences to the stage? Can this holistic approach include radical joy? Radical care? Radical love?

I am finding great inspiration from contemporary artists like South African playwright Yael Farber. In Farber's anthology *THEATRE AS WITNESS; Three Testimonial Plays from South Africa*[15] I see her work shining a light toward theatre that can be truthful *and* healing. In his forward, Archbishop Desmond Tutu writes:

> Between 1996 and 1999, South Africans across our land gathered in makeshift halls to tell their stories. For many it was the first time they would put words into the world in an attempt to describe indescribable events. Just as important were the witnesses who came to listen ... for there is a capacity to heal the human heart in the act not only of speaking—but in finally being heard.
>
> ... Theatre is the ambitious sister of Testimony. It strives to heal through truth."

For me, Farber's work shows truths on stage that are vulnerably honest, yet do not linger in pain. Instead, the work brings a person's full self to the stage, as a part of restorative justice. Her work is similar to Lola Arias, Ping Chong, and The Telling Project, in that community members perform their own stories. What makes Farber's productions so special is her ability to also bring poetry, dance, ritual, and magic to the stage. In her play *AMAJUBA: LIKE DOVES WE RISE*, five performers tell their stories of growing up during apartheid, and as they do, the ensemble uses music, choreography, and imagery to create a chimerical dream world. This dreamscape embodies the interior, emotional landscape of their lived experiences. It ritualizes their relationship with the elements through dances that take place in large basins of water or on mounds of sand. The pedestrian text is lifted with these physical moments of transformation—a bowl becomes a house becomes a stage and goes back to being a bowl again. Farber's is work that can only be theatre.

Her process takes care to protect her collaborators, and her questions allow for much more beyond "tell me what happened." In an interview with Amanda Stuart Fisher, Farber describes her approach:

> Memory is seldom effortlessly accessible, linear, comprehensive or even necessarily compelling when told. In my experience, an individual's story will first emerge in a very two-dimensional narrative, driven by dates and dry accounts of watershed moments.

After this initial narrative offering Farber then asks participants about more innocuous moments that in no way relate to any particular moment of trauma. For example, she will ask what color someone's dress was on a certain Christmas. These questions are not about unearthing secrets, but rather about uncovering someone's more expansive memories so that the participants are not only defined by the traumatic event. In addition to these interviews, in rehearsal Farber and the participant/performers devise creative exercises together: Singing childhood songs, writing letters to loved ones, etc. At the top of each session, she asks everyone to tell her what they dreamt the night before. She listens deeply, trusting the tangential and rambling nature of discovery, and in six short weeks she goes from the very first session with a group to the opening night performance. Working quickly allows Farber and her collaborators to rely on instinct—sculpting, composing, and writing a world of both realistic *and* ecstatic truth.

THEATRE AS A CIVIC ACT OF LOVE: RIMINI PROTOKOLL AND OUTBOX

There really are so many different kinds of truth, depending on the methods and mechanics one uses to find and then share them. Another group of artists I am turning to for inspiration is Berlin's Rimini Protokoll. Founded and lead by three directors—Helgard Haug, Stefan Kaegi, and Daniel Wetzel—this is a production/theatre/performance company that nearly defies description because the content covered is incredibly diverse, such as:

- examining aging through the lens of Formula One race car driving,
- tackling climate change by holding a conference where none of the keynote speakers actually attend but instead audience members read keynote speeches,
- a geological survey of shifting plate tectonics via the design and implementation of a "non-embassy" in Taiwan,
- and a tour of urban spaces outsourced to a call center in Calcutta, India.

These are just a few of the 27 projects Rimini Protokoll has available for touring at the time of this publishing. The one thing that all of these works have in common is that the performers are not professional actors, but rather what Rimini Protokoll calls experts. These experts are the very real stakeholders in the topic; they are the individuals whose lived experiences are being explored on stage. Haug, Kaegi, and Wetzel, separately or in various configurations, shape these experiences into cutting yet delicate, sharp yet soulful scripts. These scripts are framed with exceptional technological craft and an acute sense of composition. It is lecture, community theatre, *and* high art at its best.

I've never encountered another group of artists capable of including so much complexity, depth, and layering into one single production. An example is the moving and informative *Granma. Trombones from Havana.* Four people—experts, in Rimini Protokoll terms—who were born and raised in Cuba share their families' histories, connecting particularly to their grandparents. They perform different types of lecture demonstrations about their four grandparents: An animator who works for a Canadian company that he's never met tells us about his grandfather, who was a leader of the Revolution and one of Fidel Castro's first ministers; a historian who teaches at the University of Havana tells us of her grandmother, a seamstress selling clothes to the US military on Guantanamo; a professional singer and trombone player tells us of her grandfather, a founding member of a band that traveled to play for Cuban soldiers fighting in Angola and Syria; a software engineer shares the stories and life of his grandfather, a soldier in Castro's army. As each expert shares family photos and mementos, a thread develops and connects all four: The hunger and fight for social justice, the dream of a utopian future, and the inevitable corruption of such dreams. It's a love letter to family, a masterful lecture on Cuban history, a memorial of the values of socialism, a crushing prosecution of the failure of socialism, a prayer for a just world, and it leaves the audience with more questions than answers. Through a series of interactive moments in which audience members are invited to play baseball with the cast using a rolled-up sock and a plastic water jug—the actual items used during the Special Period when rations were so limited that there weren't even baseballs or bats to be found, much less soap and food and gasoline—the script is able to connect the sociopolitical struggles in Cuba with the actions of the audience's own grandparents. The play was performed for a German audience and the connection between Cuba's fate and the actions of European governments hits home. Throughout the performance we watch the cast accomplish something seemingly impossible: The expert who is a professional musician teaches the other three to play the trombone (they mastered the instrument in less than a year, the time it took to develop the piece) and together they underscore the entire performance.

Granma. Trombones from Havana deals with such vital questions as power, revolution, distribution of wealth, poverty, power*less*ness, and the loss of one's faith in utopia. And yet, this is not an interrogation. This is a love letter to being human, to the instinct in all of us for equity, and the enduring nature of hope, faith, family, and art.

Setting aside the impulse to prosecute and instead centering the theatre of listening on love ... is this, perhaps, where our artform is going? It's certainly restoring my faith in the radical act of listening. And when I met the work of OUTBOX my faith was restored even more.

OUTBOX is a contemporary theatre company in the United Kingdom that collaborates with LGBTQIA+ artists and communities. Their mission statement says it all:

> We love:
> karaoke, regional gay bars, Audre Lorde, sticky dancefloors, leather, Real Housewives, black queer liberation, novelty T-shirts, Kylie, Christina Veneno, Fenty fashion shows, Pet Shop Boys concerts, TransVegas, Crocs in sport mode, Ocean Vuong, Jose Esteban Muñoz, Missy Elliot videos, Gays The Word, Alexander (Lee) McQueen, Harpies, rave flyers, smoke and mirrors, Peeping Tom, Cipher Press, rottweiler puppies, ancestry, protest, Leslie Feinberg, chaos, WAP, Buddies in Bad Times, overalls, cat TikToks, Lena Waithe, bath bombs, graphic novels, Elektra Abundance, pin badges, James Baldwin, tote bags, mesh tops, Janelle Monáe, durags and bandanas, carabiners, Jeremy O. Harris, Spongebob, disco, leading with love.
>
> Our work is led by and for those who don't see themselves represented.
>
> We are never far from:
> a mirror-ball and a glitter-drop.

Their most recent work, *GROOVE*, is set on a dance floor—a place of "protest, identity, belonging and desire"—and is based on multi-generational testimonials of LGBTQIA+ people. During the pandemic they created the Brighter Project, which is an online resource supporting the development of LGBTQIA+ writers telling their own stories. As Mika Onyx Johnson, an OUTBOX associate artist, describes in marketing for the release of the *BRIGHTER booklet,* a collection of writings that came out of this project, "It was really important for us as an organization that we really pushed this idea of a brighter queer future and joy and hope because it's been such a bleak time for a lot of us." The production that OUT-BOX is probably best known for is *And the Rest Of Me Floats,* which is about "the messy business of gender." The cast is from trans, non-binary, and queer communities, and their autobiographical performances are a collage of styles and forms—stand-up, testimonial, rock concert, and disco party. The production leans into the metaphor of change and invites the audience to change *with* them, not because of them. Their intention is to dance with their audience—metaphorically and quite literally. Time Out's 2019 review of the London production declares, "A whole history of community surges electrically through the production's 75 minutes as it never pauses in one mood for long. 'And the Rest of Me Floats' sticks up two fingers at the bigots while blowing a kiss."

CIVIC ENGAGEMENT OF THE FUTURE: NIKKI YEBOAH

The future of theatre centered on *really* listening and *really* seeing is in good hands. There are so many expansive thinkers out there doing real and deep listening. One is Nikki Yeboah, a playwright, oral historian, and professor at the University of Washington in Seattle. She makes plays based on oral histories such as *THE (M)OTHERS,* which is about four mothers living in the Bay Area of Northern California who had children killed by police. The dialogue is verbatim excerpts from Nikki's interviews. She is currently working on a new Verbatim play, *11th & Pine,* about how the community memorializes and remembers the Capitol Hill Occupied Protest (CHOP)[16] of 2020. I interviewed her about her approach and where she's headed.

KJ: When we met and then I read your work, I got really excited to talk to you, particularly. I have a lot of questions for you about the future of listening.

NIKKI: The future of listening.

KJ: Yes. I'm just thinking, where do we go next?

NIKKI: I love that question. I don't know if we ever mastered the past of listening. Do you know what I mean? *(laughs)*

KJ: *(laughs)* Well, yes.

NIKKI: There's a future in that time moves on, but futurity in the sense of "we've done this thing, what does 3.0 look like?" I don't think we mastered the thing to begin with. I'm surprised every time I teach my students how to listen. It's so strange to me that the idea of not interrupting someone, even with an affirmative—because people think that if you are interrupting someone to affirm them, that's a good thing—but the idea of just giving someone space to say whatever, feel whatever, without having to be like, "No girl, but you're beautiful"—to strip that all away and just allow a person to be and just to experience them being, it's always the first time for a lot of people.

They come back changed as a person. That I listened. I really listened for the first time. I spoke to my mother, and I really listened to her. That kind of transformation, I don't take for granted, and I don't know what the future of that is because we're still wrestling with the act of that simplicity of it. In one sense, that's how I feel about it. That we still just have to be in the present before we can even consider that question. In another sense, I'm also really interested in thinking about—a lot of the time when we do this work, the people that do it are doing it for altruistic reasons but are often different from those that they interview. I'm also curious about a future in which we're more comfortable with that difference, less avoidant of that difference.

I think a lot of times my students wish that difference wasn't there. There are two things they want to do. They want to avoid it, like, "I'm going to interview people like me because I can't interview 'those people.' They're so different." The other way that looks is "I'm going to go in there, and I'm going to interview everyone because we are all just human beings at the end of the day." I think it would just be lovely to just be okay with that we're different, and what does that really mean? They assume what it means is all negative.

There are some great things that come out of being different from the person that you are talking to. Their desire to explain things to you, their desire to bring you into their world because they know that you are not in it. That's so powerful for an interviewer. It's so powerful.

KJ: What you're saying makes me think about our instinct to smooth things out.

NIKKI: We smooth things out to make it more comfortable for everyone involved. It's not just us, it's not just a selfish act. It's not just like, "Oh, I don't want to be uncomfortable." You also don't want the other person to be uncomfortable, the person that you're interviewing. A lot of us, yes, we got into this because we're empathetic people and building and crossing bridges is a part of our identity. It's who we are. That, I don't have any problem with, but I do think there's a first step to listening that is not about bridge building just yet. Just hear it, just be in it, just live with it, be in that discomfort, and don't force the smoothness. Let it happen in a more organic way.

KJ: How did *11th & Pine* come to you?

NIKKI: I had just moved to Seattle, and I was on Capitol Hill at this lovely cafe having an expensive brunch, mimosas flowing. I was feeling great. We're sitting outdoors. In the midst of this, my friend looks at me and says, "This is where it all happened." I was like, "What are you talking about?" She was like, "This is CHOP. You're sitting where it happened."

I looked around me and it felt—I had never seen such an immediate erasure. I had never experienced such an immediate erasure of something. I looked around, and there were no signs. You would never know that something this momentous had happened where you were. It was very unsettling because it was now just an upper-middle-class hangout. It's the exact opposite of what the radical action had been about.

That's what drove me to ask, "What did happen? Why have I been in the city, been existing in this neighborhood, and have never encountered it or talked about it with anyone?" So I followed that curiosity.

There were two things left: There was a garden that had been set up during the protests, and there was a mural that was on the street, a BLM mural. I just found out today that the city is removing the garden. It's a garden. Do you know what I mean?

What's the word I'm looking for? It's the shallowest entry point into this topic. A garden is inviting to all.

KJ: I'm curious about who memorializes. Do the people who've gone through the experience end up putting up the memorial?

NIKKI: That's so interesting. I have never asked that question. In the case of CHOP, it was the people that went through the experience, but that's being eroded. The garden was started by them. The painting of the BLM sign was started by them. Those things, they fade, and so they have to go back every year or two to touch it up. Now, when they go back, it's institutional. The city pays for that. I can't imagine the city's going to do that forever. Who's going to sustain it? Even when a memorial happens organically, who sustains it?

KJ: I was reading your bio, and I love the term "alternative records of Black life." Can you tell me more about that? What is your definition of "alternative" and where did that came from?

NIKKI: I am Ghanaian. I was born in Ghana but left at the age of six. A lot of my knowledge of Ghana wasn't from being raised there. My mother, when she left, really wanted to erase that. She left and wanted to be gone. It wasn't until later in life that I felt like, "Oh, okay, I want to connect with my culture." A lot of the ways in which I accessed that was through books written by British people, White British people.

There are many directions this could go, but one of the ways in which it went is that a lot of the books weren't about contemporary Ghana. That's not the interest of a White British, either a colonizer, if you're looking at books from an earlier era, or a contemporary researcher. Quite often, it's about traditional practices. There's very little of the everyday life of, what does an average Ghanaian in 2023 do? It's more what does the average Ghanaian in a village in 1952 think about their God. There's a denial of the contemporaneous.

KJ: An impulse to build a diorama of a past rather than a reflection of today.

NIKKI: That's right. It felt like if there were more records of their lives built by those from there that I had access to, I would be able to see. I wanted to know what people think now, what they're doing now, but they were so hard to find. We were often researched, but not the researchers, for example.

Also, it felt like the academy ... We do research, we extract it, and we go; and *they're* not going to read that book or that article or visit the archives at Northwestern—that has the largest African archive in the United States. They're never going to go there. They're never going to have access to the knowledge you built about them. They're never going to know what you said about them. That was weird to build a record of a people and they not know what the record is, necessarily. Alternative for me just meant ways of, first of all, doing the thing and then also archiving the thing. Or not even archiving, but storing the thing that was accessible to those who lived it.

KJ: When working on THE (M)OTHERS, how did you approach the women you interviewed?

NIKKI: With them, I started with an organizer. Once you have someone that's at the center of it, if they trust you, they will introduce you to others. I interviewed an organizer. They got to know me, what I stood for, etc. Then they allowed me to interview them. Then they introduced me to someone else, and that person would introduce me to someone else, and so on and so forth after having had a positive experience.

They are very guarded because they've been interviewed before by people who were—first of all, they're interviewed by the justice system. They've told their story in court. They've told their story to police officers. The interview is not necessarily freeing for them as we sometimes like to narrate. Part of the radical act of listening is this idea that, in listening, you are creating a valuable space and a necessary space for people to share. With them, they did not want to share.

The people who have listened to them in the past have been people that have used that knowledge to then criticize them in some way, use that knowledge against their child in some way to show the child was deserving of what happened to them. Have used that knowledge to create a kind of exposé. People who have listened to their stories haven't necessarily treated them with the care that they had expected and that these stories deserve. They didn't trust me just because I had created a space for them to share, no. I actually set up this process where they would pre-interview me so that they could get to know me and feel okay sharing their stories with me.

Based on the pre-interviews, they would then agree. This happened after I had messed up before. Anyways, they had pre-interviewed me. They were like, okay, you're a person I can trust. I'll do the interview with you. Then based on that experience, they would then say, "Okay, I know another mother." Because they work together. They have to. It's very isolating this experience, so they create new families with each other. That's what happened.

Eventually, I decided I didn't want to interview many, many, people. This wasn't about numbers. I felt like there was a lot of stuff about numbers. When people talk about this—1,000 people killed by the police every year, and Black people are x percentage more likely to be killed; Latinos, x percentage more likely to be killed; et cetera, et cetera—all of these numbers at a point become meaningless.

After the fourth person, I decided, if people want to be interviewed by me, that's great, but I think it would be best for me to focus on the four and really allow the audience a deep and intimate knowledge of who they are. I think that's what's necessary right now. I just interviewed four people and then stopped there and wrote the piece.

KJ: That makes so much sense. When they got a chance to interview you, which I am stealing by the way, did they ask you, "why do you want to do this?"

NIKKI: Oh yes. That's the first question.

KJ: What was the answer?

NIKKI: At the time—this is interesting for me in retrospect, because I feel like I did it again with *11th & Pine*, but I had just moved to the States. I'm Canadian, Ghanian Canadian, and I had just moved to the States. It was 2016, I want to say. That was what everyone was talking about when I came to the States, and that was a fear from my family: "You're a Black woman moving to the States at this time? Are you sure that this is the right move for you? Are you sure you don't want to stay here with us where you'll be safer?" I remember saying to them, "But I'm moving to California. It's super liberal there. I'm not like going to Alabama or something." I really believed it. Then I got here and realized that someone had been killed on our very campus. Later I realized that another student had been beaten by the police on our campus and then committed suicide after. A student of my department.

It doesn't get closer than that. When I wrote the play, it was actually supposed to be a one-off thing for our community. I interviewed women in the Bay Area, mostly San José, and it premiered Mother's Day weekend in San José. It was supposed to be that one time. I just wanted to start a conversation about how this is at our door.

KJ: You mentioned the phrase "in retrospect." Do you have ideas now of what you would have done differently?

NIKKI: I mentioned that phrase because I realized that whenever I move to a new place, I do a documentary theatre work as a way of navigating my relationship to the place, as a way of navigating my fears or questions, as a way of navigating the unknown. I've moved a lot in my life. I think it's my way of building roots, of creating roots to a place, getting to know the people where I will be living.

In retrospect, there's so much I would change about what I did, though. For example, listening in smaller chunks, smaller interviews spread out across time. I think I would have done that differently. You don't have to listen all at once, even if they want to share it with you all at once. It's a lot. Also, realizing that you embody the things you hear, they live in your body—a greater awareness of what it then does to your body once those stories are in there. That's when my insomnia started, for example. Being more attuned to what these stories do to you as well.

KJ : I've been thinking a lot about reflecting trauma and sharing those stories. We've been hearing from students here. We put out a survey about the kinds of shows we should be looking for next season. A lot of the actors came and said, "My body cannot carry another character who's had violence acted upon them right now."

NIKKI: We had a similar thing happen at U-Dub last year. There was a kind of reckoning with that. It's true, actually my newest—the play I'm working on now—there was a necessary wave of these narratives, do you know what I mean? There was such a period of time where the trauma of Black and Brown people was ignored. I do feel like it had its place in time. This was necessary. From 2014 on, to have ignored these narratives would have been unethical, immoral. It didn't feel right to just keep smiling through it all when you feel the world falling apart. You wanted to acknowledge it.

KJ : Back to that first question of mine about, my pondering on the future, what does the future of the form look like when we're all sensing there are so many important stories to tell, but we're also sensing that the community that is performing the work needs some radical joy as often as radical listening?

NIKKI: No, I'll say what I'm working on now is a work based on gossip. It's just fun gossip that I get from my mother and her friends. I'm creating a fictional work out of it based on these interviews, these gossip interviews that I did with them. I feel like the future is to be responsive. It needs to be responsive to our present. We're all saying we're tired. It's enough. We need to be represented in our fullness. This can't be our defining contribution to the archive. Listening to stories of joy and/or intrigue and/or fun and/or just allowing us in our fullness to exist. I think should be in our future. It has to be.

NOTES

1. Hammond, Will, and Dan Steward, eds. *Verbatim, Verbatim: Contemporary Documentary Theatre*. London: Oberon, 2008, 62.
2. Martin, Carol J. *Dramaturgy of the Real on the World Stage*. Basingstoke, England: Palgrave Macmillan, 2010, 78.
3. Piscator, The Political Theatre, p. 93.
4. www.oratoriosociety.org.
5. Shepard, Richard F. *Peter Weiss, Visiting Here, Talks About his Auschwitz Trial Play. The New York Times*, 22 April 1966, S. 30.
6. Favorini, Attilio. Voicings: *Ten Plays from the Documentary Theatre/Edited and with an Introduction by Attilio Favorini*. 1st ed., 137. Ecco Press, 1995.
7. Library of Congress: https://blogs.loc.gov/headlinesandheroes/2022/08/living-newspapers/.
8. Sarah Guthu, coordinator.
9. "Richard Norton-Taylor: Verbatim Plays Pack More Punch than the Papers." *The Guardian*, Guardian News and Media, 2014, www.theguardian.com/stage/2014/oct/22/richard-norton-taylor-verbatim-tribunal-plays-stephen-lawrence.
10. "Adapted and Redacted by Richard Norton-Taylor with additional material by John McGrath." p. 41.
11. The value which I learned from working with Anne Bogart and the SITI Company. Anne emphasizes the "exquisite pressure" in her rehearsal rooms, training, and writings.
12. "Richard Norton-Taylor: "Verbatim Plays Pack More Punch than the Papers." *The Guardian*, Guardian News and Media, 2014, www.theguardian.com/stage/2014/oct/22/richard-norton-taylor-verbatim-tribunal-plays-stephen-lawrence.
13. Cantrell, Tom. "Scenes From the Inquiry: Tribunal Theatre and the Act of Listening. *Research in Drama Education: The Journal of Applied Theatre and Performance* 28, no. 1 (2023): 143–59.
14. Rivers, Wilga M. "Testing and Student Learning." Paper Presented at the International Conference of the Association of Teachers of English to Speakers of Other Languages, Dublin, Ireland, June 29, 1973.
15. Farber, Yaël. *Theatre as Witness: Three Testimonial Plays from South Africa: In Collaboration with and Based on the Lives of the Original Performers/by Yael Farber; Foreword by Desmond Tutu; Introduction by Amanda Stuart Fisher; Interview between Amanda Stuart Fisher and Yael Farber*. London: Oberon Books, an imprint of Bloomsbury Publishing Plc., 2008.
16. Organizers also use "Capitol Hill Organized Protest" as the official name, replacing "Occupied" as an acknowledgment that the city itself occupies First Nation land.

BIBLIOGRAPHY

Brown, Mark. "Blair to Face Trial by Theatre over Iraq War." *The Guardian*. Guardian News and Media, 2007. www.theguardian.com/politics/2007/jan/08/uk.arts.

Brittain, Victoria, Nicolas Kent, Richard Norton-Taylor, et al. *The Tricycle : Collected Tribunal Plays 1994–2012/Victoria Brittain, Nicolas Kent, Richard Norton-Taylor, Gillian Slovo*, 78. London: Oberon Books Ltd, 2014.

Conkle, E. P. (Ellsworth Prouty). *Federal Theatre Plays. Prologue to Glory*, by E. P. Conkle. *One-Third of a Nation*, edited by Arthur Arent. *Haiti*, by William Du Bois. New York: Random House, 1938.

Curtis, N. *Nicolas Kent and Richard Norton-Taylor on Their New Grenfell Play*. Evening Standard, 2021.

Favorini, Attilio. Voicings: Ten Plays from the Documentary Theatre/Edited and with an Introduction by Attilio Favorini. New York: Ecco Press, 1995.

Flanagan, Hallie. *Arena; the History of the Federal Theatre*, by Hallie Flanagan. New York: B. Blom, 1965.

Megson, C. "Half the Picture: 'A Certain Frisson' at the Tricycle Theatre." *Get Real* edited by Forsyth, A. London: Palgrave Macmillan UK, 2009.

Gökarıksel, Saygun. "Beyond Transparency: the Communist-Era Secret Police Archives in Postsocialist Eastern Europe." *Archives and Records* 41, no. 3 (2020): 236–53.

Green, Jesse. "'Is This a Room' Review: A Transcript Becomes a Thrilling Thriller." *The New York Times*, 2021. www.nytimes.com/2021/10/11/theater/is-this-a-room-review.html.

Mally, Lynn. "The Americanization of the Soviet Living Newspaper." *The Carl Beck Papers in Russian and East European Studies* 1903 (2008).

McDermott, Douglas. "The Living Newspaper as a Dramatic Form." *Modern Drama* 8, no. 1 (1965): 82–94.

Piscator, Erwin, and Hugh Rorrison. *The Political Theatre/[by] Erwin Piscator*. Translated [from the German], with Chapter Introductions and Notes, by Hugh Rorrison. Eyre Methuen, 1978.

Rubenstein, David. "A Conversation with Anna Deavere Smith." Annual David M. Rubenstein Lecture. Cambridge, MA: American Academy of Arts and Sciences, 2019.

"Theatre/Hearing Aid: Paul Taylor on Richard Norton-Taylor's Half The Picture at the Tricycle." *The Independent*, Independent Digital News and Media, 1994, www.independent.co.uk/arts-entertainment/theatre-hearing-aid-paul-taylor-on-richard-nortontaylor-s-half-the-picture-at-the-tricycle-1423061.html.

Weiss, Peter. *Aesthetics of Resistance*. Durham and London: Duke University Press, 2020.

PART II
Interviews

8

LEIGH FONDAKOWSKI, *THE PEOPLE'S TEMPLE*

One artist who has made a significant contribution toward building bridges between people is Leigh Fondakowski. Leigh is a playwright, screenwriter, author, director, and most recently, the host and producer of the podcast *Feminist Files*, starring Jodie Foster. Leigh is the head writer of *The Laramie Project*, a co-writer of *Laramie: Ten Years Later*, and an Emmy nominated co-screenwriter for the film adaptation of *Laramie* with HBO Films. Leigh's other original plays include *I Think I Like Girls*, *The People's Temple*, *Spill,* and *Casa Cushman.* Leigh is the author of the non-fiction book *Stories from Jonestown* and is currently adapting the book to television with Margo Hall.[1] I asked Leigh about their process and about making *The People's Temple*, which was based on extensive interviews with survivors of the mass murder-suicide at Jonestown, a remote settlement in Guyana that was built by the San Francisco-based Peoples Temple, led by Jim Jones …

KJ: I fully realize that this might be a question that doesn't really have an answer, but have you noticed any patterns in what projects you're drawn to, which ones you select to work on, and which you don't?

LEIGH: Well, I became interested in this kind of docu-style or interview-based style when I was a young theatre artist and I saw the work of Anna Deavere Smith. Now, Anna Deavere Smith's work is very particular in that she's such a tour de force as a performer. And so, the pieces really are as much about her as they are about the subject matter.

But both pieces that I saw as a young artist, *Twilight: Los Angeles* and *Fires in the Mirror*, I was really struck by the form. The art form allowed me to feel the breadth and scope of these dramatic events through the lens of all these different people that she interviewed, and I was very taken with it.

And so, I set out to do a similar thing with *I Think I Like Girls* where I started interviewing queer women, lesbian women, growing up gay in America.

KJ: When was that? Mid-'90s?

LEIGH: Yeah, it was early or the middle '90s. It was before we went to Laramie.

And then when Matthew Shepard was killed, you know, Moisés[2] had approached the company and said, "Do we, as theatre artists, have a role to play in this national conversation that's happening for the first time about hate crimes?"

That was when it became more concrete that there was a real responsibility and a real relationship between this national conversation and an artistic life. It was the first moment where I felt like, "Oh, this is the role of the artist." To participate in these conversations. Not just stand on the sidelines, or have your work only in New York, but to actually engage with society and societal conversations.

And then from there, to be honest, the projects really kind of just showed up.

My rules of engagement are to not say yes or no, but to go, to do a little searching, and see, you know, if something grabs me.

In the case of *Jonestown*, that was a commission from David Dower, who was then the artistic director of Z Space in San Francisco. He saw our production of *Laramie* in Berkeley, and he was like, "Oh, this is how we could tell the story of Jonestown." And he came to me, and asked me if I wanted to work on it.

I was like, *(very wary)* "Jonestown?"

KJ: Intense.

LEIGH: Very intense. Coming off of Matthew Shepard. But I talked to the first person and—not to sound too Pollyanna about it—but there's just a moment where I feel called to the material, called to respond. So, one of the first interviews I did was the son of Jim Jones.

And the son of Jim Jones completely defied every expectation that I had about what he would be like, what the conversation would be like, what these, quote-unquote "cult-y" people would be like. I thought, "Wow, I didn't really know anything about this story."

So, I took it on. And that was huge, a five-year project, even longer than *The Laramie Project*.

But then after that, I was somewhat cautious, because, as you well know, like once you start, you're engaged for a long time. You're talking to people and, you know, trying to find like, drama and story and trying to figure out this structure, and then also feeling this responsibility to have all these perspectives and to have a balanced view.

It's just so many things, right? It's going to be a big chunk of your creative capital and your life.

KJ: It's a *huge* commitment. But with the right project, can be rewarding too, right?

LEIGH: It's very exciting when you have these moments where it's pure poetry. Like somebody speaking right from their heart, and they have a turn of phrase or a way of articulating something that's just so beautiful and so potent.

Or when drama just leaps out, you stumble upon something that's just like all this inherent drama, explosive and dynamic. And it's something you didn't makeup. It's something you discovered. Something that you've found along the way in the conversation.

That still is ... I did an interview last week for this podcast, and I felt high.

I was remembering why I've gone to such lengths in my career to have these interviews and these conversations and have the work based on them.

You feel changed at the end of the conversation. The other person is changed at the end of the conversation, and you covered this territory together. You know, it's a, it's a form of intimacy that is rare in everyday life.

KJ: Was there anyone that you interviewed that left a deep imprint in a challenging way? Or, you know, you mentioned walking away feeling high from an interview. What are the other feelings you've had when you've interviewed people?

LEIGH: Yeah, that's, that's an interesting question. I mean, with *Jonestown* it was always kind of mixed, because, you know, they had been through so much.

We spoke to this one survivor. This man who witnessed his baby being injected with poison. And we knew that he had been an eyewitness to, you know, the murders in Jonestown. Like a lot of people, they "drank the Kool-Aid" and they all committed suicide. But many, many, many people were murdered, and that was a little-known fact of the story. So, we wanted him to tell us that story, because we kind of needed it for the play, you know?

And so, we had all these different conversations with him. And it was maybe like, the fifth or sixth time we had gone and interviewed him. Each time, he's kind of like, "I'm gonna tell you the story. I'm gonna tell you the story." And then he just wasn't able to, and then this last time, he just bared his soul and told us all the details, and it was horrific. And he was sobbing. So, we got the story that we needed from him. But it didn't take away his pain. It didn't. It didn't lessen his burden.

There are moments where you realize that the theatre is very transformational and the process of dialogue is very transformational. And then there's just some pain that's just going to be there forever. And there's no salve. There's nothing that you can do.

Did I just commodify his pain to make this product? Is it gonna, you know, come to something good? Why did we just put him through this?

It's kind of, you know, a feeling of like that—a feeling of incompleteness. Not being able to do anything with all his pain, other than bear witness to it. And it had a kind of stickiness to it that—

KJ: Did that stickiness continue as you considered putting it in the play? Like, was there—

LEIGH: Well, we put it in the play, and in the end, the play ... It was interesting with *Jonestown*, the play was pivotal in the arc of the community of survivors. And the function that it served, was that—it premiered in Berkely[3]—Tony Taccone[4] at first did not want to do it. He was like, "This is some dark shit." You know?

And basically, his back was up against the wall. Because he couldn't *not* premiere it. This is the theatre that *should* do it.[5] And in his heart, he knew that.

So he finally said, "All right, I know I have to do it, so I'm gonna do it." But what happened in Berkeley was that the survivors all came, and the audience, the Berkeley audience, and the press at the time, the press that had covered Peoples Temple, it was like the first time that the survivors felt like they were being heard and not judged.

And I think that was, you know, a testament to our work to a certain extent, my collaborators Margo Hall, Greg Pierotti, and Steve Wangh. But it was really a testament to that community and that audience that Berkeley Rep had been cultivating for all those decades. They didn't say, "Oh these crazy cultists. Why are we listening to those stories?"

They, they came to hear.

And the press, which was interesting, did a kind of "mea culpa," where they were saying, "Okay, we were part of this, too. We held Jim Jones up as a pillar of our community. And we had a part to play in this too."

KJ: Wow.

LEIGH: So, it was a really interesting moment. That was kind of like the shift inside the survivor community of feeling that it was safe to tell their stories. And then they went on to talk to all these other people, and all these other projects came of it. But the play was kind of like a Rorschach test, for "is society ready to see these people as human beings and not these crazy cultists who followed Jim Jones and 'drank the Kool-Aid?'"

In the end, the play never made it to New York. It had a short life after Berkeley. It was at the Guthrie, it was in Chicago and other places, but it never moved to New York. It never got published. By commercial standards, it was not a success, but by any kind of spiritual standard, personal achievement standard, it was—it served a very important function in the life of the survivor community, which, I think, was David's intention from the beginning.

KJ: But this kind of building a play for a specific time and a specific place and a specific people, even if the play may not go beyond that moment. What would you call that?

LEIGH: I don't know what to call that art form. I mean, I just think of my work really just as theatre. I don't call it Documentary Theatre or any kind of theatre. It's just, you know, it's just theatre, you know, based on real events, kind of as far as I take it. But I do think it's interesting.

When we premiered *Spill*,[6] in Baton Rouge, at Swine Palace in Baton Rouge, a lot of the people coming to see it had literally never seen a play before. So, the first and only play they'd ever seen was a play about their lives and themselves, which is, I don't know, just kind of cool.

KJ: Have you gone back to that first, um, interview? That first show that you worked on, *I Think I Like Girls*?

LEIGH: I haven't. But I thought about it. I've really thought about it, because it just was such, you know, was such a moment. And I had interviewed both my parents. So, my mom opened the first act, and my dad opened the second act. And both my parents have passed now. So, I have thought about getting back in there, um, but you know, it's possible.

KJ: Do you have—do you consider there are any occupational hazards in what you do?

LEIGH: Uhhh. Occupational hazard. Being on the road? I don't know. Being on the road a lot. Being separated from, you know, family at maybe crucial times, because you're immersed in something else.

And I don't know if it's an occupational hazard, but it is definitely a choice to, um, I don't know. People talk about—I don't know why this is coming to mind, but—you know people talk about, slow, what do they call it, slow fashion? Where it's like, we're not going to have fast things that are mass produced that only last a year. We're going to wear things that are high quality for a long time, because the earth can't sustain it anymore, right?

KJ: Right.

LEIGH: And I sort of feel like the career I chose, or the career that chose me, was definitely one where there was a slow arc in the development of the project. "We're going to go through this. We're gonna learn everything we can learn. We're going to study this. We're going to form these relationships. We're going to travel around. We're going to do this thing." It's a very slow, slow approach to art making.

KJ: That's something deep. Um, this last question—I have stolen this from you. I heard you say you did this, so now I am using it as well... Is there a question that I should have asked you that I didn't?

LEIGH: What I always say to people is that if somebody agrees to talk to you, there's certain etiquette and certain techniques you can study and all of that, but if a person agrees to talk to you, there's a *reason* why they've agreed to talk to you. And your job, as a listener, is to sort out why that is.

And so, in that way, the process teaches you what the ultimate outcome wants to be. Like, the artistic outcome is one that is shown to you, rather than one that you prescribe.

There's something about the uncertainty of the process. There's certainty in knowing that if someone agrees to talk to you, they have a reason why. There's a certainty in that. But there's also an uncertainty that you have to be comfortable with, in letting it come to the surface.

Even if it doesn't come to the surface in that very first meeting, it's going to come to the surface at some point, if you stay present and keep your heart and your ears open.

NOTES

[1] https://leighfondakowski.com.
[2] Moisés Kaufman, founder of Tectonic Theater Project.
[3] Berkely Repertory Theatre, Berkely California.
[4] Artistic director at the time of production.
[5] Because People's Temple began in San Francisco, most of its members were from the Bay Area.
[6] Fondakowski's play about the 2010 industrial disaster, the Deepwater Horizon Oil Spill, AKA the "BP oil spill."

9

LES WATERS

Les Waters is a director and theatre maker who has had an extensive career and influenced countless artists. His Broadway productions of Sarah Ruhl's *In the Next Room (or The Vibrator Play)* and Lucas Hnath's *Dana H.* were critically acclaimed. He's worked closely with playwrights such as Charles L. Mee, Anne Washburn, Naomi Iizuka, Will Eno, and Caryl Churchill. He is also one of the reasons there are so many theatre makers making plays based on real people and real events. As a young artist, he worked with Caryl Churchill and Joint Stock Theatre Company on *A Mouthfull of Birds* and *Fen*. Both premiered in London, and *Fen* opened in New York at the Public Theater in 1983. In the 1990s, Les was on faculty at the University of California in San Diego, where he taught a class on the Joint Stock method of making plays based on conversations with real people. Students in that class, including Anne Kaufman and Steve Cosson, went on to lead the current wave of Investigative Theatre in the United States. From 2012 to 2018 Waters was the artistic director of Actors Theatre of Louisville, where he helmed the Humana Festival, one of the most influential American new play festivals of its time. I had the privilege of working with Les on the world premiere and four following productions of Chuck Mee's *Big Love*—Les directed and I performed the role of Thyona.

I asked Les about working on *Fen* ...

KJ: Can you walk me through that whole process? How did that idea start? How did you find people to talk to?

LES: Well, the idea ... Caryl Churchill and I pitched a project to Joint Stock. We both worked for Joint Stock on *Cloud Nine*. I was the assistant director on *Cloud Nine*—the production, not the workshop. And we wanted to work together, and we pitched an idea about women who worked on the land, farm workers.

And partly it was because many of my mother's family for many generations were agricultural workers. And I'd read a book called *Fen Women* by Mary Chamberlain, who was a socialist feminist historian who interviewed women who worked in the Fens, which is a particular area of England. And they, Joint Stock Theatre Company said yes to us doing it. We knew we had to go to the Fens to talk to people. So, I think it was Caryl, myself, and Annie the set designer.

KJ: Annie Smart?

LES: Yep. And six actors, five women, and one man. So, if you've got six actors and five are female, you've made some pretty important decisions about the event. And we went to live in a village called Outwell, which is near a village called Upwell.

And we moved up there. And we didn't know anybody there. We started walking through the village on our own or in pairs. And we asked people—could we talk to them? I mean, we were very upfront. We said who we were, you know, and that we were interested in making a piece about the people who lived in this area.

KJ: Did they ask you why? And did you have an answer?

LES: Most people would say, nearly all of the women would say, "You don't want to talk to me, you should talk to my husband." And people would say, "Yes, I'll talk to you, but you won't mention me by name in it, will you?" And we agreed to that. Nobody signed anything. Which I suppose if we did that now it could well be an issue. Oh, I remember I was asked several times, and I would say, "Well, my mother, you know, my mother's family were land workers from further north." And people would either talk to us for like 10 minutes or three hours.

KJ: So, as you're listening to people, and this is in '76? '80? What year is this?

LES: Early eighties, I think.

KJ: Did you use a recording device? A tape recorder?

LES: No, no. We made a decision not to record anybody. I've always found that when I'm interviewed, I speak differently if I'm recorded. I begin to perform in a very loose sense to the recording device. So, our decision was not to record anybody. We came up with a list of basic questions like, what's your name? Where are you from (which was a big deal in that area)? What do you do? That seemed to cover everything. I think there were five or six simple questions. And then, one big, big question. Like, if you didn't do this, what would you like to do? Or, what would be your dream?

KJ: Oh, that's a lovely. What is a good question? What makes for a bad question?

LES: I think at some point in the earliest stages of it, the more the question is based on a particular fact, the easier it is. So, what's your name? "My name is Les Waters, but on my passport, it's Leslie Waters. But everybody calls me Les, but my family called me Leslie. It's also my father's name; my grandfather was called Charles Leslie. My father called me Herbert until I was six years old. True. I don't understand why." The one simple question opened up a door. Do you know what I mean?

Or somebody could just say, "My name's KJ." End of it.

KJ: That's interesting, because it gives you a clue as to, is this gonna be a three-hour conversation? Or is this gonna be a 15-minute conversation. And of course, we're looking for the longer conversation.

LES: Yes. And the thing was, what we endeavored to do, and what we struggled to do, was not to ask questions with conscious value judgments built into them. There was something the other night on the news in the Bay Area about a particular car crash somewhere. And there's somebody standing by the side of the road looking completely collapsed. And the reporter said, "This tragedy must have traumatized you." And, and the person then started to talk about how they've been traumatized. That question defined what the person would say. We were trying very hard not to do that. And we would practice it on each other. So, I can remember one afternoon sitting with somebody in the group. And we would practice interviewing each other without trying to ask leading questions.

KJ: So, you would ask simple questions, and you would listen. You didn't have a recording device; you just had the questions you'd agreed to in your back pocket. And you didn't go fishing or try to ask leading questions, and then you'd walk away. And would you write it down? Would you share it with each other?

LES: Yeah, we'd walk away and go somewhere and write down everything we could remember. I mean, not necessarily in the order of the interview, or chronologically. Usually, you remember the first thing people told you. And then your mind begins to jump. But constructing an actual narrative is quite tricky. We would write down as much as one could remember, take a step back from it. Have a break and, you know, have lunch, go away and do stuff. Look at it again. Add things that we remembered. Put question marks by things—any particular phrases that people used we thought were interesting. And then every evening in the place we were staying, one, two, three, or more of us would sit on a chair and say, "My name's KJ." And just start talking, trying to talk as that person, without doing an impersonation, without doing the local accent. We'd just talk, and sometimes people would have the notes in a notebook on their lap or on the floor, and the person presenting would talk as the person they interviewed, and the rest of us would ask them questions.

And that—you can't remotely claim it's objective. Because it's not recorded. But there's some imaginative process, there's some creative process going on—you're editing it.

KJ: Right, so you're leaning into the fact that the memory and the transpositions, and all of that is a creative act. So, it's already becoming fiction.

LES: Yes.

KJ: But I think the fact that you lived there, that you're careful about not asking leading questions—so there was an imprimatur of these real lives on you, that you—

LES: I think the huge value to people who do this kind of work, however it's defined, is that the people who do the interviews and then perform them have some kind of extraordinary ownership of the material. You know? Because they were there, they witnessed it. They understand it. And then, with, *Fen*, the whole thing was then transformed again by Caryl.

KJ: Right. She would listen to these sessions.

LES: She would listen. She and I made notes about what everybody did. Then Caryl wrote *Fen* in just six weeks. Then we had six weeks to rehearse. We did a three-week workshop, two weeks in the Fens, one week in London.

KJ: Wow. So, step one: asking people questions. Two: reflect what you remember them saying thru sharing with the group. Three: the playwright fictionalizes what she hears in these presentation sessions. *Cloud Nine* was built in sort of a similar way, yes?

LES: *Cloud Nine* was based, built by them [Joint Stock] wanting to do a workshop on sexual politics, and they interviewed people, and they talked to historians, and they talked about their own sexuality.

I think the final line of *Fen* is, "My mother wanted to be a singer. That's why she would never sing," is actually me. Is me talking to the group about our families and agriculture, because my mother's family were agricultural farm workers. And my mother was extremely deferential. And my mother wanted to be a singer, and that's why she never sang. She never sang. That's my mum.

KJ: Lovely. The reason that I'm writing this book is because I had a real crisis of faith in my art in the last couple of years. You know, I've always been rather sentimental, romantic, and maybe naïve about this art form. But I really believed everybody has a beautiful story. Just take the time to listen. And you know, it's important to listen to two sides of an argument. And then I just stopped wanting to hear from people. I just didn't want to listen anymore. And I feel like I've lost the capacity to listen. I feel like my hearing is going and, emotionally, I am struggling. Have you ever had that? Do you think you could go back to a place and live in a town and just ask farmers about what they do?

LES: Asking me today? Yeah, I think I could do it. I think if you asked me last year, if you asked me when Trump was elected? I mean a lot of the time I'm angry. And yes, I often think my own art form is completely pointless. And I should put on big boy pants and go and do something else that would have an immediate effect. Yeah, but I think I could do it now. I mean, when I left Actors Theatre in 2018, Annie and I drove from Louisville to California. Well, I didn't drive, Annie did. And I've never been across the middle of the country—Wyoming and places. And my overwhelming sense of it was like, it had been abandoned. It looked like America got up and left. And I mean, the landscape is deserted. We were in Cheyenne, Wyoming, and Annie went to bed and I went for a walk round Cheyenne, Wyoming at nine o'clock in the evening. It was deserted. Downtown was deserted, and it went: pizza parlor, bar, Thai restaurant, drug addiction clinic, drug addiction clinic, thrift store, pizza parlor, drug addiction clinic, drug addiction clinic.

And I did think then it may be really interesting to go and talk to people. I don't know how I'd be if I sat down in a room and somebody told me all liberals were the Antichrist, Obama was from Satan, and Trump was our Savior. But part of me is like, that kind of fierce listening, you have to do when people tell you things that are unacceptable to you. Maybe. It may be interesting to find out.

KJ: Fierce listening. That's the phrase I needed to hear.

LES: Yeah, it's just really hard to listen.

10

STEVE COSSON, THE CIVILIANS

Steve Cosson is the founder and artistic director of the theatre company The Civilians. Steve and The Civilians, who, on their website, describe what they do as "making new work at the intersection of the theatrical and the real" have a remarkable body of work including *Gone Missing*, with several United States and United Kingdom tours culminating in a one-year Off-Broadway commercial run; *This Beautiful City*, about the Colorado Springs Evangelical movement; *The Great Immensity*, about climate change; *Another Word for Beauty*, created from a residency inside Bogotá's national women's prison during their annual beauty pageant; and *Pretty Filthy* created from months of immersion in Los Angeles' adult film industry.

My own introduction to the Joint Stock interview technique came from Steve. I was a Civilian[1] back in the early days of the company, and Steve invited me to a workshop. What he shared with me changed my life and has informed nearly 20 years of work. Steve began his own foray into investigative theatre when he was getting an MFA at the University of California,

San Diego (UCSD) and taking a class with theatre maker and director Les Waters.

KJ: I interviewed Les about Joint Stock. And I thought maybe we could start there. That era at UCSD led to so many artists making work based on conversations with real people.

STEVE: Yeah, yeah. It's a whole interconnected family tree. My introduction to this kind of work was with that Joint Stock class with Les. I'd always had a passion for documentary film. But certainly not in the world of theatre.

The archetypal Joint Stock process is basically: A workshop phase, within which some kind of interviewing process happens. That gets shared with the group. Then that material goes to a writer, and a writer creates a play. In Les' class, we mostly worked on the first phase of the process. Les picked a subject, we went out into the San Diego area and found people to interview.

Part of the learning experience is, how do you go out and connect with an interesting person, or a person that you want to talk to? We took no notes, didn't use any recording devices, would have the conversation and then try to immediately go somewhere and transcribe everything we could remember, and would then at some point return to class, present the interview from memory, and essentially be that person. The other members of the class could ask us questions, and we essentially relived the conversation. Then the class, led by the writers, edited the material together into a presentation.

The year that my class did the project, our subject was the very rich and the very poor of San Diego. I chose the very rich because I figured it would be harder to find those people and get them to talk, and I wanted the challenge.

KJ: And how did you approach them?

STEVE: This was sort of the first thing that really clicked for me that I realized that I liked figuring out how to connect with people. The way I went about it is, was a little bit sneaky. I went to development directors, you know, the fundraisers basically at the La Jolla Playhouse, and one of the museums in La Jolla, and said that I was doing a class project about philanthropists and wanted to talk to them. I think I learned one thing, which is, you know, actually showing up with something unusual is usually novel and interesting to somebody. You know? It's a, it's an unusual ask, it's like, "Hey, do you know somebody who's really interesting? Who would talk to me?" And in both cases, they said, "Oh, I know somebody who'd be great. Let me make a phone call."

KJ: In those early days, Steve, that was sort of like the wild west where we were doing anything to get an interview. Are you still as wily about finding somebody to talk to? Or are you more transparent now about why you're asking questions? Or does that even matter to you?

STEVE: Oh, yeah, ever since I've been more transparent. I think, for every other project where I've needed to interview someone, it's because we are making a show.

KJ: It's interesting that this clicked for you, gaining access—you've had an incredible track record. I mean, the people that you were able to connect with for *This Beautiful City*,[2] alone, was impressive. What you found interesting is the thing that most people are afraid of, getting a stranger to talk to them.

STEVE: I was going to say, there's an art to it. It's not really an art; it's really more of a process. If you start with the notion that you need to go up to a stranger and convince them to sit down and talk to you, then yeah, that is challenging and is intimidating to anybody. But I think the instinct that I had is, it's networking, it's a process of who can you make contact with. Who can be a helper to connect you to the next person who still might not actually be a subject for your show, but that next person is going to be a connector to the people that you actually want to talk to?

It's no great mystery. It's how journalism happens. It's how most things happen. It's human relationships, one person making a connection with another, building a sense of trust.

And I think the thing, one of the things that clicked was—I was really surprised, like, "Wow, I sat in this man's house for three hours as he talked nonstop. He didn't care at all about, like, what the premise was of me being there." You know? He just had somebody interested in what he had to say.

It is the weird circumstance of showing up, just to do an interview for a theatre project that can make it work because in many cases, you show up in this person's life as someone without an agenda. Or at least seemingly not to have an agenda. Your agenda is to listen to them and have that feed into this work of theatre that you're going to make. And you know, there may be certain things that you want to find out about. But I think if you can create that dynamic with the other person, where you are this creature that has shown up from the blue, that just wants to listen to what they have to say. I mean, how often is it that you have somebody just want to listen to you that is not going to ask for anything in return? You know?

KJ: Yeah. So, then you're sitting there for three hours, and he's talking, and you're not using a recording device. So, you walk away, and you write everything you remember from the first person, correct?

What, what tricks, or what muscles have you learned are required to listen in a way that you actually capture what that person said?

STEVE: I will say, after the first few years of the Civilians, we did start using recording devices. When we weren't recording, one part of it is being present when you're doing the interview, and not worrying about trying to remember, not worrying too much about what you're getting from the interview, your attention is in the moment. And, whatever questions you ask are very responsive to whatever has just been said by the person. And if you've been present throughout the interview, when you go to write everything down, you start from the first thing that you can remember and just put your mind in the interview, and then just let one thought go to the next. And it's quite remarkable how much you actually remember.

The other remarkable thing is how quickly you get better at it. We did, we did some projects where we were presenting from memory, but we were also recording and then transcribing, which was a slow process. Eventually, we got the transcriptions. And I could compare what came out from memory in the interview in the rehearsal process, versus what was in the transcript. And sometimes things would be out of sequence, but remarkably accurate. And you know, I don't know what that means exactly. But I think that for a lot of our human evolution, things—stories, epic poems—were communicated orally and remembered and passed from person to person. So, there's capacity in the brain, to remember.

KJ: Yeah, and I wonder if what's required above all else is just a desire to absorb somebody else's experience in a profound way. I'm writing this book because I am at a personal crisis where I'm struggling with the ability to listen to people, which is kind of a problem when we're professional listeners. I feel like right now, with everything in the world, my brain feels like a jar full of bees, and I don't know if I can just set everything aside and simply listen.

Does any of that ring true for you? Can we listen anymore?

STEVE: I think we can. I would say that one of the things that I really yearn for, during these two years of social isolation ... if I could be doing a project where I was interviewing people in person, I almost always found that to, to bring me back into the world. Part of the strain of isolation and interacting with people by phone or Zoom is you don't have that physiological experience of shared presence. This is stuff that's above my paygrade that other people know much more about than I do, but I can say, from my experience of it, if I'm doing a project where I'm interviewing several people a day and spending a lot of time outside of my head, in listening mode—and in a particular kind of listening mode, of being genuinely curious, of letting go—that your attention is off yourself and it's on this other person. And it's very freeing and liberating. And that's what hopefully comes across in the work and why the theatre is compelling. That it actually makes reality real for you again.

And it's not just the pandemic. We have egos, and egos make us think of ourselves as separate. And, and then, you know, we live in an increasingly individualized society and have all sorts of forces that encourage us to think of ourselves as separate. So then other people become objects of our consciousness, as opposed to other subjective experiences sharing the world with us. And, I think it's very easy to get stuck in a prison of your own mind. When you are stuck there, other people become less real to you.

KJ: That's amazing. Everyone becomes props in our own personal reality show. And then what we're trying to do with, with this kind of theatre, is bring people together to, in a room, *experience*, you know, because like, we're, we couldn't be further away from the reality television show. I'm starting to suspect that theatre's closest cousin is actually graphic novels. Because we build a series of panels, and then the audience fills in the gutters to make those connections. But where I'm going with this is that it's so interesting that investigative and documentary theatre, as you say, makes reality real for us again.

You made a piece at such an important time for all of us New Yorkers: *Gone Missing*. It's simple, it's elegant. It talks about big things without talking about big things. And am I right in remembering that you built it in the midst of the attack on the World Trade Center, and us being in New York, you being in New York, the company being there, and trying to come to terms with that moment of crisis—is that right?

STEVE: *Gone Missing*'s really the second show that we started working on. The very first one was done right in the midst of 9/11. I think our first rehearsal was within a week after the attacks of September 11.

KJ: And that show was?

STEVE: *Canard, Canard, Goose?*

KJ: I loved the beginning—the cast sings or says, "We listened to some people. And we made a show about it. We had a lot of snacks," You're really transparent about the process at the beginning of that show.

STEVE: In a weird and ridiculous way, we were doing a parody of ourselves as a theatre company in our very first show. Usually something exists and is in some way important. And then you can parody it. And we neither existed nor were really important, and we did the parody anyhow. It just seemed to be what made sense at the time.

Gone Missing started to evolve in 2002. And part of the impetus for that was we were still very much in a state of grief from the losses of the attacks. And, at the same time that grief was being manipulated for political ends. There was a distinct feeling that our legitimate grief was getting hijacked and manipulated and weaponized for the neo-cons to do whatever they wanted. This is not to say that *Gone Missing* in any way is a very political show. Just to say that the original impulse came from a very simple idea: Can we as a company take on loss, memory, and grief on its own terms? To be, to be alive is to go through a series of losses. I don't think it's a show that necessarily had any kind of political impact, but on a more emotional level, I think it did. It came from an interest in, in detoxifying grief.

KJ: In *Gone Missing* you were sharing stories of loss that were, on first glance, superficial—the loss of my family's attention, when I hide in the closet and nobody knows I'm there, or the loss of a shoe, a favorite lipstick, the little things. Did you know that that's what you wanted to focus on? Or did that come about as you started interviewing people?

STEVE: You mean the objects? That was, that was one of the first rules was: we are going in through a side door. It was designed mostly as a comedy that creates some space to allow an audience to feel grief. We purposefully went on a circuitous path. I think that there also is—there are profound ways that we experience our more complicated inchoate emotions, through our relationships to objects. Our basic question was, "Tell us about something that went missing that for some reason was important to you." So, there's some emotional charge between the person and the thing, which opens the door to get into some of the more complicated stuff that goes on inside of us. And then the show ends with a, with a sequence that is, at least in my mind, is pretty explicitly about 9/11.

KJ: You made this work in connection to what, at the time, felt like the hardest thing we were ever going to have to go through. And now we're living in, well, an even more difficult time. Is there a way to capture this moment? Is there a way to use this kind of artmaking to stay healthy and sane?

STEVE: There has to be some way. In a sense, like every work that comes out of this time is speaking to this time in some way, whether directly or obliquely. I found it a particularly challenging time to think about how to do documentary theatre that directly engages any of the issues that are at the forefront of the news or at the, at the heart of the complexity of the moment.

It's hard to get the distance and separation from what's happening in such a way to figure out what's going to be an effective artistic intervention.

I mean, if it's just like with, with COVID, like, who wants to watch a documentary about what it's like to live through lockdown? We lived through lockdown. Don't need to watch the documentary. You need something that's going to actually illuminate the moment or give you some kind of experience to help metabolize the experience.

I think one of the biggest questions with this kind of work is how do you go from the investigative process into actually making that into a show?

KJ: If you were to make a brochure that had six bullet points, or five bullet points for that, what would you include?

STEVE: That's a good way of asking the question. I've written fully verbatim shows, and I've also written fictionalized narratives that draw on the research. I think both the investigation and the resulting play need to center around an unanswerable question. Going through an investigative process, you and the people that you're working with go on a journey of discovery. You learn things. You then are surprised by things. You form ideas that then later fall apart when contrasting information comes in. And, and often, that is the scaffolding for the play itself. You're seeking to give an audience something of a parallel experience in 100 minutes.

KJ: And you lean into the complexity rather than trying to simplify it?

STEVE: The same way that a traditional narrative play takes its protagonist into a problem and then the problem gets more and more complicated and the protagonist has a harder and harder time getting out of the problem. They solve one problem, and then it creates a bigger one.

And in a non-narrative piece the basic rules of play structure and dramaturgy still apply, whether there's a narrative or whether there isn't.

And, that asking, yes, what the conflict—what are the, what are the opposing forces? How is that changing over time? All of those questions are then the guideposts for structuring and making the work.

NOTES

[1] What artistic associates with The Civilians call ourselves.
[2] By Steve Cosson and Jim Lewis from interviews conducted by associate artists Emily Ackerman, Marsha Stephanie Blake, Brad Heberlee, Brandon Miller, Stephen Plunkett, and Alison Weller, with music and lyrics by Michael Friedman. World premiere in 2008 at the Humana Festival of New American Plays.

11

SARA ZATZ

Sara Zatz joined Ping Chong and Company in 2002 and leads the company's community engagement work. She is one of five members of the artistic leadership team, a leadership model established in 2022 upon the retirement of founder and artistic director Ping Chong. Since 1975, Ping Chong and Company has worked continuously, across the country and all over the world, making "theater and art that reveal beauty, invention, precision, and a commitment to social justice."[1] The *Undesirable Elements* series is one of Ping Chong and Company's flagship programs. It focuses on presenting theatrical events based on interviews and features community members performing their own stories about place and people, culture and community.

KJ: You've been collaborating, writing, and directing the *Undesirable Elements* pieces for 20 years.

Has anything changed for you?

SARA: I started with Ping as a kind of assistant and mentored with him and grew in the process, learning from him, and then, ultimately bringing in my own practices as well. And so, my entire journey with *Undesirable Elements* has definitely been an evolution.

And I think that the creative process and the listening process have definitely evolved. One thing that has changed gradually over the years—and it was partly how I positioned myself when I started doing the work independent of Ping—was kind of questioning my own place in the listening and the power dynamics of interview-based theatre as a White artist working in and with communities that were not, that I was not of, and recognizing the different dynamics that I had from Ping, when it was the two of us working together.

And so, one of the things that has changed in the *Undesirable Elements* methodology is, not always, but mostly, trying to build a creative team where one of the co-creators is either part of the community that we're working with or shares identity with the community.

That is one way that we've rethought what the power structures look like in terms of inviting people to tell their stories, and who has agency.

I think, with *Undesirable Elements* we've always talked about the idea that it is intended to highlight people who haven't had a chance to speak publicly. So even within a community, when we invite people to tell their stories—if we're working in a small town, the partner organization might instinctively put forward, you know, the head of the Chamber of Commerce, or that person who's the activist leader of that group. And we're not refusing that, but we're trying to look for the person who maybe doesn't have that public-facing platform. So, I think with the world that we're living in right now, and that question of listening, I think it's still very much about who has a platform to speak, and who has a place to be heard.

KJ: And if you were to write a, if you were to make a little brochure on how to find people whose voices are not being heard, how do you do that?

SARA: So, one of the things that makes UE [the *Undesirable Elements* program] not unique, but you know, a little bit different than some other interview-based work is that we are always working with people who are telling their own stories. So, they're not being represented by actors. And often that does come through the relationships with the partner organizations.

Right now, we're in conversation with the Justice Beyond Punishment Collaborative around doing a project, that we're calling "UE adjacent." It's not going to be a typical *Undesirable Elements*. It's being led by another artist, Kirya Traber, who does a lot of interview-based work, with whom I've worked closely. So, she's the lead artist, informed by *Undesirable Elements*. Ping Chong and Company is going to be the co-producer.

In the conversation we had yesterday, we were talking about, "How do we identify folx impacted by incarceration?" And still, even within that group, you know, who are we looking for who maybe isn't already a leader in the movement or isn't already someone who's had a documentary made about them? They have a coalition of independent organizations, and so they, the partners, are looking in their networks in terms of asking for folx.

In terms of inviting everyday people to be part of a project who aren't theatre people, it's just a lot about availability. Making sure that it's possible for people to participate, because if you're telling your own story on stage, but you work nights, and you have to take time off of work, then how do you account for that?

When UE first started, it was housed a lot in regional theatres, and they—the regional theatres—sometimes used actors who were telling their own stories, but were, you know, actors by training. There was often a very broad call for participants. This is going back to the time when they might actually, literally put an ad in the newspaper.

Now, we're working with the host or partner organization which hopefully already has deep relationships. We do info sessions, we do meet and greets, and more sort of workshops, so that people can come and experience a little bit of the methodology before deciding if it's something that they're interested in.

KJ: So, the lifespan of a project: The first step is the partnership. Then, through the partners, an all-call, and then you have info sessions and workshops. So, people can get a sense of what you're doing. Then what's the next step? Do you audition? Does everyone who wants to be a part of it become part of it?

SARA: What you just recapped is the direction that we've been going, that sort of open call. It's not always that way. And sometimes, if the theme is really specific, the partner organization might pre-identify people.

So, we've done an open call where 25 people apply to be part of it. And we're working with six or seven. We've also done projects like *Say My Name, Say My Name: Stories of LGBTQ Youth from New Orleans* where we were working with a group of trans youth of color in New Orleans who are working in anti-policing. And that was in partnership with BreakOUT!,[2] a youth-led community-based group dedicated to fighting the criminalization of LGBTQ youth of color in New Orleans. And they were like, "These are the people that are part of our organization. These are the people who are part of this process." So that one was very much internal to that organization.

So, it can depend on the specificity of the project and how the partner works with its own community members, but, broadly speaking, once we have the partner, and the partner usually is very hands-on in terms of identifying the theme and who the community members might be.

There's usually a kind of application questionnaire—now it's a Google Form—where we include all the information about the project: This is what the time commitment is. This is what the expectations are. This is the pay that people will receive because everyone's always paid for their time. The more information we can put out there upfront the better. This usually happens up to six months before the actual performance begins. The full planning process usually takes about a year to a year and a half before we actually get to the performance.

So, people can fill out a Google Form. That sort of identifies why they're interested, and there's also a basic questionnaire that has, you know, a little bit of background information like: Who are you? What is your relationship to your community? What do you do with your time? Where did you grow up? If you didn't grow up here, um, what brought you here? And what are some things that you, um, feel positive about in this community? What are some things you'd like to see change? And often but not always we ask people for a sort of timeline of their lives, in broad strokes. So sometimes people will answer a lot in a narrative question, and sometimes they won't, but when you get the pivotal moments of someone's life in a timeline, it gives you a great launching-off place for the interview. Sometimes we get that later.

As my work with *Undesirable Element*s has evolved, I've also learned to see the limitations of asking people to put forward in writing a lot about who they are and where they come from, because that's a lot to ask in terms of vulnerability and sharing when you haven't built that trust yet, or because, you know, that's not always everyone's best form of communication. And so, we've also shifted to either, you can record your answers, or you can call and just have this conversation over the phone. Or if there's a point person with the community organization, you don't have to fill this out at all. Just give them your basics. And we can arrange a meeting.

We don't want it to feel like a test.

So usually, we have people do that initial questionnaire, and then we select a group to interview and get one-on-one conversations. That gives us a sense of people's personalities. That gives us a sense of their comfort level in telling these stories. It's not really an audition, but you do want someone who can feel comfortable being on stage and speaking in front of an audience and also sharing the rehearsal space with other people.

And we do work with people and coach, performance coaching. But no one needs to do anything performative in order to be part of the consideration.

KJ: So, you have your cast then. Can you talk me through how you, um, tease out the stories?

SARA: When Ping started it, it was really like "what does it mean to be from Austin?" or "what does it mean to be from Milwaukee?" And they were very broad in kind of cultural scope, with a core geographic connector. Right? So, it really was, "we're all so different, but we live in Austin."

Then as the project has evolved, we've had partners request more specific themes, where people may all be very different, but they have some kind of shared, lived identity that may be cultural, it may be experiential. Some of those have been—a piece that we did with all survivors of child sexual abuse, *Secret Survivors*. Um, we did a piece in, the last piece before the pandemic that I did was in March of 2020 in St. Paul, *Face to Face: Hmong Women's Experiences*. We did a piece in Dearborn, Michigan, *Undesirable Elements/Dearborn*, that was Arab American Muslim women—that's three shared identities, but they're still all very different. So, depending on, you know, how specific or how broad that theme is, that will help inform the interviews.

We always try and get a scan of everyone's whole life experience. If you are a survivor of abuse or trauma, you're obviously so much more than just your trauma or your survivor experience, and so we try to get a sense of what made you the person that you are. What gave you resilience? Who were the community members, the people who helped you? Those are some of the questions we might tease out. And we do interview people individually, but also ask the group, you know, collective questions.

With a project like *Secret Survivors*, which was initiated by survivor/advocate Amita Swadhin, we wanted to really create a sense of safety for people, so we first did a lot of collective workshops where we would do a group conversation around certain themes, and then from there we did one-on-one interviews.

The other way we've done it is, do the one-on-one interviews first and then bring people together once the cast is formed for group conversations.

KJ: Are you the one that's organizing it into a script?

SARA: Yeah. One of the things about *Undesirable Elements* that I think is, distinctive—I mean, everyone does interview-based theatre differently—is that it's not a collectively devised process, right? We take the material; we curate it and edit it and collate it.[3]

Some of that structure is formed as the experiences are told chronologically, and so each person kind of has their own personal arc. Sometimes the storytelling will go back hundreds of years, to include people's ancestors.

Sometimes, if we're looking at Native or Indigenous stories, we will try and crack the kind of Western time paradigm and do some mythology and origin stories: "How did our people arrive in this land?"

If someone is telling an immigration story, one person might have ancestors that who came on the Mayflower, and one person may have an ancestor who's Native American. We're trying to find out what were the forces that brought people to land in that community. It's always told chronologically. So we are pulling people's key life moments and those forces like, "my family fled Iran in 1978, and they were on the last plane out of Tehran, and they arrived in San Jose." So, being able to incorporate some of the history, so there's some kind of narrative history, as well as the personal storytelling.

Once we have it pieced out, put in chronological order, you start looking at the overall ebb and flow and you might see like, "Oh, well, that person doesn't have anything from 1992 to 2010. Where's their voice in this moment? Maybe we need to go back and find a story to add in for them."

And because people are interwoven, they're also sharing in each other's storytelling. So it's not like monologue, monologue, monologue, but I'm telling a story of, you know, my seventh-grade math teacher, and someone else is telling a story of the time their sister ran away from home, and someone else is telling another story about how they moved, and that all happened in 2002. I might become the voice of that person's sister, and they might be the voice of the math teacher. And so it's not a play in scene dialogue, but someone will say, "my mother said to me" and then that other person will be the voice of the mother.

KJ: That's re-, that's such a great effect.

SARA: It allows people to have stage time even if it's not their moment.

The first couple of rehearsals are table reads, and there's a lot of editing that happens. So we put the script together, and then they [the participant performers] come in, and we try to have them experience it together for the first time because it's so interwoven. If I only showed you your parts, um, it wouldn't make sense.

The first reading is always really beautiful and really powerful as people both discover their own story reflected back to them, but also other people's stories in context.

Then we do a lot of edits. And we literally go through page by page—there are two kinds of edits: One is just pure accuracy—"oh, at that time I was living in El Paso, not San Antonio"—things that are just facts that are easy to change. The other edits are like, "that entry doesn't really feel right to me, can we talk about it?" We invite the cast members to give us feedback. We ask them not to rewrite it themselves, we ask them to tell us what doesn't feel right and then try and fix it. Sometimes that takes a couple of passes.

KJ: And am I right in understanding you also give them the right to retract anything that they said?

SARA: Yeah. In the interview I always say, "If there's something you don't want to talk about, just tell us, and we won't even ask you about it," or "If you want to tell us about it just so we understand who you are a little bit better, like: 'in order to understand me, you really need to know about this relationship with my sister, but I'm not gonna talk about it on stage.'"

So then at the first reading, we've had people say, "Wow, I know I talked about that in the interview but when I see this on the page, I really don't know if I'm ready to talk about that." And the other way around. We've had people say, "Oh, you know, I didn't think I wanted to talk about my sexuality publicly, but I saw this person did, and now I feel more confident to do it," or, "You didn't choose to focus on this, but I really feel like this is missing, can we please get that in?" And there's a little bit of negotiation that can happen because we are trying to find the balance of that individual story with everyone's stories.

I have evolved in my editing over the years to edit heavily before I bring the script forward because it's much easier to add in than to take out.

KJ: So then when you're in rehearsals, when you're working on moments of intensity, um, do you have any—or do you feel it's important not to have any—rituals or clinical approaches to prepping people to share these intense moments?

SARA: Absolutely. This is something that I've committed to bringing into the development space. I've learned a lot over the years from other practitioners; I always have a community agreements or room agreements that guides our process.

We create them somewhat collectively. I usually bring in a set that is our standard and then invite the group to add to them. We revisit them every single rehearsal, and recommit to them every single rehearsal. They talk about consent and safety and boundaries and what we owe each other as a community, but also, what do we get to *not* share with each other as a community? And also addressing anything that might come up in the room. It's a practice that came to us during the work with BreakOUT! in New Orleans because that was part of their community organizing practice. They basically said, "You know, if Ping Chong and Company wants to be in the space, this is part of what we do," and I saw how grounding and helpful it was.

We always do check-ins at the top, to see how everyone's doing. We usually do a check-out at the end, but not always depending on timing. I like to, after we've worked through the material, whatever that day looks like, we usually do some kind of closing circle, and we do a fair amount of warm-ups and games, for community building and for fun.

We try to do body stretches and body awareness, and then depending on the project, I always try to say upfront to everyone, including the partners, "We are artists. We are not therapists. We do not have a social work degree. We do not have clinical training in trauma," although I think I have a lot of lived experience in holding space for people, and have done work around trauma-informed practices. But I think it's always important for people to know that we are not promising a therapeutic outcome—our goal is to not create or recreate any kind of harm—but that our skill is in art and community building.

That being said, we talk a lot about what do you need to feel safe in this process. And as we get towards the presentation, I'll talk to people about "who are you inviting to see this? It's okay. You don't have to invite your mom if you don't want to. You don't have to invite that teacher if you don't want to." You know it's a public event, usually, so you can't always control for that, but it's not your obligation to share this with the world, even though you're doing it publicly. I usually ask, "Who will make you feel really supported? Like, invite that person to the dress rehearsal. Make sure that you have someone there for you." And also, what are you doing, in between [rehearsals] to take care of yourself? We talk a lot about self-care outside of the space, like, "What are your practices? Do you have a Yoga practice? Do you have a therapy practice? Do you have, you know, just a set of friends that can support you?" And we talk about this as the show comes to an end too, because you've put all this emotion and energy into it. So, what do you do when it's over?

KJ: With *Secret Survivors*, that was a public performance that anyone could come to?

SARA: Yes. The first version, the workshop version, was invite only, and we set it up so every person in the cast invited, like, five or six people to support them that they wanted to share the material with.

Another thing that I like to try and do with folks who feel very vulnerable and nervous is to make sure that at some point—not too early—at some point there's an open rehearsal where they at least get that feeling of being in front of an audience before you even get to the dress rehearsal.

KJ: So you're helping your collaborators and cast members and company members prepare for the work ahead. What about the audience? Have you had times when an audience is triggered in the—

SARA: Um, yes, so with *Secret Survivors*, I was very concerned about the well-being of the audience and how to support their experience.

And so with *Secret Survivors*, we invited—both in the development process and in the audience sharing—um, trauma-informed social workers to be on hand. And so, during the workshop and storytelling time of *Secret Survivors*, before we did the one-on-one interviews, I had a friend of mine, Jen Warner, who's a trauma-informed social worker and psychotherapist, to come in to be on hand for the cast members in whatever way they needed her to be—as a resource and emotional support—on their terms and they made the decision in that room that they actually didn't want her to be in the room, but just nearby.

So, she stayed in the other room while we did the work. And then I think a few of them checked in with her, just to kind of quick check-in afterwards, and she shared some resources, and then, years later she actually became a cast member in another project, *(Un)conditional* that we did in Portland, Oregon, which was about living with chronic illness, telling her own story. So that's a wonderful thing about *Undesirable Elements:* Sometimes people come back in different ways.

When we got to the presentation of *Secret Survivors*, we had three or four trauma-informed or trauma-based therapists available to the audience where we identified them at the start of the show and said, "If anyone needs to leave of course you can leave. And if you need to check in with someone, there's these people in the audience," and you know they raise their hands, and we had some designated spaces ahead of time, and several audience members took advantage of that. And we created a resource sheet for a follow-up, so that if they weren't needing to check in with someone at that moment, but things came up afterwards, they had some resources to go to.

KJ: So, you're taking care of your company members and your audience, what about you? Do you have any advice for fellow theatre makers on how to take care of themselves?

SARA: This is a very important question. Just one other thing, before answering that question—these resource sheets. As I have gone through additional projects that deal with different kinds of trauma, I encourage our partners to create a resource guide that they can put out on the table at the, at the theatre, and people can grab, you know, just for any kind of community-based resources.

And, I'm a fan of a content warning, you know, and so different theatres have different responses to asking for content warnings, but I think it's good to say "this show addresses blank blank blank blank blank, and if you need more information, please contact us to learn more." you know. I don't want to send people scurrying and say, "Oh, it's going to be so traumatic." But I'm a fan of, know what you're getting, and you can decide for yourself if it's the right fit for you.

Ok, for me, um, I am in therapy, *(laughs)*. You know, I've been doing this for 20 years, so now I'm in mid-40s. My overall energy level is less than it used to be. I need more sleep than I used to need. Um, I think it's just really—self-care is becoming, almost like a commodity concept, but I think it's really important that people, you know, "put on your own oxygen mask before you help others."

But like I do feel if I'm going to be holding space for other people, I really need to make sure that I'm creating some space for myself.

I would probably tell practitioners to just make sure you're taking the same advice that you're giving your cast members. Like, if you're telling them to drink water and find someone to check in with, and to make sure that they're creating space for themselves, just make sure that that applies to you, too. I think, having two people at—two co-creators—is really helpful because you can tap out if you need to. If you're like, "Hey, I am just so drained," or "I know I'm gonna need a night off," you can plan with that other person to run rehearsal.

And I think snacks are really important, and hospitality is really important. I think it's something that gets under-recognized in theatre spaces because people say "Oh, we don't have the budget for snacks," but always having food in the rehearsal room is a very good idea.

It should be fun, and it should feel that your space and your time and your bodies are respected in the space. You want to make sure that it feels like something everyone should look forward to going to. Not like, "Oh, God! Now I have to go to rehearsal."

Um... I'm answering all these questions about making space for other people and not for myself. *(laughs)* So I, I have to work on making more space for myself, in these, in these things, but, um, I think the best, the best advice I could give myself would be: Do the things that I tell other people to do, and make sure you're leaving enough time for it, and for me.

NOTES

[1] https://www.pingchong.org/about/company.
[2] A youth-led membership organization focused on ending the criminalization of LGBTQ youth of color.
[3] "We" means Sara and her writing partner(s).

12

MARK VALDEZ, SERVING COMMUNITY

When I review Mark Valdez's career, I have to keep reminding myself that all this work was actually accomplished by just one person. (And I bet he would say it was not just him but a community of collaborators.) Here's a small sampling of the many contributions Mark has given the field: As a company member, associate artistic director, and interim artistic director of Cornerstone Theatre Company (discussed in Chapter 3) Mark devised and directed adaptations of classic plays for and with various communities of California. He then expanded his own work across the country, working with arts organizations including Trinity Repertory Company, Alliance Theatre, Native Voices, ChildsPlay, and Center Theatre Group. Mark initiated funding opportunities and programs such as Cedar Riverside's Project 154, which was a collaboration with health providers to use personal narratives for patient advocacy and health. He founded and was the executive director of the Network of Ensemble Theaters, a national organization of theatre companies. He was the 2019 recipient of the Johnson Fellowship for Artists Transforming Communities and is currently the artistic director of Mixed Blood, a 46-year-old theatre considered a creative core of Minnesota's Twin Cities.

KJ: Has your listening changed over the years?

MARK: Absolutely.

> I think when I was younger, I was listening for what I wanted to hear. And I think now, I'm listening out of genuine curiosity and interest in learning. And listening to others helps me see them.

KJ: How do you ask questions to get a better view of someone?

MARK: This is tricky because it's complex, how do you not make it anthropological? How do you not make it, "I'm going to study you. I'm going to learn about you." You know what I mean? That feels like bad listening. Especially when you enter the communities that I enter, people have been "studied," and people have been kind of extracted.

> So, for me, just saying, "While we're here, I'm going to be fully in front of you, and I will meet you where you, wherever you are." Creating space to occupy however they want it to be occupied, and being okay with that. And that's not to say being neutral, because I also feel I owe it to them to be myself and sometimes say, "Actually, I'm going to push back on that because ..." you know? That comes out of love and respect, not out of reciprocity. It's not argumentative. It's present.

> When I was starting out, I think there was a part of me that just enjoyed the argument, and I might push back on something just because I thought, "Woah, look at me, I'm not afraid to call this thing out," you know? Now, that matters less. It's more, "Hey—tell me more about that because I'm not sure if I agree."

KJ: So, for you, the listening is a conversation, more of a dialectic? "I'm gonna offer something that might be counter to where you're going. And then we're going to see how the conversation flows?"

MARK: Sometimes. But I really do try to center the speaker, I'm not approaching it like "we're just going to have this dialogue." That's not true; I am the least interesting part of the conversation.

So, I'm going to reciprocate. I'm not just going to sit here and interview you, but I'm actually going to engage in the dialogue, but—but—I'm going to give you the space, and I will insert myself as appropriate, but the space is yours. Because I'm usually making the invitation to talk, and because of that, I want to host a positive, safe, curious space.

KJ: Yes, yes, that's beautiful. And you said you meet them where they are. Do you mean, figuratively and literally meet them where they are?

MARK: Both. Correct. "Where are you comfortable? Where's convenient for you? I'll meet you there," in the literal sense, and in the figurative sense of, "Oh, these are your beliefs, these are your experiences? Cool. That's where we'll start."

We're doing a project right now in the Iron Range of Minnesota, and the Iron Range is about a two-and-a-half-hour drive north of the Twin Cities.

And when I go up there, I have yet to encounter another person of color when I'm there. This is a place that's distrustful of outsiders. So, there's no blending in. I walk into the room, and they know that I'm not from there. I'm a person of color, I'm from the big cities, I'm from the outside, all the things. And that one has been difficult, slow, the process of just building trust, or just getting people to talk. It's taking a whole lot of time.

KJ: Did you have a day when you took a step forward with that community?

MARK: I did. There's a candy store owner; it's the oldest candy shop in the state of Minnesota. And I went in, and I just was like, "Hey, I'm here. We're working on a play. We want to collect stories. You can be in it." All of the things. And they're like, "Oh, you know," there's always the jokes of "oh, well, I'm not, but you know my wife will do it," or, "my kids will do it." You know, and then they were just so welcoming in a way that people hadn't been. And we sat down, and I talked to the father and son, and then they were just like, "Well, you know, here's a person, I can connect you with them, because they'll be more apt if they hear from me."

And that's when it starts to ripple out.

KJ: How do they feel about how you're going to represent them?

MARK: There's skepticism. And I get it. I've never been in a community where most of the people aren't concerned about how they're going to be depicted.

I think that's just a human response; that makes sense. I think there's a genuine love for your home, for your hometown, for your home community.

And they're just trying to be protective of their home, which I understand. And I always reassure them, "you're going to give input, we're just meeting. It's a first date. We don't ever have to do this again, but maybe if you have fun, we can come back."

I also think that people are not used to having somebody take an interest in them. I think it's actually a radical act to take an interest in another human being. And just listen and be curious, and hold what they share with you.

KJ: How do you get feedback from them?

MARK: We'll share a draft script. We have everyone's emails and we'll just say, "Hey, here's the script. We're so excited to share it with you. If you don't have time to read it, not a problem. We're also going to do a reading of it in your community on these dates.

And we'll do a little video of it. So, if you couldn't be at the reading, there's a recording of some sort. We put it out in places, just random places, like the library or the historic society, or something. "Hey, here's a thing, and here's a page of context. And here's a pen!" And people will just doodle, or people will write, you get the mix. I'm not going to pretend everything is genius dramaturgy. But you take it all. It's all good.

If you put it somewhere convenient, at some point somebody's bored, and rather than scrolling through your phone, you can just peruse these pages. And hopefully, it's engaging enough.

KJ: Have you had instances where, after somebody's come to a reading, they've said, "That's not me. And you can't use my stuff anymore."

MARK: No, that has not happened. As you know, my artistic practice is Cornerstone. And so it is all informed by that. And there were times in Cornerstone's history where people would just say, "Oh this is wrong. You got this wrong. And here's what happened." And then usually Alison Carey[1] would add it in, "Great!" you know, "let's add that perspective in." Um, there were instances where people have said things like, "You know, this is a bigger deal in the play than it actually is in my community, it just feels like you've blown it up in a way that makes me feel uncomfortable."

KJ: Do you have any guidelines that help you navigate the real vs. the poetic?

MARK: I'm a fan of the adaptation. The beautiful thing about adapting an existing play is that the conflict, everything is already built in. And so, it's just a matter of, how does this collective group who are here participating in this project want to represent that? And what does that mean in this local context? We are all equally approaching something from the same place and making meaning of it in a way that isn't putting any one person in the spot of being "the bad guy."

We did *Blood Wedding* and the death character—the beggar woman—we asked: "What does that look like here in this community?" And it was great to just ask, "Who is scary? What is scary? What is death? What does that look like locally?" We were in a farming community, where there's a lot of land and there's a lot of, of meth manufacturing that pops up, and people will just go into a large field where nobody will see you and cook up some meth. And so, they said, "That, what it looks like here."

KJ: Oh, so you adapt that scene from Lorca's play, and you put it in this meth trailer in the middle of a field.

MARK: Exactly. It gets incorporated into the adaptation.

The community members led us there. I, or the playwrights, would have made up something not as interesting and not as honest, right? The adaptation lets you do that.

I think I'm afraid of the responsibility of a wholesale new piece. There are just more ways to get it wrong. Because then you have to find the conflict, you have to find the dramatic arc, and somebody has to be the bad guy—for lack of a better word—or to be overly reductive. And then, who am I as an outsider to this community to say what it is? It loses nuance. It loses the actual complexity of community dynamics. Where the reality is, it's much more complicated than that: We're good *and* bad. In the writing of a new play, you know, you make tons of choices to make it theatrical, to make it dramatic, to make it into an interesting narrative, and um—

KJ: Is it important to you that the audience know it's *Blood Wedding*?

MARK: Yes. A few years ago, I had this revelation: I have been writing myself into the canon. I just kind of realized, all of these plays that were not meant for me, are not about me, I have just been inserting myself, and I've been inserting people that look like me into what was somebody else's tradition.

And in some ways, that's been my career in the field. I'm just going to say, "I'm here."

KJ: And instead of saying like, "I'm gonna make this new thing that is in orbit with the canon" you're just saying "No, I'm just gonna take the canon and remake it."

MARK: Yeah.

KJ: So, your youth was Cornerstone. And then you developed many works on your own, and now you're leading Mixed Blood. Where does Mixed Blood take your way of working and how you listen?

MARK: I moved here, and because I'm an outsider, I was trying to figure out—the board was very generous, and they let me program my first season—but then, I was stuck. Because, an artistic director sets the tone, you make a statement. And I had all the bad ideas: "I'm going to do these plays that can be edgy and all cool, and we'll do these things with social justice, and I'm going to do a musical. Nobody's going to expect a musical." And then

I thought, "What, what am I doing? I know nothing. I have no right to be programming any kind of dialogue, conversation, because I know nothing about this area. I don't know what people care about. I don't know what's important. I don't know what the conversation is." And then I thought, "How do *I* learn that?" And then I came up with this idea to commission: 12 artists to work in 12 neighborhoods.

This was a way of building relationships with artists. This was a way of just entering the community with some humility and some respect and some curiosity, and they've been fantastic.

And we've been building relationships with other organizations and partners. And all of our partners have said, "Can we continue this work together? Can you come back? What else can we do?"

I think it demonstrated a genuine need and interest in theatre-based, theatre-centered, story-centered collaborations working in communities.

We commissioned a range of artists from a tattoo artist, to a chef, to a poet, a synchronized swimming group, an ice-skating group—

KJ: Oh, my gosh.

MARK: Part of it for me is also stretching what theatre is. I want to do more than just plays, and I want people to think, "Oh, you might come see a play, but you might come see a performance at a swimming pool."

But people here have no context for it. I didn't give enough context to why and what, and I think we've alienated some of our audience members and some of our supporters because they have a 47-year history of seeing plays. They understand, "I get my ticket. I show up. A play happens. I go home." And now, it's like, "This week you're in this neighborhood," and "What is it? What am I showing up for?" "It's *all* going to be synchronized swimming?" "No, it's gonna—" "Well wait a minute—what? Why?"

I came to the realization that it's not going to happen in this one season. It'll maybe happen after we've been doing it for three years.

There's no magic phrase. There's not a magic email. There's not a magic video. We tried all of these things. It's just going to take repetition. It has to just become familiar, and we have to stick to it long enough that it becomes less foreign and less weird and less scary and less unknown, and just trust that in time people will start to understand what we're doing, and if we can repeat the message over and over again over a long enough period of time in different ways, that folks will start to catch on.

People ... when they get it, they get it, and they get excited. And we just need to stick with it long enough that it works.

KJ: You have this whole other side of your career as a listener, which is that you started and led the Network of Ensemble Theaters, and in that role you were listening to the field.

Tell me about the role of listening in that context and if that has changed for you.

MARK: That was particularly hard because no community is a monolith, and the field certainly is not a monolith. And especially a membership organization, there are a lot of voices in the room, you know, that have no problem speaking.

And so, part of it was just: How you slow it down? What are the questions to ask?—become really important, you know, when you're looking at the macro of the United States.

KJ: I think business leaders, and leaders of all sorts of different fields, are all in a moment of paying attention to how you ask questions. For you, what were the questions that had traction? What were the questions that led to chaos?

MARK: The things that were obvious, like when you ask, "What do you need?" it's always, "Well we need time, space, money." That doesn't go anywhere. It's like, "Great. Can't help you on any of those things, but good luck." Right? So, let's just put those aside, and ask, "What can we do together that we couldn't do alone?" "What is the thing that we could *only* do as this coalition?" Because you can do so much by yourself, but what are the things that require this group? And then the realization is that as you build community, you build capacity. And so, the more community that we could build, the greater our capacities became, certainly as a national organization.

A lot of it was just how to practice and how to support relationship building.

KJ: Is there a question that I should have asked you?

MARK: I think a lot about the role of the artist. And I've been thinking about ego. I think it is a total act of ego to look at a blank page and say, "I can put something on that page." Only a massive ego will do that, to say, "Art doesn't exist here; I'm going to put art here."

And that's not a bad thing, right? There's the unchecked toxic ego that we can agree is bad, but there is the ego—maybe ego's not the right word—but I think about the presence of the artist, especially in this listening work. Because ultimately, we're editors and we're curators, and we will decide, "I'm gonna use that story. But I'm not gonna use that other story," and we have to be okay with that. What I found is that community members look to me to be the artist. And when I say to them, "What do you all want to make?" that's the worst question, because often they don't know—or they will just share what they think you want them to say.

It's this weird balance, you know. It's one thing to listen, but then what? What's after listening, you know? And I think that's when the rubber meets the road, and that's when it gets complicated. And that's when you have to juggle the ethical and the moral and the artistic and the personal and the interpersonal.

In some ways, the making space to listen is the easy part. It's the fun part; it's the really interesting part because people are just always so interesting. And then it's the work of, "Okay, now that I have this, now that I heard, now, what?"

Many years ago, we did a play with religious communities. And we created something that the community did not like, and they walked away. They said, "No. You've totally got it wrong. This is not how we want to be depicted. This is not it." And we lost all these community partners. "What do we do now?"—you know, and it was all personal and complicated.

It doesn't matter what we want to make as artists. If it is just not representing the community, then we missed the mark, because the art needs to be meaningful to the community. And we went back to the drawing board, and we had to rebuild trust. Some of it we weren't able to do. And you have to find for yourself, what is right for you, what is right for the community.

KJ: Have you ever given up too much to the community?

MARK: I hope not. I don't think so. I don't feel like I have.

There's been one moment where I really struggled. It was this one example that I just mentioned, where the community said, "It doesn't work." It was about putting queer people on stage, through the lens of a faith community that didn't view, didn't sanction homosexuality. And so, as a queer artist, I felt, "I don't know what I'm supposed to do here."

KJ: Right because they're saying "In our world you can't exist."

How on earth did you move forward and say, "I still want to represent this community?"

MARK: We took out any reference to gay characters. So, there were no gay characters in the play. But we did cast gay people, as performers. So, that's how that played out.

KJ: How did it sit with you then? And how does it sit with you now?

MARK: I think in both instances it was the right call. Then, it was particularly hard to get to. But now I think, yeah, of course, the work was about representing the community. And nobody was saying, "We have to put hate on stage" we don't have to vilify anybody, but the community just said "This is not the most pressing conversation for us right now, and it's a complicated conversation."

It's all complicated, right? You know, we can justify anything to make sense of the thing that's important to us. You know what I mean? But ultimately, the question was, "Well, why are we doing this project in the first place?" It wasn't to piss everybody off. That was actually the exact opposite of what we were trying to do. So, if, no matter what we made, if the end result was just alienating everybody, turning everybody against theatre and turning everybody away from this project, then I can hold on to whatever argument around principle I want to make, but it's not doing what we're trying to do.

Even now, I think we made the right choice. And I think we found ways to have the complicated conversation. I feel bad to this day that we violated some trust. We were just reflecting the stories that we heard, and we heard from some queer people of faith, and their perspectives were in the play. So it wasn't that we came in with an agenda. We listened, we reflected, and the community didn't want to hear that at that time.

KJ: Who knows what vibration that conversation has had with the people involved. Maybe they have space for that now.

MARK: Yeah, you know, there's a couple of participants that I've heard from in the years, and this was a long time ago, and uh, I think it's something that sticks with them. It was a moment where I think we all learned, and we all grew. I don't think they think about it every day or anything. But I feel like it was an important moment in a lot of our lives.

NOTE

[1] Alison Carey was co-founder and resident playwright of Cornerstone Theater Company.

13

CHRISTINE SIMONIAN BEAN, DRAMATURGING THE "TRUTH"

I first learned of Dr. Christine Bean's work when reading her article *Dramaturging the "Truth" in* The Exonerated: *Ethics, Counter-Text, and Activism in Documentary Theatre* for the journal *Theatre Topics*. Christine served as the dramaturg for a production of *The Exonerated* by Jessica Blank and Erik Jensen, which was produced by Northwestern University in collaboration with the Center on Wrongful Convictions. As I note in Chapter 3, *The Exonerated* was a performance of edited text from a transcript of interviews with six individuals who were exonerated from their death sentences. As the dramaturg for the Northwestern production, Christine was tasked with providing context and additional research about the real people the work was based on. In this process, she discovered that there were some complexities to one individual's history, which was not included in the play. This "counter-text" would have undermined the impact of the play—which had become a form of activism against the death penalty. In short, one of the six people represented in the play, after being exonerated for the crime of murder, was then convicted and was serving time for a second murder that predated the one at the center of their story in the play. This play, which I believe had a real and positive impact, suddenly became more complicated once it was understood that some information was not inside the frame of the play, information that made the activism at work less cut-and-dried.

To be clear, I appreciate Blank and Jessen's work and am not interested in tearing down the real value of the play. But this situation is a good example of what each and every documentarian faces when making work: We all make choices about what is in our frame and what is not, and those choices have ramifications. As Christine writes at the start of her article: "Although the ethics of documentary theatre are complicated from the start—even if the artists desire objectivity, they are always removed from the initial events and are thus constructing a version of the truth—the complexity increases when the production is remounted at a different time than the original."

I was curious to know more about how she and the team at Northwestern handled the discovery of the counter-text. Christine and I first talked about *The Exonerated* and then moved on to her current work, as associate director of the University of Michigan's CRLT Theatre Program where she and her colleagues (also known as the CRLT Players) make plays based on listening to various communities on their campus.

We began our conversation by talking about theatre that serves as a call for social justice.

CHRISTINE: Not all theatre makers agree that there *should* be a point, or that audience members should be receiving some kind of social justice call.

> Not everybody believes in activist theatre or the idea that there is a fixed truth that you could expect someone to walk away with and change their life, so, and I don't want to reify that idea that there should be only one way that we make theatre and design our art-making experiences.

> However, I do think that it is often the point for people when they're putting together documentary theatre, or they're trying

to tell different sides of a story and saying, "This is an issue that isn't talked about enough," and so our goal is to raise up those voices.

In the case of the production of *The Exonerated*, which was put on in partnership with the Center on Wrongful Convictions, which is a historical center that does the work in the actual world for people who have been wrongfully convicted—to start pulling apart the play and saying, "Hey, there's actually this, one of these people, in real life, has been, um, you know, incarcerated for a prior murder that looks very similar to the murder in the play. We don't have any information about this from the playwrights ..." I had talked with the folks at the Wrongful Convictions Center, who were partners in promoting the piece, and they were like, "Can't you just take that one out? Can't you—" and I was *laughing*, "No, we can't just change the play and just cut this character out," but they were very much like, "Hey, this would undermine our partnership, being a part of this play and using this as a gala benefit for us, in terms of getting more donors and getting more people's eyes on the issue of wrongful conviction."

We talked about it with the cast. We talked about it with the director. I put together this huge packet of all this information, and we just decided, instead, to focus on the issue of wrongful conviction contemporaneously.

So instead of having additional information on the characters who were real people and their cases as the dramaturgical presentation to the audience, what we did was we printed full window-size posters of people whose cases were currently pending in the State of Illinois, to re-center audience awareness on the actual issue.

So that's the choice that we made. We also said—and I asked the Center on Wrongful Convictions—"Hey, if people bring it up, I'm gonna talk about it, you know, after the play. If people know about this case, I'm gonna talk about what happened."

No one brought it up *ever* in any of the talkbacks, and we had talkbacks after each performance. Which concerned me, because this information is public, but no one found this information.

KJ: How many people at those performances of *The Exonerated* do you think knew they were there to see their belief systems reinforced?

CHRISTINE: I'll answer the question and then I'll meditate on it, because I think it's a good question. Writ large, for this particular audience, which was largely subscriber-based in Evanston, Illinois—it was a joint production between the Northwestern University School of the Arts and Next Theatre—and I think it was largely the older white subscriber base, and then also students. So, you have these sort of poles—the academic student audience, and the subscriber base of the theatre—which I think was sympathetic to the message in the first place.

I don't think we had a lot of people who were like, *(gasps)* "I had no idea that this was an issue." And probably zero people who were like, "Oh, we shouldn't be talking about this. I actively oppose the giving of time and air to the issue of wrongful conviction."

So, and in that sense, the preaching to the choir thing was very real. We were asking ourselves, "What are we using the theatre for in this case?" I'll give you a short anecdote from one of the post-show speakers who we had arranged through the Center on Wrongful Convictions, who was a formerly incarcerated person who had been wrongfully convicted. An attendee had asked, "Well, what could we do?" Most of the time people are thinking, "I'm gonna donate. I'm gonna get involved in this way." But our speaker said, "I need you to serve on juries when you get jury duty. I need you to actually be a part of the civic process. I need people who understand how racism operates in the system, to be a part of the system and don't wrongfully convict folks in the first place."

I remember that—this is almost ten years later—I remember that like it was yesterday, I thought, "This is exactly right. You're trying to call people into being ethical citizens."

I understand the point of view of, "Oh, theatre is overly moralistic," or "it is preaching to the choir." But at what cost are we *not* going to focus on social problems issues, you know? And I don't think *all* theatre should be social problems issues. But *some* theatre should be about social problems. They should help us think about what it means to be a citizen in the world. And if that helps us be more ethical, I think it should.

I know not everybody agrees with me. But that's that's kind of where I am at the moment.

KJ: Heard. And it makes me think that maybe there's a reason why choirs go back to church to be preached at every week.

CHRISTINE: One of my good friends and collaborators, Sara Armstrong, says, "the choir needs practice," which I think is another way of saying what you just said, that there's a reason people go back to hear the choir. We need to be reminded of how to, how to, quote unquote, to "be true."

But I'm still drawn to DJ Hopkins' formulation of the counter-text, so this idea of dramaturgy being a counter-text, something that *opposes* the text or *complicates* the text or *pulls apart* the text in some way. Often documentary theatre does have moralistic ethic blinders on, right?

KJ: Right.

CHRISTINE: "This is the story, and this is the only way to view this issue."

KJ: Yeah.

CHRISTINE: When, in some cases it can be really valuable to say, "Hey, this isn't as cut-and-dried as it looks." I think that it's very valuable to introduce complexity. It might introduce better critical thinking and a better, uh, you know, state, when an audience goes away and chews on things and is thinking about things after the fact. Wouldn't they chew on it more if it was complicated? If it was hard, if it challenged a belief system? Perhaps? I mean, that's often how learning works.

KJ: Can you tell me what you do at the CRLT?

CHRISTINE: Essentially, we make activist applied theatre with a social justice bent, and we work predominantly with audiences in higher education: we work with faculty, we work with graduate student instructors, we work with administrators, usually on trying to examine issues in higher education around inequity and trying to help people be more equitable wherever they're located in the university system.

So in that sense, you could think, "That's about as moralistic as you can get" *(laughing)*. We have a specific set of goals that we're trying to get people to arrive at. We're trying to move people, who all have different roles and identities, along a learning continuum to examine—from their own positionality—how they might shift the inequitable status quo that does disproportionate harm to so many people. And at the same time, it doesn't work if it's just sort of, you know, all one-sided preaching to the choir: "Everyone who does X is bad, and everyone who does Y is good." Life is so much more complex than that.

We work with different playwrights, but it's predominantly my collaborator, the director of the CRLT Theatre Program, Dr. Sara Armstrong, who is the playwright who puts these plays together.

As the dramaturg for all of these different plays that are applied theatre, I'm often thinking about, "What is the message we're telling? Who's portraying this? What are the, um, racial and gender politics that we're displaying here? How might people be interpreting this, and how can we introduce more nuance, more thought, in terms of how we're moving people along?" Because people respond very negatively to things that seem black and white because the world isn't black and white.

KJ: Do you start—does the company start with a question, or with an answer?

CHRISTINE: I would say we tend to start with a problem that maybe doesn't, have an easy answer, you know, but it's the problem that we're grappling with. So, if it's something like, well, I'll give you this example because we worked with an external playwright—Jordan Harris—on a play that's called *How Do We Begin: A Historical Reckoning with Anti-Black Racism at U-M*.

It looks specifically at the problem of anti-Black racism in higher education—and I know some of our public schools in the

United States couldn't even put on a play like that, in the current climate. Well, at Michigan we can. And so, we did this deep dive into the history of racial politics in admissions at the university and then put together, essentially, a historical play with different vignettes. It's not a straight play. It's a series of different allegorical vignettes that tell this story. The answer isn't there. But the problem is, which is this: In Michigan, we say we're devoted to equity and inclusion in our practices, and Michigan frequently touts that. And so, the play asks, "What does it mean to tout that, if we have this historical problem and this contemporary residue that lives into the present, and we haven't changed it ... What does that mean?"

KJ: Do you know who you're performing for before the making of the piece?

CHRISTINE: Almost always. Sometimes it's a request that comes in. Sometimes it's something that we're driving, for a specific population.

KJ: Who is your audience?

CHRISTINE: Our audiences are typically folks at Michigan or in higher ed. So, we'll be invited to come to external universities as well, or conferences. I would say, graduate student instructors are usually the earliest-stage academic folks that we work with, and then we work with administrators and tenured faculty and instructors of all kinds in the university system. We don't typically work with undergraduate students.

Something we try very hard to do is not perform things that ask people to take responsibility for something they aren't responsible for—or have a more *constrained* responsibility for due to their role. We're often saying, "Hey, here's an issue in our community. And we want you to take responsibility for that in your role."

I'm not gonna tell undergraduate students, for example, that they need to change the organizational climate regarding sexual harassment. They don't have the levers of power to do that. If I were to design something for undergraduate students, it would look very different, likely, and it would be pitched toward the levers of power that they *do* have.

So, we're attentive to who the audience is and what we're trying to get across to that audience member, maybe way more so than most theatre makers. Since it's applied theatre, we're doing a specific kind of intervention.

KJ: What is, this is such a, um, a naïve question: what is your definition of applied theatre?

CHRISTINE: Oh! No, it's not naïve! I think people have very different, um, what do you say, philosophies on applied theatre. So, my definition of applied theatre would be: theatre for a purpose. You're using the theatre toward a goal. We are speaking from true experiences; we are speaking from the experiences of our performers and our community members for a purpose of instigating social change in the academy.

That's our, that's our goal as a company.

KJ: Wow, what an amazing and amazingly focused mission.

CHRISTINE: That's a great way to put it. It is a very focused mission. Yep.

Something that is really nice about being a theatre company that's creating its own work—and we're not publishing that work outside the university, so it can always somewhat be in flux—if an issue changes, or we learn more information, we're not in this kind of quandary around, "Hey, this is published play. We paid rights for it. We have to perform it as written." We are frequently in a revision process.

KJ: Who conducts the interviews?

CHRISTINE: Predominantly, the director and me. So there's, uh, Sara Armstrong, who I've mentioned before, uh, the director of the CRLT Players, and I'm the associate director. So we're the academic team that'll do the qualitative interviewing if there's qualitative interviewing, the reading and research compilation if we're drawing on studies or we're drawing on published research. Sometimes we will get research assistants; sometimes we have grad students who will help us or we have other interlocutors who we can work with from the university.

And we always involve a performer voice—so, folks who are cast, folks who are in the play, even if it's not a fully devised piece. We're always asking, "Does this feel true? Is this right? Does this feel like something you can say?" Because a lot of the time we're working on issues of the politics of representation. And if you have people who are outside your visible identities or your realm of experience, you want to say, "We're getting this from research. Does this feel like it's true to your experience, or where you're coming from?"

KJ: If you were to make a little brochure of pro tips for interviewing, what would you put in it?

CHRISTINE: Oh, that's lovely! I would say, explain the ethical boundaries of the project. And, pay people. We always try to pay/compensate our subjects who we're interviewing for projects. Ensure that there is a protocol, but you can also be flexible to where the conversation is going. We have a protocol *and* it can shift.

KJ: We all understand it's an observer-created-reality, so the questions that you ask will influence that person, and where they, how they leave the interview and spend the rest of their day—

CHRISTINE: You're right

KJ: You might possibly trigger—

CHRISTINE: Absolutely. You're right. And I think it's challenging for our performers as well. What are the expectations on the community members, and the ethics of doing this work, and the kind of pain points that you ask of people—and so, I don't say you personally, KJ—but that *we* ask of our community and our performers? And so, when you were saying that there are triggering aspects of the work, there's a toll that it takes not only on staging, but on the performers' identities, who you ask to come in and carry this weight continually, you know, over time, day after day. So that's something that we're thinking about—often the plays, the plays that exist, that diversify, quote unquote, right, "the repertoire," are incredibly difficult and painful for performers of color.

Why can't joy be a counter-text? Does documentary theatre always have to be difficult in terms of emotional weight? Even within the weighty subject matter, where are those points of release and expression of other things?

So, if you were thinking about telling stories and telling narratives, there are different stories to tell that express joy and positivity that don't, uh, reinforce a kind of white supremacy or, the majoritarian identities.

KJ: You've been hearing a lot of stories, and you've been paying attention to a lot of ... cracks people fall into.

CHRISTINE: As a white woman who holds a lot of majoritarian identities—you know, highly educated, have a PhD, like all these ways that I've acquired privilege, or born into privilege and acquired privilege—there is no way to take responsibility for those privileges without listening, right?

I'm just speaking from my own personal point of view there, and I'm not saying that that is true of everyone, because it's not, because all of our positionalities change what that looks like and how that operates—some folks already know a lot of things based on their experiences!—but I think that the point of one's experience only extends so far without listening, and if you're not listening, then that becomes an enclosure for your own sense of morality, your own sense of ethics. You're just closed off, based on what your own experiences have been.

I think the radical act of listening starts to puncture, well, I don't want to say puncture holes, but maybe like open out the doors of what that enclosure looks like and feels like. I don't think that *only* what we do when art making. I don't think that's *only* what we're doing is opening doors, but I think in some ways we are.

We are opening doors for some people to new ideas, allowing them to participate in an experience they wouldn't otherwise have been in. Even if they're in the "choir," there are all kinds of ways that listening to something, and being present for something, and being called to accountability with something—which I think we could talk probably more about the idea, like all these beautiful words, "whole presence," "witnessing," um, "accountability"—there are so many good things that theatre does in that way.

And, I think it's a good way to reframe what listening is because I think most people are like, "Well, yeah, I'm listening to you right now." But ... am I actually listening to you? Am I allowing it to change my being and my understanding? And am I going to do something differently coming out of this conversation? I think people maybe don't think of listening in that way enough. And maybe that's a gift that theatre practitioners can give, is reframing what listening is.

BIBLIOGRAPHY

Bean, Christine Simonian. "Dramaturging the 'Truth' in the Exonerated: Ethics, Counter-Text, and Activism in Documentary Theatre." *Theatre Topics* vol. 24, no. 3 (2014): 187–97. Web 2018.

Hopkins, D. J. "Research, Counter-Text, Performance: Reconsidering the (Textual) Authority of the Dramaturg." *Theatre Topics* vol. 13 no. 3 (2003): 1–17. Project MUSE. https://doi.org/10.1353/tt.2003.0008.

14

IDRIS GOODWIN, TELLING THE STORY

Idris Goodwin is a true renaissance artist. He began his career as a rapper, then became a playwright, essayist, poet, educator, thought leader, keynote speaker, and is currently the artistic director of Seattle Children's Theatre. He is a Pushcart Award nominee and a 2021 United States Artist Fellow. He was featured on Def Poetry Jam and even performed on Sesame Street. Idris has written many plays including *And in This Corner: Cassius Clay*, about the teenage Muhammed Ali, which was produced by Stage One Family Theatre in collaboration with the Muhammad Ali Center in Louisville, Kentucky; *This is Modern Art (based on true events)*, co-written with Kevin Coval and produced by Steppenwolf Theatre Company, which is a discourse on what is considered vandalism, what is art, who decides and why; and his most recent work, *The Boy Who Touched the Sky,* commissioned by Seattle's Children's Theatre and the Alliance Theatre of Atlanta, inspired by Jimi Hendrix's childhood.

DOI: 10.4324/9781003437154-17

I wanted to hear from Idris because he has a knack for attuning to real moments and real people and then transforming them into fictional works of art that are uniquely his own.

KJ: I'll start with asking how do you listen, and has your ability to listen—or your art of listening—changed over the years?

IDRIS: Well, in a few different ways. I think a lot of it has to do with patience and being married with children, definitely, that has greatly advanced my patience, which has improved my listening.

I think there's been a shift in my pedagogy as an educator, which to me is very tied to my identity as an artist. To me, there's no separation of the two. My pedagogy, used to be so much about selling myself and looking for affirmation. I find a lot of times that people who don't know how to listen are just uncomfortable. There's a un-comfortability with themselves, and so they feel like they always have to prove something or have to show they know something or make people like them.

I think I got over that kind of stuff. Also, if a person is choosing to engage with you and speak to you, that's a gift. They're giving you their time, they're opening themselves up to you, and so it's a transference of energy. If you're not listening, then you're cheating yourself out of that energy someone is giving you and information someone is giving you and wants to give. I think once I realized that, I became voracious for learning things I didn't know and getting energy from other people, and how comfortable can I make someone feel, all of that stuff. It became about the art of conversation.

Then I think, innately, I'm an audiophile. I learn most through sound and oratory—that's always been a big thing for me. There's that. Then, finally, and I think most significantly, I have increased my understanding of my neurodivergency. I've been struggling with ADHD for over 30 years. It went untreated for the most part, and I'm finally looking it in the face, and I've been getting treatment for the last year. The more I understand how

I'm wired, the more I'm able to make the right adjustments and also understand how I might be coming off to others. That has, I think, improved my listening as well.

KJ: You've made work about different subjects like the life of Muhammad Ali, or a relationship between graffiti artists and the institution of "high art." Is there a role that listening to yourself plays in your process?

IDRIS: Well, yes. In multiple ways. One, I am in constant self-reflection. Part of being neurodivergent, having ADHD is like, it is *Twelve Angry Men (laughs)* at all times. The conversations are all over the place. That's one. Two, in terms of my work as a playwright, I'm writing "time art"—I'm writing an event. I'm writing poetry, it's lyric. Hearing my work back to me is a key part of the process. It's always been this way because I started out as a rapper. I was like, "You got to hear how it sounds. Does this flow? Are these rhymes working? Is that corny?" Listening is integral. When I fly out to other cities to see my plays, my son asked me the other day, "Why don't you just watch a video?" Well, because I have to hear it. I have to hear it with an audience. I've got to know if it's funny. I've got to know if the timing is right. I've got to know where it feels stale. All of that, that is a key part of the aesthetic for me.

KJ: Did you ever come across a subject that you couldn't listen to?

IDRIS: Oh, well, definitely. These days, anything having to do with brutality to children or people of color—There was this movie about Emmett Till, that was out a while ago, and I thought, "No. Not seeing that." I still haven't seen *12 Years a Slave*. At the same time, people choose those sounds. People choose to engage in those kinds of stories from the particular angles that they do and so I don't particularly—It's just not something I want to judge anybody else about, but I just don't want to see it.

KJ: We're at a place where suddenly in an effort to be more inclusive, artistic leaders are putting hard stories on the stage, and the people that those stories are intended to be about are now saying, "We don't want to hear that. We don't want to see that."

IDRIS: Yes.

KJ: God bless theatre. I love it very much, but we're always so far behind the curve.

IDRIS: Yes.

KJ: I'm wondering, how do we create a body of work for the next 50 years? Is there a way forward that involves joy and hope that is still speaking to a moment? That we can sleep well at night knowing that we're still artists?

IDRIS: To me, end of the day, it's about: what are the choices and negotiations that you make with yourself as a creative? Me, personally, I'm interested in joy right now in all aspects of my life, including the joy of writing in and of itself. I don't particularly wish to give more of my energy and thought to writing stories about certain things, but at the same time, there are some things that are always going to appear in my work no matter what. I get what people say when they're like, "We want stories about joy." I get that on a superficial level, but no story that's worth a damn is one thing. I don't particularly give much to that binary, to be honest with you, of stories of Black trauma versus stories of Black joy. I don't really I get it. I get what people mean conversationally and colloquially. For me, it's just that you could focus on the more joyous aspects of a particular person's life and experience in terms of tone, versus not.

I think joy is, definitely, something I am actively after in my own life. Certainly, working in TYA.[1] I think that's much of what draws me to TYA. There are, definitely, some thornier subject matters that are on the workbench too.

KJ: Do you have opinions or ethics around who can tell what story?

IDRIS: That's a good question. Anybody can tell whatever story they want. The question is just, is it going to ring true? Is it going to ring true? Are people going to be into it? You know what I mean? I think, again, we waste so much time in theatre, man.

KJ: *(laughs)* Say more.

IDRIS: We make family business public business. There are far too many conversations that we have in the saloon that are becoming media articles that don't need to be. The stuff is not headline news y'all, to people who aren't in our little town of 500. There are not that many of us working. There are not that many of us because everybody else wised up and pursued a different, more sensible career. Yes, of course, read the room. Of course, there are some things that are also obvious, but everything is not one, two, three, black-and-white. Sometimes it's like this is a director and a writer who've worked together for 20 years. Yes, this person is not Cambodian, but these are two artists who know each other well. It's like ... this director who's not Cambodian, yes, maybe you don't have this person be the keynote speaker of the Cambodian Theatre Artists Festival, but if this Cambodian playwright and this non-Cambodian director have a great working relationship artistically, who cares? Great. That's beautiful.

Part of what we're doing is about learning and teaching, as well. Also, no one artist of color speaks for all the other artists of color. What do I care if this person who is not Black wants to direct my piece? Should this theatre company have reached out to all these other Black directors? In general, yes, but I'm also like, "Reach out to those Black directors for *Christmas Carol*." Also, stop doing *Christmas Carol* but reach out to that Black director to do something. You feel me? There's something inherently, weirdly, strangely reductive in the, "Okay, the Chinese go do the Chinese show." That feels foul too.

There's got to be some intersectionality. There's got to be some fluidity. We use those old words only when we're talking about gender and sexuality, but also, in this work we do, which is intersectional. Theatre, in and of itself, is intersectional. Storytelling and performing arts, culture, it is all intersectional. It is all intersectional. I'm a Black man who comes from stolen African writing in English in this very Western form.

I'm not working in some West African tribal form. You know what I'm saying? I'm working with a form that was banging in my head from years of "English" class. Again, much like the joy versus trauma thing, I just think these ... We're talking about corporate ethics and operational stuff. That has nothing to do with the process. When we have these conversations, that's what we're talking about.

We're talking about the business part of it, which is frankly quite uninspiring. You've decided, I've decided, I want to, actually, get paid for my writing, so I'm going to go into the writing business. Nobody told me I had to go into the writing business, I chose to go into the writing business, right?

I could have opened a car wash and been a car wash entrepreneur who writes plays and gets great joy and satisfaction out of that, and who could have built a little theatre right next to my car wash. The car wash subsidizes the theatre company, and I'm able to do the work I want to do and work with the actors I like. I could have done that, and I might mess *(laughs)* around doing that.

KJ: It sounds kind of good. *(laughs)*

IDRIS: Right. Anyway.

KJ: When you're dealing with real people or real events, what's the balance between just reflecting shards of what you see and hear vs. needing to cover everything? And what does it mean to be "accurate"?

IDRIS: It's an impossible situation, to be honest with you. There is one project that I'm working on now, but we are choosing to first do as an audio documentary before we start fictionalizing anything, because we were talking to all these relatives and family members, and so, it's like, we're going to make our process a product because I'm thinking, "Get it all out now."

KJ: Oh, that's interesting.

IDRIS: Then we'll talk about, perhaps, "Okay, what's next? Do we want to make a play." Honestly, KJ, that's probably my last one. It is too much. I don't even really like having the conversations with people post-show, where they say, "He used to drink egg creams not soda and it was, actually, in '53, not in '54." I'm like, "Y'all, I'm a storyteller, and I'm telling one version."

IDRIS GOODWIN, TELLING THE STORY 241

With Ali, people were tripping about, "Did he actually throw his medal away?" I'm like, "He said he did." "I know, but did he really?" I'm like, "He really said he did." I'm like, "Fam, this is not journalism." I had another guy who was a journalist who had written extensively about my subject, and he was like, "You didn't get this," He goes, "Well, I'm a journalist. I'm a journalist." He is like, "I'm just saying. I'm a journalist." I'm like, "I am *not* a journalist." I've got a room of second graders that I have to entertain for 70 minutes.[2] We have different objectives.

I think when we get into these estates and stuff, we've got to be clear with folks. You have your objective as an estate; you have your objective as a family member. I'm interested in this person and really the public's understanding of them, but I'm using this person's history or—using, maybe not the right word—but engaging with this person's legacy as a way to really make connections with things happening now.

What else are these legacies for? What is history for? Why do we lionize certain people? It's all a story. It's all storytelling. Of course, no one's going to know everything. Of course, not. No one expects that.

You know what I mean? It's just too much.

I'm from the hip-hop generation, and really the hip-hop I came up on was so influenced by the downtown art scene, which was embracing pop art. We don't look at Andy Warhol's work and think, "His Marilyn Monroe is not the story of Marilyn Monroe." We know we're looking at Andy Warhol. His individual style is engaging with this legacy known as Marilyn Monroe.

That's where I come from—sampling. Yes, you recognize this James Brown, but this is my record. I'm just engaging with James Brown on this record. It's past this tired uninspired thing known as the jukebox musical. No disrespect. I know there's a lot of hard work that goes into those, but for me, I just find them a little uninspired. It's a check, right?

I don't mean to come off flippant, but I'm just speaking from where I'm at right now.

My big thing right now is I try to encourage writers to write like themselves, or at least try to explore what that means. My pedagogy is very much about style, the development of a style and why, being informed about it. It's really about writer confidence, creator confidence. This is relatively new for me because I think all these years I didn't really, actually have a pedagogy. I think I was just immersing. I was just showing up and trying to just be myself in a room. I like this stuff. Maybe you guys will like this stuff.

I didn't really have a pedagogy. Now I do. That's the cornerstone of it. It is about you, but it's about what you value, prioritize, and your abilities as a storyteller. Always going back to, "What is it you're trying to say?" And trying to create spaces and nurture spaces where writers can influence and support each other thoughtfully.

KJ: Does what you, you're consuming, in your daily life, play into that? What you're listening to, what you're reading or watching, does that inform your point of view in your art?

IDRIS: I'm maybe conflating what you're asking, but I think as a writer, you've got to listen to yourself. You've got to listen to yourself, but also you don't have to obey yourself either. You've got to at least hear yourself and what you're feeling.

Yesterday, I started saying something to someone and I stopped and she was like, "Well, I'm thinking blah, blah, blah." I said, "You know what? I still don't think this is the way, but I'm going to hope to be wrong about this."

KJ: That's so good. This project you mentioned, what a great idea to do an audio documentary. Step one is we're going to hear the thing. We're going to capture this person. We're going to chronicle this event. Then bouncing off of it in later work ... I mean that's so Greek. You can make a lot of work out of the same collection of audio recordings.

IDRIS: Yes. Totally. My co-writer, Kevin Coval—who I wrote *This Is Modern Art* with—same thing. He went and engaged with all these people and got interviews and stuff, and we started trying to transform them, but I'm like, I, actually, think it would be better this time if we just live in the true stories, if we live in the recordings.

KJ: It has to be a recording, versus putting it into a play or a movie because we're actually hearing the real people. Is that the idea?

IDRIS: Yes. Audio documentary, just hear them. You're still making the same choices. You're just not writing all the dialogue. You know what I'm saying? You're taking the chunks, and all of that. It also immerses you in the source material because I didn't do those interviews, he did. Also, I've made documentaries too. Documentaries are like, you never remember everything you had. It's all in the logging. To me, you can go do the interview. That's the easy part. The hard part is knowing all the stuff you've got and figuring out what the thread is. That's the hard part. That's where the writing of it actually, really happens. You've got to know what you got first, and then what's missing. Then you've got to go do another interview. You have to find some creative way to fill in the holes of the story. You're still telling the story, but you're engaging with, you're just closer to the different experiences, which again, helps alleviate that tension around like, "Whose story is this and why are you trying to recreate the job?"

NOTES

[1] Theatre for Young Audiences.
[2] Idris' play, *And In This Corner: Cassius Clay* was written for young audiences.

15

LARISSA FASTHORSE, TY DEFOE, AND MICHAEL JOHN GARCÉS

Larissa FastHorse is a citizen of the Sicangu Lakota Nation. She is an artistic leader, consultant, choreographer, playwright, and writer for film and television. A MacArthur Fellow and recipient of the National Endowment for the Arts Distinguished Play Award, Larissa's plays, such as *What Would Crazy Horse Do?*, *Teaching Disco Squaredancing to Our Elders: A Class Presentation*, and *The Thanksgiving Play* have been seen across the country, including on Broadway. When I asked Larissa if she might grant an interview, she said yes, *but*, "I would want to have my collaborators in the interview as well. Decentralizing the voice of who speaks for the work is essential in any discussion of it. My most frequent collaborators are Michael John Garcés and Ty Defoe. If you are thinking specifically of a part of the body of work that I've participated in, let's find the correct additional voice to discuss it. Or just include them both. But talking about listening and community engagement by myself goes against my ethos." This is such a great example of why I wanted to include her approach in this book—she's the first to say that the work is not about one artist and it certainly doesn't happen in a vacuum.

Ty Defoe, who is a citizen of the Anishinaabe and Oneida Nations, is an interdisciplinary artist whose work has been at Lincoln Center, the Metropolitan Museum of Art, and the Park Avenue Armory. Ty has won a Helen Merrill Playwriting Award, a Grammy, and many fellowships including MacDowell and the Kennedy Center's Next 50; has worked in film and television and also teaches.[1] Larissa and Ty co-founded Indigenous Directions, "a consulting firm for companies and artists who want to create accurate work about, for and with Indigenous Peoples."[2] In other chapters I discuss Michael John Garcés' work with Cornerstone Theatre, where he served as artistic director for 17 years. Additionally, Michael has written plays and directed other's work across the country and internationally, including New York Theatre Workshop, INTAR Theatre, La Mama Experimental Theatre Club, the Edinburgh Fringe Festival (Fringe First Award), and Teatro Lo'il Maxil for Sna Jtz'ibajom *(The House of the Writer)* in Chiapas, Mexico. Michael and Larissa have collaborated with Cornerstone Theatre Company on the trilogy *Urban Rez, Native Nation,* and *Wicoun*. At the time of this interview, all three were about to go into tech rehearsals for the world premiere of *For the People,* written by Ty and Larissa and directed by Michael. *For the People* is not documentary or verbatim theatre—the play is clearly fictional, but the making of the work was centered and rooted in several layers of listening: Listening to people from Indigenous communities, listening to each other, listening to the work, and then going back to the communities to listen again and again.

KJ: How's the play going?

LARISSA: I think on the new play production side, it's going well. But we're also in this in-between world of reminding people we're still the community engagement artists, and so it's been an interesting push and pull of them saying, "We don't want to bother you. We want you to focus on the art," and us saying—I literally said in a meeting last week—"I really don't give a fuck about the art. I give a fuck about the community." The community is forever. The art is six weeks, then it's done.

TY: We have been in process here at the Guthrie starting in 2016. Through conversations with individuals inside of the institutions, taking risks on seeing a need that was not happening at the institution. The work is both decolonization, and indigenizing, and values inside that kind of work. So since then, we did the project in 2017 on a piece titled *Water is Sacred*, and then in 2018, we created another piece titled *Stories from the Drum*, that were the stepping stones to this work. It took a great deal of work to get an inch of change because of the insidious nature of historic colonialism and how that still plays out today.

Then, from there, out of all the atrocities that happened during the pandemic, funders were taking notice of how to create a direct line toward serving artists. It matched our charge working directly. There was a direct need for disparate communities—who did not have access to things like healthcare—it was like system upon system upon system, and here we are making the charge of this work of amplifying Indigenous voices for this community in particular through all of these years. So, the process to me kind of talks about rematriation and reparations towards narrative reparations of telling the stories of beings who deserve their stories to be told within an institution that may need to mitigate a specific type of democracy. Beings including the people, including the land, including the water that's surrounding this giant building that's literally a blockade between the water, the people, the earth, etc. So how do we, as artists, open these conversations to foster reciprocal relations with hope that signals itself to future generations? Even if we move the dial of progress to shift culture two inches, we have made a difference.

LARISSA: I think we're all grappling—the three of us, separately and together, are grappling with, where do we have to say, "Okay, this is now up to this institution." We have enough depth and knowledge in this work, in this community that we could just call people to fix whatever comes up, but we need the institution to do it. And so we're in this constant dance of, is this something good for the community for us to jump in and fix this with the community, and where is it we need to let the Guthrie—the institution—succeed or fail in this community, you know? Outreach and connection. So far everything that Joe Haj and the Guthrie have done has indicated that they are a very trustworthy partner to the best of their ability in the very large institution they're in. The opening of our first rehearsal was transformatively different than any other opening of any first rehearsal for these guys in the recent past, since Joe's been here I'll say, I don't know about before. It was just, it's so different. It was all open to community, it was all elders, it was all community focused process, etc., etc.

TY: The untrustworthy partner is colonialism. It's literally everywhere, like racism. Some of the systems we helped put in places are a Native Advisory Council, so it is not just us three sitting in a room giving these "best practices." This is a rotating Native Advisory Council that comes from not only the Twin Cities but the surrounding reservations and area. We don't physically live in Mni Sota Makoce; we are visitors, even though we have ties to this community, we don't sleep, cook, eat our food here. As contemporary people, I think there's something to be said that we're also creating circles of accountability for ourselves as ephemeral artists who are working with something that is here today but then gone tomorrow.

KJ: I appreciate your work because you resist any notion that community is a monolith. Tell me about your process when it comes to representation and breaking through monolithic expectations.

MICHAEL: In terms of the diversity of the community and the complexity of representation and the sort of inevitable need to make choices and, you know, that is just a process of ongoing listening and conversation. Right? It really is at the core of the work.

We had a group of kids in rehearsal yesterday, and they came to a pretty chaotic rehearsal. We were staging a fight without a fight choreographer. We're sort of figuring out the trajectory of things. Then we changed the script around it, and we sort of blew it up, and Larissa had been gone for a week, and she came in with all sorts of, horrible critiques and complaints, about what we had done ... No I'm joking but she had some cool ideas and we sort of blew it up, and we were playing with it—I only cite this, not because it's atypical of anything, but because it's an example of listening and a lot of conversation and an organic response to what is often a really rigid process of staging a fight—"You will (blank) it, and you will (blank)." Right? and we were doing the opposite, and, you know, on Tuesday our fight choreographer will come in and take our shape, institute some things for safety so it's replicable and things like that. But I think what was interesting about it was that it was a microcosm, an example of the ongoingness of all of us listening to each other.

And you know our room represents a lot of—we have mostly Indigenous guests. We have one White person in the play. And some of them are local, and some of them are from other places, right? So in terms of the cultural context of all of us, it's pretty diverse. All that's to say that there's sort of an ongoingness of listening that doesn't stop throughout the process and it doesn't stop after opening. I haven't been with the project from the beginning, but the making of the play has been in response to a conversation with the wide diversity of people in the communities here in Minneapolis, of asking, "if we were to make a play at the Guthrie, what should it be?" And then even after I came on board, we still did story circles. We did some live story circles, which were really kind of amazing and had a big impact on the play. We've had several readings that everybody was invited to come see and respond to. And the response process continues.

There's no "no's" from us to what people tell us they want. It's never "no" because the process is ongoing. One of the kids was like, "how much do you change things?" Essentially, the idea is, if you make changes in the script to accommodate who's in the room, how much are you willing to change your vision? And I said "Vision is not a static thing. Vision is like a dream." It's an amorphous thing, it's something we're shooting towards. We as artists intuit and understand and have a rigorous practice around vision. But the vision is not, "I've blocked this guy to walk from here to here. That's my vision. and if it doesn't happen that way my vision is somehow compromised." Or, "This line has to be these words in this order in this sense ..." You know, the vision is constantly changing those things to find the most perfect or the most exciting or the most whatever version of your vision as it continues to evolve in your own practice. And, honestly, every process should be somehow community-engaged. It's ridiculous not to be. We're just more conscious of it, and of course conscious of it in a sort of deeply stratified, oppressive system that excludes, right?

There's fear of perception and making mistakes. The fear of making mistakes is our single biggest obstacle, really, I think.

KJ: The fear of making a mistake? Or is it the fear of insulting somebody who is left out or misrepresenting something?

MICHAEL: The fear of insult, the fear of saying or doing the wrong thing, the fear of being the person culpable in some way—people don't want to be culpable. But the problem with change is you have to be culpable. You have to make the mistakes, and then you have to acknowledge the mistakes, and you have to learn from the mistakes. However painful the process that might be, you know change means things change. And I think at the end of the day people kind of want to change so that things remain the same somehow and that's not how it works, you know?

Theatre is a culture of siloing, right? And colonialism is absolutely based on siloing in order to preserve capital, right? Cultural capital, material capital, etc. ... And so, it's really a fearsome thing to try to change, and it makes people feel insecure. I mean look, it makes me feel ... Like we don't know what we're gonna do in rehearsal on Tuesday, right? It's fucking scary, right? When we have tech coming up, but that's on purpose, right? Because if you're listening then you don't know what the other person's gonna say, you don't know what's gonna come out of that process. You literally have no idea.

KJ: And listening requires waiting, and that is indeed scary. And to tell an institution and a system that is focused on production that you have to wait is hard and scary.

LARISSA: That's legitimate, right? It's legitimate to be scared. Especially if you've always worked in a context where you know what's gonna happen. So, something we're reminded of daily here, by folks at the Guthrie, is that they don't do new plays. They do very few new plays. So this is a new process, so it's legitimately scary, to have to change what they're doing just to do a new play is already scary. We need to acknowledge that and hear their fears. Yeah, we are asking you to do something different, we know this isn't something you do, but then in addition we're all bringing constant questions: Why do you do it this way? What is opening night? Why can't people come and go from the theatre? We want community here, we want to rehearse in the community, we want ... You know, just constantly asking, why do you do it this way? Why can't we do it like that? What if we leave all possibilities—what are the possibilities, if we leave all possibilities open that we can legally do? Let's find out what people's ultimate dreams are and see if we can do that, you know? And so, we're constantly asking.

Back to your question about script stuff and telling the stories—there is a freedom we have because we do not do docudrama. We're creating a fiction, one singular fictional story. I can't imagine the responsibility of folks that do docudramas. It would, like, break me, I don't know. We're creating one fictional story, so we get to have that freedom. So, one fictitious character ... It's amazing to me, every time, 50 people will come up and say, "Oh, that was me." You know? Because it was a fictional character. And so, they *all* can identify themselves in that one character. Whereas if it was a docudrama, then it's one person's story.

MICHAEL: You synthesize the multiplicity of perspective and viewpoints, and it also allows us to just be doing "A" story versus "The" story. And that's hugely important. In no way shape or form are we pretending this play is *the* story or *the* community, which we have no right to define and really no right to tell. So that's super helpful.

KJ: What about for yourselves? What comes to mind when you think about your own mistakes?

LARISSA: I'd say, in general, one of the things that we have learned very acutely in the last few years is around just picking who to invite to listen to the listening. It's so much harder to teach other people to listen than we thought. We thought that just because they're fellow theatre artists, or just because they have the same political viewpoint on life, they're fellow supporters of the kind of art we love and make, etc., we just thought that a little bit of context would be enough, but it absolutely was not. To the point of being damaging and to where we had to come in and repair things with community. We underestimated how difficult listening is to most folks, and how damaging questions can be—like endless questioning, questions that were sucking things and wanting things and taking things—

MICHAEL: It's the extractive-ness of it right?

LARISSA: Yeah!

MICHAEL: We seek not to be extractive, which is very hard. We're an extractive culture, so it's very hard for people to make this—

LARISSA: Admiration even, could be extracting—

MICHAEL: Absolutely. Which becomes objectification easily. That was a learning process for me, certainly, to witness people I admire and I respect sort of really not get it, but with all the good intentions in the world. And obviously there's a constant process of policing ourselves not to fall into it, right? There has to be this constant self-inquiry: am I falling into this pattern, process, way of being because it's what I'm being taught to do by everything in the dominant culture?

KJ: It's a false equivalency, to think everyone should be able to give you feedback.

If you made a brochure on how to find the right listeners to bring into your room, what, what would be in it?

TY: This question around assuming good intentions for others who might not understand Indigenous protocol and frameworks for cultural experiences, who might hold a whole other set of values that they can't even see or understand. When you go to a gym for a workout, you warm up before you begin. It's like a conditioning of your mind, or heart, and/or body to be tuned in. To notice patterns. To know change. To listen not just to hear, but to understand. Otherwise, you are asleep and not alive to awareness.

LARISSA: This seems obvious, but it so isn't: the community is always right. If you're going to do this work, the community is right. There's no wrong. They are never wrong; they are always right. So, it doesn't matter that they don't say what you want them to say. It doesn't matter if they say something offensive, doesn't matter if they say what you don't expect, doesn't matter if they're not giving you what you want because you're already wrong if you're going in wanting something. The community is right. You have to have zero ego. It has nothing to do with you. The community is always right. No matter what happens, no matter what's said, because the community is just being the community. If you're only truly there to listen, there's not correcting, there's no how you felt. It's just the community is right, because the community is the community.

If you're not coming in with a heart of service, then, don't come. And people think they are but they're actually, 90 percent of the time I'd say, people are actually in service of themselves. And yes, we are, obviously, at a base level, we are too—it's how we make our living. But I think there's the lack of ego you have to have to walk in and just be of service. You know, I watch Michael cleaning rat poop off of risers for children instead of being in the room doing fun things. It's so humbling, but it means everything to the community. It means everything to the process, and when people see that they know that that human is trustworthy. I think artists want this work to be something else when really the work is cleaning off rat poop. It's serving meals. It's driving grandma around all day and missing all the fun meetings, and missing the ceremony because you're driving grandma around.

I keep saying this but it's true: If nothing happens, nothing happens. And I think that's also very hard for listeners. They're always trying to get to something. The process is it; we're done.

Like, showing up today, and cleaning up rat poop, and gluing on a bunch of little balls on dog ears for children—that's it, we're done, we've succeeded today. And tomorrow we might get to do more. Or maybe not.

TY: Larissa, you're reminding me of, with listening, there is more than one truth that exists in the community—in terms of the monolith question. Multiple truths can exist at one time, so how do you listen when it's multiple people saying conflicting things?— It's deep listening. sometimes there is not one answer to anything.

MICHAEL: It's absolutely right in those moments in which there's multiple contradictions—there's not a community standing there telling you "This is how it is" and it's just one thing, it's an infinite thing that's telling you contradictory things, and you have to say "yes" to all of it and then live in that and proceed forward in that and practice in that, as opposed to this idea of choosing one and deciding that's the determinative "right."

LARISSA: I would also say, do your homework. Listeners, don't just show up at a community. That's what kept happening. People show up and are like, "Teach me! And tell me all your ways." I think people don't realize—I'm sure it's true in other communities I can only speak to Native communities—how triggering that is. Especially, you know, for a non-Indigenous person to come into our community and want to be taught. They want things that A.) They haven't earned and B.) Just wanting things from us is so triggering. We're dealing with centuries of that, and it ended up being stolen and taken and used against us, and so, yeah, do your homework, do your own freaking homework!

TY: Tensions will happen, that's inevitable, and it is important, especially when you're making drama and you're making theatre, you're making playfulness, you're making all these things, that tension is so important; and I was thinking a lot of a piece I was working on once, where the grandmothers were actually in direct conflict with youth as it relates to changing the gender of characters. They were specific it had to be, a female-identified individual in a particular piece, and the youth were like, "Well, that's not how we identify. We are, you know, changing." So, this began a conversation with this idea about changing genders and talking about gender binaries between generations etc. Folks came together with these conflicting views that were being discussed in public with individuals that were not of that community, right, who were non-Indigenous, and they were sort of somewhat fearful. There was tension from them about witnessing what was going on, "people inside the culture" maybe not agreeing, but that conversation was really important because here you have the youth who are the carriers of nation, culture, community, etc., saying, "No, this is how we want this to happen, how we want to identify." When elders are saying "Well, if this happens it's gonna get lost," but that conversation is so key, and that's how culture shifts and changes, I think, so the tension is very important.

MICHAEL: And I think we make work in the tension.

TY: Yeah.

NOTES

[1] In the fall of 2023 FastHorse, Defoe, and Garcés all joined the faculty of Arizona State University's Medieval and Renaissance Study Program as Professors of Practice.

[2] From Indigenous Directions' website: https://www.indigenousdirection.com/.

Index

Note: Page references with "n" denote endnotes.

11th & Pine 165, 167, 171

Ackerman, Emily 26–28, 31, 105, 199n2
activism: against death penalty 224; political 143–144
An Act of Killing 129–130
Actors Theatre of Louisville 51, 185
Act Prohibiting Importation of Slaves 127
Adelphi Theatre (New York) 152
Aeschylus 54, 65
The Aesthetics of Resistance (Weiss) 145
After Sorrow 120
Agitprop Theatre 150
AKA Jane Roe 112–113
Alberini, Cristina 22–26, 41–42
Ali, Muhammed 235
Alliance Theatre of Atlanta 213, 235
All My Puny Sorrows (Toews) 48
"all sides of a story" 121–124
AMAJUBA: LIKE DOVES WE RISE 161
ambivalence 117–118
American naturalism 116
American realism 116, 151
American Records 33
American Theatre 28
Amplifiers 104–108
And in This Corner: Cassius Clay (Goodwin) 235, 243n2
And the Rest Of Me Floats 165

animated film 131
anonymity, in interview 75
Another Word for Beauty 191
Aquinas, Thomas 48
Arena; The History of the Federal Theatre (Flanagan) 149
Arent, Arthur 151
Argo 95
Arias, Lola 97
Armour, Lou 97
art: public 148–149; sequential 115
Atomic Energy Commission (AEC) 114
Auschwitz-Birkenau death camps 144

Baha Mousa 153
Baldwin, James 137–138
Barracoon: The Story of the Last Black Cargo (Hurston) 127
Battle of Ia Drang 128–129
Bauer, Fritz 147
Bean, Christine 224–234
Belber, Steven 97
belief systems 8, 68, 227
Bergman, Ingmar 145
Big Love (Mee) 186
Billington, Michael 142
biographical film (biopic) 95
Black Watch (Burke) 101–102
Blair, Tony 153
Blake, Marsha Stephanie 199n2

INDEX

Blank, Jessica 52–53, 224–225
Blitzstein, Marc 139n2
Blood Wedding (Lorca) 102, 217
Bloody Sunday 153
"Blue Blouses" 150
body language 74
Bogart, Anne 50, 66n6, 172n11
Bowie, David 9
The Boy Who Touched the Sky (Goodwin) 235
Brando, Marlon 144
Breaking Bad 7, 11
BreakOUT! 203, 208
Brecht, Bertolt 135
Brechtian technique 151
"Bridge Show" 64
BRIGHTER booklet 165
Brighter Project 164
British Parliament 152
Brown, James 119
Bryden, Bill 101
Bulbul, Nawar 86–90
Burke, Gregory 101
Burnett, Carol 8
Bush, George W. 133

California Institution for Women 57
Called to Account (Kent) 153
Cantrell, Tom 156
Capitol Hill Occupied Protest (CHOP) 165
"Capitol Hill Organized Protest" 172n16
Capps, Ron 107
Carey, Alison 217, 223n1
Carillo, Juliette 64
Casa Cushman (Fondakowski) 177
Castro, Fidel 163
Cavett, Dick 8; abilities as talk show host 9–10; impromptu interview 17–19
Ceaușescu, Elena 98
Cedar Riverside's Project 154 213
Center on Wrongful Convictions 226–227

Center Theatre Group 213
Chamberlain, Mary 186
Chicago Repertory Group 133
ChildsPlay 213
Chinoiserie 120
Christmas Carol 239
Churchill, Caryl 185
Cincinnati King 106
Cinema Verité 96–97
civic engagement: of the future 165–173; listening as 141–173
Civic Repertory Theatre 139n1
The Civilians 99, 191–199, 199n1
climate change 121–122
Clotilda 127
Collins-Hughes, Laura 100
The Color of Justice (Norton-Taylor) 153, 155
Combat and Operational Stress Control (COSC) 31
comics: and gutter 115–116; as sequential art 115
Communist Party of Germany (KPD) 143
community: defined 57; participants 57–58
A Complicated Sadness (Toews) 48
comprehension 48–49, 137
Conard, Conard Goose 99
context and listening 9
cool medium 108–109
Cornerstone Theater Company 52, 54–58, 62, 65, 102, 120, 213, 223n1, 245
Cosson, Steve 66n7, 99, 185, 191–199, 199n2
Coval, Kevin 235
culture mapping 56
Culture of Desire 50
Cynn, Christine 129

Dafoe, Willem 49
Dana H. (Hnath) 99, 185
Dearborn 205
Declassified UK 152
Defoe, Ty 244–254, 254n1

deliberate sequence: and comics 115; ethics of listening 115–116
Demme, Jonathan 66n2
Deshima 120
Deveare Smith, Anna 159–160
The Devil's Highway (Urrea) 71
Didion, Joan 128
The Dinner Party Download 10
Division Street: America (Studs) 132, 134
documentation of interview 73
Dramaturging the "Truth" in The Exonerated: *Ethics, Counter-Text, and Activism in Documentary Theatre* (Bean) 224–226

eavesdropping 75
Edinburgh Fringe Festival (Fringe First Award) 245
editing process 110–115
Eno, Will 185
ethics of listening 92–124; "all sides of a story" 121–124; certainty or ambivalence 117–118; curatorial modes 104–108; deliberate sequence 115–116; editing ethics 110–115; medium 108–110; transparency 92–104; *see also* listening
Evening Standard 157
The Exonerated (Blank and Jensen) 52–53
extreme human injury 43–45

Faber, Yael 160–162
Face to Face: Hmong Women's Experiences 205
false equivalency 121–122
Fast Cheap and Out of Control 94
FastHorse, Larissa 244–254, 254n1
Federal Refugee Resettlement Program 78
Federal Theatre Project (FTP) 139n2, 149–152; Living Newspapers 150–151
Feminist Files 177

Fen 185, 189
Fen Women (Chamberlain) 186
Fiksel, Mikhail 100–101
The Files 157
Fires in the Mirror (Deavere Smith) 159, 178
Fisher, Amanda Stuart 96, 109–110
Flanagan, Hallie 149
Flanner, Janet 17–19
Folman, Ari 130–131
Fondakowski, Leigh 97, 177–184, 184n6
For All Time (Sanchez) 52, 58, 62, 64–66
For the People (Ty and Larissa) 245
Foster, Jodie 177
Frankfurt Auschwitz trials 144, 145, 147
Freie Volksbühne theatre of West Berlin 144
Friedman, Michael 199n2

Gagliano, Rico 10
Galloway, Joseph L. 128–129
Garcés, Michael John 62–63, 64–65, 244–254, 254n1
Gasbarra, Felix 143
generous listening 69
Gillespie, Dizzy 129
Gilligan's Island 8
Going, Going, Gone 50
Gone Missing 191, 196–197
"The Good War": An Oral History of World War II (Studs) 132, 138
Goodwin, Idris 120, 235–243, 243n2
Google Form 203–204
Granma. Trombones from Havana 163–164
Gray, Spalding 48–49
Great Depression 132, 149
The Great Immensity 191
Green, Jesse 158
GROOVE 164
Grotowski, Jerzy 157
The Guardian 117, 152

Gussow, Mel 49
Guthrie Theater 76–77
gutters 115–116

Half Straddle 158
Half the Picture 98–99, 153
Hamlet (Shakespeare) 51
Hammond, Will 113, 142
Hard Times: An Oral History of the Great Depression (Studs) 132
Hare, David 117, 142
Harrison, George 9–10
Haug, Helgard 162
Heberlee, Brad 199n2
Hébert, Julie 64
Hendrix, Jimi 9, 235
Herzog, Werner 95, 111
Highway 47 (Sanchez) 12, 16–17, 103
Hitler, Adolf 144
Hnath, Lucas 99–101, 185
Hodges, Betsy 77
Hoggett, Steven 101
Holiday, Billie 133
Holocaust 145–147
Home (Rushdie) 79
Hopkins, Harry 149–150
Hotel Rwanda 95
hot medium 108
The House of Broken Angel (Urrea) 71
House Un-American Activities Committee 144
Howard Bay 151
Hubbard, Freddie 129
human justice 55
The Hummingbird's Daughter (Urrea) 71
Hurston, Zora Neale 127–128
Hussein, Saddam 152

Iizuka, Naomi 64, 185
immigration 77–78
IndieWire 130
Indigenous Directions 245
The Inner Chronicle of What We Are—Understanding Werner Herzog (Linden) 95

In Spite of Everything! (Piscator and Gasbarra) 143
INTAR Theatre 245
interviews: anonymity 75; avoiding eavesdropping 75; body language 74; documentation of 73; instincts 74–75; people of Minneapolis/St. Paul communities 77; play about Minneapolis/St. Paul communities 80–90; play based on 76–77; process 28–30; situational awareness 73–74
In the Matter of J. Robert Oppenheimer (Kipphardt) 114
In the Next Room (or The Vibrator Play) (Ruhl) 185
Into the Beautiful North (Urrea) 71
The Investigation (Weiss) 110, 144, 145–146, 148
Investigative Theatre 70, 185
Iraq-Iran war 152
Is This a Room 158
I Think I Like Girls (Fondakowski) 177, 178, 183

Jackson, David 97
Japanese Americans 132
Jensen, Erik 52–53, 224–225
Jiang Qing 98
Joffé, Roland 66n3
John, Little Willie 106–107, 118–119
John, Mabel 107
Joint Stock Theatre Company 185, 186
Jones, Philly Joe 129
Jones, Thomas S. 33
Joplin, Janis 9
Jory, Jon 51
"journalistic-adjacent" principles 106
justice 60; failed judicial system 61; human 55; restorative 63, 67n13
Justice Beyond Punishment Collaborative 202
Justice Cycle 52
Justifying War (Norton-Taylor) 153

INDEX 259

Kaegi, Stefan 162
Kaufman, Anne 98, 185
Kaufman, Moisés 97, 178, 184n2
Kazan, Elia 150
Kent, Nicolas 152–154, 156–157
Kerry, John 8
Khmer Rouge 49
Kiang, Jessica 130
The Killing Fields 49
King, Jessica 111
King, Rodney 159
King Records 106
Kipphardt, Heiner 114–115
Kirk Douglas Theatre 99
Koenig, Jerzy 142
Kossola, Oluale 127–128; *see also* Lewis, Cudjoe
Kraus, Dan 97
Kurup, Shashir 64

The Ladies (Washburn) 98
La Mama Experimental Theatre Club 245
Laramie (film) 177
The Laramie Project (Fondakowski) 97, 177, 179
Laramie: Ten Years Later (Fondakowski) 177
Lawrence, Stephen 153
Lebanese Christians 130
LeCompte, Elizabeth 48–49
Lennon, John 9
Lewis, Cudjoe 127; *see also* Kossola, Oluale
Lewis, Jim 199n2
LGBTQIA+ people/writers 164
LGBTQ youth of color 203, 212n2
LIFT (London's International Festival of Theatre) 97
Lin, Maya Yang 148–149
Lincoln 95
Linden, Tom van der 95
listener: non-judgmental 14, 18, 31, 76; professional 1

listening 1–3; alternative approach to 68; as civic engagement 141–173; and context 9; and reconciliation 47–66; and time 9–10; and trust gaining 9, 60; without agenda 60; *see also* ethics of listening
Living Newspapers 150–151
Loftus, Elizabeth 21–22
long-term memory 22, 25
Loomer, Lisa 112
Lorca, Federico Garcia 102
Los Illegals (Garcés) 64

Mailer, Norman 18–19
Marat/Sade (Weiss) 145
Marcos, Imelda 98
Margo Hall 177, 181
McCarthy, Joseph P. 144
McCloud, Scott 115
McGrath, John 99, 154
McLuhan, Marshal 108
medium: cool 108–109; ethics of listening 108–110; hot 108
Mee, Charles L. 185
Mee, Chuck 186
memory 22–26; extreme human injury 43–45; long-term 22, 25; and narrative 40–41; and neuroscience 21–22; and place 40; short-term 22; and storytelling 40–41; and time 40; traumatic events 24
mental illness 48, 51
Mercein, Jenny 116–117
Meyerhold, Vsevolod 150
Mid-America Theatre Conference (MATC) 53
Middle Passage 127
Mika Onyx Johnson 164
Milk 95
Miller, Arthur 150
Miller, Brandon 199n2
Miller, Henry 18–19
Minefield (Arias) 97–98

Minneapolis/St. Paul communities: interviews of people from 76–77; play about 76–80; refugee resettlement 77; Syrian Refugees 77
Minnesota Department of Human Services 77
Mitchell, Joni 9
Mixed Blood Theatre Company 102, 125n5, 214
Molina, Judith 144
Moore, Harold G. 128–129
Morris, Erroll 94–95
A Mouthfull of Birds 185
Muhammad Ali Center, Louisville, Kentucky 235
Myatt, Julie Marie 64

narrative: and memory 40–41; structure 2, 51, 100, 102
Nash, William P. 31–33
Nathan, Syd 106
National Public Radio's All Things Considered 131
National Theatre of Scotland 101
Native Nation 245
Native Voices 213
natural disasters 43
Navy SEALs 43
Need Your Love 106
Network of Ensemble Theaters 213
New Deal 133, 149
New Journalism 128
Newnam, Brendan Francis 10
New York Theatre Workshop 245
non-judgmental listener 14, 18, 31, 76
Norton-Taylor, Richard 99, 152–157
Notes and Tones (Taylor) 129
Nuremberg 153
Nuremberg Trials 153

Obama, Barack 77–78
O'Connell, Deirdre 100–101
O-Dark-Thirty 107
Odets, Clifford 139n1, 151
On Being's Better Conversation Guide 69

On Being with Krista Tippet (Tippett) 68, 91n1
O'Neill, John E. 8
One-Third of a Nation (Arent) 151–152
Onstad, Katrina 48
Operation Iraqi Freedom 133
Oppenheimer 95
Oppenheimer, Joshua 111, 129–130
The Oresteia (Aeschylus) 54, 65
Oslo 115
Otero, Ruben 97
THE (M)OTHERS 165
Outbox 162–165

Parramatta Girls (Valentine) 122, 124
Paul, Philip 106, 118
The People's Temple 177, 184n5
The Performance Group 48
Performing the Testimonial; Rethinking Verbatim Dramaturgies (Fisher) 96, 109
The Permanent Way 113
Perón, Eva 98
Pierotti, Greg 181
Ping Chong 200
Ping Chong and Company 120–121, 200, 202, 208
Piscator, Erwin 143–145; theatre as political activism 143–144
place, and memory 40
Plunkett, Stephen 199n2
poetic testimonial: theatre as 160–162; and Yael Farber 160–162
Pojagi 120
political activism: theatre as 143–144; and Theatre of the Eighth Day 157
Polley, Sarah 66n1
Portus, Martin 123
posterior cingulate cortex (PCC) 25, 41
post-traumatic stress disorder (PTSD) 24–25, 32
Pran, Dith 49
Pretty Filthy 191
prison abolitionist 63–64
prison sentences 51–52, 57

professional listener 1
public art: and Maya Yang Lin 148–149; as theatre of memorial 148–149
Public Theater (New York) 67n10, 185
public trial, theatre as 145–148
Puttnam, David 66n3

Rai, Sukrim 97
Ratsabout, Saengmany 80–83
realism: American 116, 151; of Konstantin Stanislavski 150
rebellion, theatre as 157–158
reconciliation, and listening 47–66
ReEntry (Sanchez and Ackerman) 26, 31–34, 42, 105, 118; as military leadership tool 34–40
refugee resettlement 77–78
Refugee Resettlement Program 77
restorative justice 63, 67n13
Reuler, Jack 125n5
Revolt of the Fisherman 144
Richter, Max 131
Rimini Protokoll 162–165
Roach, Max 129
Roe (Loomer) 112
Roe, Jane 112
Roe v. Wade 112
Rogers, J. T. 115
Roosevelt, Franklin D. 133, 149
Royal Shakespeare Theatre 145
Rubenstein, David M. 159
Ruhl, Sarah 185
Rushdie, Salman 79–80
Ryan, George 52

Sagastume, Gabriel 97
Satter, Tina 158
Say My Name: Stories of LGBTQ Youth from New Orleans 203
"Scenes from the Inquiry: Tribunal Theatre and the Act of Listening" (Cantrell) 156
Schanberg, Sydney 49
Schechner, Richard 48
Schiller, Daniela 22–26, 40–41

Schindler's List 95, 145
Seabees (Naval Construction Battalions) 43
Seattle Children's Theatre 235
Seattle Housing Authority 152
The Second City 134
Second World War *see* World War II
Secret Survivors 205, 209–210
Shakespeare, William 51
Shepard, Matthew 97, 178
The Ship (Bryden) 101
short-term memory 22
Simone, Nina 129
SITI Company 50, 172n11
situational awareness 73–74
Sixty Minutes 158
The Skin of Our Teeth (Wilder) 151
Slovo, Gillian 152
Small Lives Big Dreams 50
Smith, Bessie 137–138
Soans, Robin 109
Sobol, Hannah 78
social media 156, 158
Someday (Myatt) 64
Sophie's Choice 145
Spill 177, 182
Stafford-Clark, Max 113
Stage One Family Theatre 235
Stalin, Joseph 144
Stanislavski, Konstantin 150
Star Tribune 77
Steard, Dan 142
Steppenwolf Theatre Company 235
Stories from Jonestown (Fondakowski) 177, 179
Story Circle 55–57
storytelling and memory 40–41
Stritch, Elaine 144
Stuart Fisher, Amanda 161
Studs 131–139; death of 134; humor and showmanship 133–134; WFMT interviews 137; during World War II 133
Studs Place 133–134
suicide 39, 48, 51

Sweeney, Nick 112
Swimming to Cambodia (Gray) 49
Syrian Refugees 77

Taccone, Tony 117, 125n16
Tactical Questioning 153
Tadashi Suzuki 66n6
Takers 104–108
Talking to Terrorists (Soans) 109
talk therapy 40–41
Taylor, Arthur 129
Teaching Disco Squaredancing to Our Elders: A Class Presentation (FastHorse) 244
Teatr Ósmego Dnia (Theatre of the Eighth Day) 157–158
Tectonic Theatre Project 97
Telling Project 121
Terkel, Studs *see* Studs
Terrors of Pleasure (Gray) 49
The Thanksgiving Play (FastHorse) 244
theatre: as civic act of love 162–165; as civic mirror 159–160; as economic and political engine 149–152; as poetic testimonial 160–162; as political activism 143–144; as public trial 145–148; as rebellion 157–158; as social media 158
THEATRE AS WITNESS;
Three Testimonial Plays from South Africa (Farber) 160
Theatre of Fact 142
theatre of memorial 148–149
Theatre Topics 224
This Beautiful City 191, 193
This is Modern Art (based on true events) (Goodwin and Coval) 235
Thompson, Hunter S. 128
Thornton, Leon 33
Three Truths (Iizuka) 64
Tiffany, John 101
The Tijuana Book of the Dead (Urrea) 71
time: and listening 9–10; and memory 40

Tippett, Krista 68, 72, 86, 91n1, 136; common questions 70; elements of work 69–71
Toews, Miriam 48
Tomé Land Grant 10–11
Too Much Water (Sanchez) 51, 66
"torture porn" 78
Touch and Go (Studs) 133–134
Touch of Water (Hébert) 64
Tower 108–109
Traber, Kirya 202
traditional journalism 128
transparency: for audience 92–96; ethics of listening 92–104; for people representing 92–94
traumatic events 24–25, 75, 123
Tribunal Plays 98, 152–157
Tricycle Theatre, London 98, 152–157
Trinity Repertory Company 213
Trojan War 54
trust: and listening 9, 60; suggestions for earning 13–16; and transparency 13–14
Tutu, Archbishop Desmond 160
Twilight: Los Angeles (Deavere Smith) 159, 178

Understanding Comics (McCloud) 115
Understanding Media: The Extensions of Man (McLuhan) 108
Undesirable Elements (UE) project 120–121, 200–202, 204, 205, 206, 210
Urban Rez 245
Urrea, Luis Alberto 71–73, 86
Urwintore 146
US Housing Authority 152
US Navy 43

Valdez, Mark 102, 213–223
Valentine, Alana 118, 122–124
Vallejo, Marcelo 98
Value Engineering: Scenes from the Grenfell Inquiry 156

Verbatim: Contemporary Documentary Theatre 113
Vidal, Gore 18–19, 127; United States of Amnesia 127, 131
Vietnam Veterans Memorial 148
Vietnam War 132
violence 61–62, 66

Waiting for Lefty (Odets) 151
Wallach, Eli 144
Waltz with Bashir (Folman) 130
Wangh, Steve 181
Washburn, Anne 98, 185
Washington Post 77
Waters, Les 100–101, 185–190, 192
Wax Museum 133–134
Wei, Jonathan 121
Weiss, Peter 110, 144; theatre as public trial 145–148
Weller, Alison 199n2
Wells, Orson 139n2, 150
Wetzel, Daniel 162
We were Soldiers Once ... and Young; Ia Drang—The Battle That Changed the War in Vietnam 129
What Would Crazy Horse Do? (FastHorse) 244
The White Album (Didion) 128
Wicoun 245
Wilder, Thornton 151

Williams, Tennessee 144
Winner, Reality 158
Wolfe, Tom 128
Women Talking (Toews) 48
Woolery, Laurie 58, 61, 63, 67n10
The Wooster Group 48
Working Classroom 12–13, 17, 19n1
Working: People Talk About What They Do All Day and How They Feel About What They Do (Studs) 131
Works Progress Administration (WPA) 133, 149–150; Federal Project Number One 149
World War I 143
World War II 132, 133, 142, 144, 156
Writers Guild Initiative 107
Writers Guild of America 107

X's and O's (Sanchez and Mercein) 116, 117

Yeboah, Nikki 165–173
Yoko Ono 9
You Are Here (Sanchez) 84–90

Zatz, Sara 121, 200–212
Zero Dark Thirty 95
Zhivaia Gazeta (Living Newspaper) 150–151

For Product Safety Concerns and Information please contact our EU representative GPSR@taylorandfrancis.com
Taylor & Francis Verlag GmbH, Kaufingerstraße 24, 80331 München, Germany

www.ingramcontent.com/pod-product-compliance
Lightning Source LLC
Chambersburg PA
CBHW071815300426
44116CB00009B/1327